ROUGH EDGES

xo
Sarah &
Marion

ROUGH EDGES

SARAH J. MARRON

NEW DEGREE PRESS

This is a work of fiction. Any references to historical events, real people, or real places are used fictitiously. Other names, characters, places, and events are products of the author's imagination, and any resemblance to actual events or places or persons, living or dead, is entirely coincidental.

ISBN   978-1-63676-821-2 *Paperback*
         978-1-63730-221-7 *Kindle Ebook*
         978-1-63730-265-1 *Ebook*

A NOTE FROM
THE AUTHOR

Dear Reader,

I envision my life in two parts, pre- and post-technology. When I was growing up, we still used encyclopedias to write reports... until the internet was born.

I started online dating before online dating was even "a thing." Back when it was so new I didn't want to tell anyone for fear of judgment. Back when I was naïve and the internet didn't afford us any of the social media stalking we can use to check up on a person's background today.

My online experiences began as quick friendly interactions, usually meeting new people through the chat features of online gaming. The interactions never extended past those few minutes... until one day I met someone and felt a pull that tested my carefully constructed online boundaries.

Here's the thing about talking to someone online. The screen is a wall that blocks judgment. You share things on an emotional level that you might never share in person.

It promotes raw honesty.

In those limited moments online, you feel truer to yourself than you do walking through the motions of your daily life—craving that honesty more and more. It can be such a freeing experience that it even becomes obsessive.

I used to try to hide this period of my life, brush over it when talking about myself, feeling a little ashamed of my reality. I think there used to be this stereotype of, "You must only be dating someone online because you can't find anyone in the real world," or, "How can you love someone you've never met face-to-face?"

Maybe that still exists.

I'd come back with, "You'll never understand," and believed what I was saying was true. I still believe it to be true.

You'll never understand unless you've been through it yourself.

It wasn't easy to overcome the fear of even mentioning this other life I had. Sometimes I still cringe when the topic comes up. But I discovered that the most important thing is to know who you really are and what you really want. It's even better if you can show up in the real world and share yourself with the people who matter most to you. Without my experiences, I wouldn't be who I am or where I am today. And for that, I'm thankful.

I wrote this book with hope in my heart. The hope of detailing the highs and lows of relationships, self-discovery, and the sometimes-difficult task of coming back to reality. Whether these experiences happen online or in the real world, the emotions are universal to a point. I want to help people understand… if they've never been through anything like this.

For those who have—take solace, knowing a kindred spirit is out there.

I hope this book gives you the courage to be honest with others and to share the real you with the world. I hope Casey becomes your friend, someone to resonate with, to validate your feelings, and ultimately give you comfort that you're not alone.

Xo
Sarah

To Sarich.

PROLOGUE

Have you ever felt lost?

Yeah…

… me too.

PART I:

REFLECTION

CHAPTER 1

The sound of the bell counted down the hours left of one of our last Fridays of the school year. We could almost taste the weekend, and beyond that, our final summer before college. Break was on everyone's mind, even the teachers'. With blisteringly hot temperatures, it was cruel and unusual punishment to keep kids in a school that didn't have central air and relied solely on rotating fans to keep us from melting. Even on a good day, the heat was enough to lose focus, but on a Friday, there was no chance of productivity. Classes consisted of lights-off movie time on wheel-in TVs and Drop Everything and Read. Anything we could do that required minimal movement in our sticky, sweat-inducing, one-piece metal desks—just slide in, don't move, and slide out forty-five minutes later.

I hate this time of year.

At this time of year cliques were in full swing. They huddled together in their designated spots—the popular group dominating the rusted old swing-set that should have been taken down years ago. Girls in short-shorts that barely met the "fingertip" dress code and tank tops that blatantly ignored the "no midriff" rule perched atop their boy counterparts sporting cargo shorts and casual tees with little bird and moose emblems.

I let my gaze wander over the girls' hair, scrunched stiff with too much gel, and eyes, rimmed with dark eyeliner and bright eye shadow in a rainbow of colors. A heaviness weighed in the pit of my stomach. Of course, they were all thin and bronzed to perfection, even if it was fake. I could hear them from my place on the brick ledge, vibrating with anticipation for their summer plans. I watched, noticing the grip of strong hands on slim hips. The girls threw their heads back and squealed at each pump as the swings climbed higher in the air. I swallowed hard and snapped my head back to my little group, my eyes prickling.

I wasn't popular, but I wasn't unpopular. I fell somewhere in the middle.

Or maybe I don't fit anywhere at all.

I first noticed this feeling of isolation sometime around fifth grade. No one ever paid me much attention until I shot up taller than everyone in my class, even the boys. One day at recess, I sat with my back against the brick wall, my nose deep in a book. A group of girls walked by snickering. They all pointed, and one made a comment loudly enough that suddenly every kid in the immediate vicinity was laughing at my tie-dye Tweety Bird shirt that I had tucked over my knees. I choked back tears through the rest of the day.

When I came home, I shuffled through the door, head bowed, trying to make myself as quiet and small as possible. I just couldn't escape the squeaky floor. My mom looked up, her head tilted, and asked me what was wrong. I collapsed into her arms, burying my face in her hair and sobbing until I was out of air. After several minutes of her soothing hands rubbing circles on my back, I took a breath and spilled everything at once. She calmed me down, telling me it didn't matter what I was wearing on the outside. I was a good person on the inside and someday soon everyone else would recognize that too. I believed her and ignored the twinge every time I didn't get invited for pizza on half-days or Friday night sleepovers. I took solace in the idea that I would find my place eventually. I made a point to upgrade my style just a touch and was okay making it through the school days as the smart girl in class, helping my classmates, and eating lunch with a different group each day. I sat with whoever had the space.

If I was forced to choose a stereotype, I would pick "floater." I had acquaintances in almost every group. I just didn't belong to any specific one.

Leila always included me, though. Leila's my best and oldest friend. When my parents moved us to our neighborhood just before I turned five, she was the first person I met. One day once we were settled, my mom had brought me out to play in the field when she saw a little boy and girl out there with their mother. I was scared and hid behind her while she made the introduction. This little girl had seemed so much older and tougher than I was. She was play-fighting against her much bigger older brother as if she knew there wasn't a thing in the world she wouldn't be able to take on. She was proud and clearly not scared of anything. Pushing past her own mother, she marched right up to me, her curly chocolate-brown hair falling in front of her sparkling brown eyes and introduced herself. Then she grabbed my arm, dragged me out to team up against her brother, and charged.

Sometime between the grass stains and giggles, I forgot my initial nerves and knew that Leila would be my best friend forever. She introduced me to the other neighborhood kids, brought me with her everywhere, and we made a pact to tell each other everything. Since then, we'd been there for every big and small moment in each other's lives: first days of school, first jobs, new friends, and new boys. *Her new boys.* Despite our friendship, I was still sometimes intimidated by her overabundance of confidence, especially since I was usually lacking in that department.

I clung to the idea that I had her and my neighborhood group, and that was enough. Enough to keep me mildly happy and invited to just enough Friday hangouts to feel welcome.

At least until high school when the separation worsened.

I'd just learned how to scrunch my hair when suddenly, the fashion gods decided that straight was better. *I didn't get the memo.* The girls grew more glamorous, the groups more defined. Their bodies rounded nicely in all the right places, where mine stayed mostly flat. And I never could get rid of that last little bit of baby fat around the middle. Leila could have been one of them if she didn't despise their collective personalities. She grew into the perfect average height for a girl, just tiny enough to fit nicely in the crook of any guy's arm, with the long, lean muscles of a runner. She didn't care about trends or labels, dressing in clothes that flaunted her body regardless of the emblem on the sleeve. I didn't have any of that confidence. Despite upgrading my own wardrobe to include a few moose of my own, only affording the sale items, I could never bring myself to take off my hoodie and put my body on display. I wouldn't be caught dead in short-shorts or a tank top outside of my house.

It wasn't just appearances. When they picked up new sports like field hockey and tennis, I shrank further into myself and spent a lot of time reading. Then I discovered the internet. I overheard Leila's brother shooting the shit with his buddies about this thing and all its glory—chat rooms and multiplayer games—and asked my parents if I could use the computer that night "for schoolwork." I found another world, and *that* became my escape even more than the made-up places of my fantasy novels. Real people would talk to me in this place of no judgment, where I could be whoever I wanted. I found a space that let me make friends, people like me wanting to be themselves. It didn't bother me that I would never meet them in person. It had always felt worth it, just to feel like I belonged somewhere.

It had always been enough. Until it wasn't.

CHAPTER 2

Let me take you to the moment the obsession started.

On this scorcher of a day, us bored kids in my small town couldn't wait to get to the computer lounge. The hum and heat of the oversized, tan metal towers and fat-backed computer screens were no match for the only room in the high school with air conditioning.

Any normal day, after twenty minutes of "learn to type" challenges, we wiped our fingers clean of the layer of film that clung to the squishy orange keyboard covers and peeled them off. We were then free to do as we pleased if we stayed within the limits of creating masterpieces in Microsoft Paint or roaming the internet. The icing on the cake this Friday was a full free period—a whole hour to ourselves.

This was our only chance for connection to the outside world during the school day, and we took full advantage. Forget waiting until our parents let us have that precious hour of dial-up at night. Our teenage hormones itched to explore the depths of the internet right at that moment.

Cue the angels singing, or in this case, the Microsoft login tone.

The popular choice? None other than Myspace. Some concerned parent must have dropped the hint at one of the PTA meetings about Instant Messenger. The IT guys, tucked in the closet they called an office off the cafeteria, blocked the program. Apparently "IM" gave us too much freedom to shit-talk each other in writing. The school preferred we kept the insults verbal on their watch. I guess no one told them Myspace did the same thing, only a little more subtly.

Everyone had a Myspace. It didn't matter what group you belonged to. From the soccer jocks and cheerleaders to the band geeks and loners, Myspace didn't discriminate. The minions pulled their chairs around their queen bees to obsess over her perfectly curated page while the rest of the second-class citizens watched out of the corners of their eyes, changing their backgrounds to match the royalty.

What is it about human nature that pushes us to focus all our energy on making everyone like us?

Myspace is not where my story began. I only half-cared about impressing the popular girl with the perfect song lyrics in an attempt to move up in her top eight. I could try, but I knew it was a lost cause at this point. My eyesight softened at the sight of the trees through the window and the sun beaming through the double-paned glass. I wanted to get out. At only seventeen, I wanted more than this town and these same people could give me. I wanted to do more, know more, see more.

The sun shifted and sent a glare straight through my vision. My eyelids snapped closed, and my head turned back toward the screen. I hovered over the Internet Explorer icon, letting my index finger settle on the mouse, and double-clicked to open.

Instead of reliving my same small-town life in a virtual Myspace bubble, my guilty pleasure was online gaming on a little-known site called Miniclip. The website popped up with a burst of color and flashing graphics displaying the categories. Miniclip was a powerhouse for any game you could think of—puzzles, arcade, sports, and more. I liked the robotic mindlessness of the unblock-me puzzles and the time-crunching challenge of Tetris, but what I really loved was the multiplayer games. In addition to the strategy of outsmarting your opponent, there was a chat feature that opened a window to the world. I had the chance to be matched with anyone, international or domestic, male or female, gay or straight, young or old. It was the perfect way out—*virtually*—of my tiny-ass town where the biggest news was that Jay and Amanda broke up again… for the third time this week.

I had the ability to ask questions about different cultures and get an authentic answer. I could talk to someone living experiences so different from my own, rather than wait to read them in a history book.

I met Hanna from Alabama while bowling—a girl my own age who spent every Sunday with her grandmother cooking dinner for her family of twelve. All the way from Germany, Peter entered my racing game and taught me a bit of German by professing his love to me. At the time, I didn't find that even remotely suspicious. Occasionally, I took a slower pace and played Backgammon, matching with grandparents who warned me to be careful of the information I shared with others online. The connections may have been short lived— ten to fifteen minutes sometimes—but long enough to feel like I was pulling back the curtains and peeking into the real outside world.

Halfway through class, I matched with IllinoisBoy in a new game of eight-ball pool. It was clear from the first shot that he was good, sinking three solid balls into separate pockets on the break. I was impressed and sat up straighter in my seat.

JerseyGirl09: ur pretty good at this

I didn't wait for his reply before taking my turn. I'd played this game before and wasn't bad myself. At my moment of release, he responded. My aim shifted, and I scratched, cursing under my breath before nervously peeking over my shoulder to see if the teacher had heard. Amanda, sitting to my left, didn't even bat an eye in my direction.

IllinoisBoy: not all im good at

My cheeks burned despite the chill of the room.

JerseyGirl09: want to put ur money where ur mouth is?

On his second shot, he only pocketed the one-ball, but it was enough for him to keep shooting until he missed. My knee bounced in anticipation of his response, waiting for him to finish his turn.

IllinoisBoy: i dont think u can handle it

I lifted my hand off my mouse and placed my fingertips on the keyboard, not bothering to start my turn. A smile tugged at the corners of my lips.

JerseyGirl09: oh i think i can
IllinoisBoy: prove it
JerseyGirl09: haha fine i will

I cleared all my striped balls, except the thirteen, and missed again when his message came through.

> **IllinoisBoy:** whats ur name Jersey?

A flash of heat spilled over me.

What's my name? No one on here asks for real names.

I watched him start his turn, lining up the cue to avoid my thirteen and attack his two remaining solids before aiming toward the eight-ball. His cue was drawn back, but he didn't release.

> **IllinoisBoy:** corner pocket
> **IllinoisBoy:** top left
> **IllinoisBoy:** not gonna tell me ur name?

The cue fired forward, and the eight-ball shot into the top left corner pocket. Game over.

> **JerseyGirl09:** good game
> **JerseyGirl09:** another?
> **IllinoisBoy:** sure

He broke again, leaving me time to debate giving him my real name.

> **JerseyGirl09:** how old r u IllinoisBoy?
> **IllinoisBoy:** 19

He answered in the middle of his turn, the clock running down against him.

JerseyGirl09: r u in college?
IllinoisBoy: yes

He shot and missed.

JerseyGirl09: was that on purpose?
IllinoisBoy: no ;)

I lined up before responding but didn't take the shot.

JerseyGirl09: 17
JerseyGirl09: in high school. senior year
IllinoisBoy: how did u kno thats what i
was going to ask next
JerseyGirl09: just a guess
IllinoisBoy: what do u do for fun Jersey

A few quick clicks of the mouse and I missed. I quietly rolled the name Jersey around on my tongue, exploring the feeling. I liked my new nickname.

JerseyGirl09: go to the city

I flinched internally, a sting like someone snapped a rubber band against my arm.

Why did I just say that?

I'd gone to the city but only with my grandfather and on special occasions. I was in no way a city girl, though I'd have liked to be. Nothing moved on the screen.

IllinoisBoy: thats a far drive for u
JerseyGirl09: not rly

```
JerseyGirl09: its about an hour
IllinoisBoy: nuh uh
IllinoisBoy: Chicago has to b 12 hrs at
least
JerseyGirl09: ohhhhhhhh no. i mean NYC
IllinoisBoy: so not THE city then
```

I leaned toward the screen and smiled, rereading the last few lines of our chat over and over while his cue darted across the screen, swinging around the table and clearing his solids.

For the next thirty minutes, the usual topics ensued: favorite subjects, hobbies, and what kids in his town did for fun on a Friday night. At some point, the conversation shifted in a personal direction to family, friends, and future aspirations. We had completely forgotten about the game and were engrossed in the flow of conversation. Before I knew it, class was over.

```
JerseyGirl09: Casey... my name is Casey
IllinoisBoy: nice to meet u Casey
JerseyGirl09: do u have AIM?
IllinoisBoy: yup
JerseyGirl09: talk to u 2night?
IllinoisBoy: sure
IllinoisBoy: 8pm
IllinoisBoy: i have a feeling ur better
than anything going on around here
JerseyGirl09: KCButterfly9
JerseyGirl09: find me
```

The second bell rang. Students poured into the room letting me know that for the first time in my life, I was late for my next class.

* * * * *

Several things about that last interaction were different.

Generally, my rule online was to steer clear of any topics that could link me back to real life... you know, in case of a serial killer on the other side of that screen. I never discussed my family or plans for the future—not college, not after college, nothing.

So why had I just told a stranger that I wanted to go to school in either New York or Philadelphia? That I thought I wanted to be an accountant or do something with numbers? That I wanted to get married and have four kids, two cats, and a dog? Why had I just provided my real screen name that eliminated the randomness of being able to click that tiny "X" at the top right of the screen and remain unsearchable? And more importantly, my very real name that ripped open any semblance of anonymity I had.

Naïvely, I gave these private pieces away because of the fluttering butterfly feeling in my stomach.

He saw me. The real me.

No one, outside of my parents, had ever cared or bothered to ask me about my hopes and dreams past high school. As far as I knew, not one of my friends was thinking that far ahead. Everyone I associated with daily was focused on their dress or date for the prom and how many scholarships they would get at graduation. I was the only kid I knew thinking about how big the world was.

What exists outside of this town? What is life like in college and after?

I only had one thought on my mind. What was my purpose in this life? I wanted to make an impact on this planet. I wasn't sure how, but I knew staying put wasn't it.

Maybe I was the weird one for fixating on these things right now. Whatever it was, this stranger was the only person in my life who unlocked my need to share this passion. He seemed to take a genuine interest in what I had to say and portrayed a sense of faith in my potential, all within the span of thirty minutes. It was a heady feeling—an ego trip with intense flirtatious undertones.

It made me feel a little like the first time I had candy as a kid. You know that jittery invincible sugar rush? It's the pull of a feeling you didn't know you wanted. A feeling you want again and stronger next time.

I think that's called addiction.

I should have known in that moment how this would end, but I ignored that needling sensation at the base of my skull that said maybe, just maybe, this was a bad idea.

Nah… I'm gonna do it anyway.

CHAPTER 3

My nerves fired off like electricity under my skin. Whether it was fear or excitement, I wasn't sure.

After school, I fought an internal battle. I had mixed feelings about my plan to reconnect with this boy. I questioned whether I daydreamed the entire thing staring out that window, blinded by the sun. Some part of me knew it was real but wondered if I'd made the connection out to be bigger than it was.

Is it one-sided?

Am I the only one feeling intrigued by our conversation and hungry for more?

Maybe I was so desperate for something to happen, for something to be different, that I mistook a normal conversation for something more.

For a while, I sat at my desk in front of a blank computer. I had built the desk with my own hands the previous summer under the guidance of my proud grandfather. My desk, in my purple room—purple walls, purple carpet, and purple bedding.

Purple was my teenage attempt at rebellion against pink, to prove I wasn't a little girl anymore. I tried, as every girl does at a certain age, to show my maturity by changing my environment and appearance. I'd switched out my frilly, lacey, flower-print bedspread in favor of a dark, heavy, velvet comforter around the same time my parents had let me move our family desktop to the privacy of my bedroom. That was about the same time the computer helped me discover that I didn't have to be the same person online as I was in real life. Where the real me never wore the right clothes or said the right things, too afraid of not fitting in, the screen was like a wall to block judgment. Since I couldn't be seen, I wouldn't be seen through. It gave me confidence.

I spent a lot of time chewing on my cuticles, glancing between the screen and the keyboard in front of me, second-guessing that confidence. Tucked into my desk chair, swimming in my oversized sweatpants and sweatshirt with my plain blondish-brown hair tied up in a messy bun, I debated whether to chicken out of our scheduled meet up. Maybe he wouldn't show up and then I'd feel humiliated at my own excitement.

I sucked in a breath and splayed my hands on the desk in front of me, my fingertips red and angry from being worried at. Unfolding from my chair, I caught my reflection in the mirror across the room. I padded over, peeling off the sweatshirt on the way, and tossed it on the bench below my windowsill. At my dresser, I turned to the side, straightened my back and shoulders, and sucked in my stomach. I admired the lines of my body, my head tilted sideways. Though I wasn't tiny, thin, and perfect, my strong thighs, trim arms, and long neck were something to work with. A smile spread across my face, reaching my green eyes. I tugged my bottom lip between my teeth.

He'll show up.

I felt it vibrating through my body, humming through my blood. The connection had to be real. I convinced myself I'd take the leap. If nothing else, I just wanted confirmation that I wasn't making up some girlish fantasy. I needed to know there really was someone else out there who felt just as stuck as me. That this simple, small-town life wasn't enough. I stared into my own eyes before crossing back and tucking my leg under me in the chair.

Resting my hand on the mouse, I squeezed my eyes shut and clicked Sign On.

I was logged in.

I planned to go into this with attitude and a clear head, no matter what happened. I would assume I had made up "the spark." If it was there the first time, surely it could reignite on its own, right?

Right.

* * * * *

On Friday nights, I had unlimited time on the internet. The weekend meant my 10 p.m. lights-out rule didn't apply. I was fortunate that my parents trusted me to be reasonable. I wasn't a goody-two-shoes, but I was a good girl. Everyone knew it. They just didn't know the real me, the darker wild child, clawing her way from the inside out.

Instant Messenger announced my arrival with the sound of a door creaking open. I scrolled through my buddy list to see who was online.

Some kids had already put up one of the typical away messages:

don't cry because it's over, smile because it happened
Cool kid code for "out at a party be back later."

two roads || **diverged in a wood, and I— ||**
~~I took the one less traveled by~~
Art kid code for "hanging at the local coffee shop."

And my personal favorite:

School. Home. Out. Cell's hot if you are ;)
No code needed.

I approached the end of my online list, and it dawned on me.

Only me.

Only I had given my name and screen name. I had no idea how to find my mystery man. All the confidence I had just built up drained from my body, leaving my cheeks flushed and my skin prickled with goose bumps. I shivered, one quick movement that rattled my chair. Most people didn't duplicate screen names between platforms. I didn't know how to even begin finding him. So, I waited. I could hear the seconds tick by on the watch thrown on my dresser. I listened for what felt like hours. It was already ten minutes later than we had agreed. That was it. Ten minutes staring at my reflection may have been all it took to miss my chance. I'd have no way of knowing. I pressed the heels of my palms into my eye sockets.

"My life is officially over," I muttered with a dramatic sigh.

But then it happened. The sound of a message received.

```
itsyourboyybrett has sent you an IM. Do
you want to read it?
```

This was the easiest question of my life so far. One hundred percent unbelievably, undeniably, yes.

```
itsyourboyybrett: hey its Brett
```

This must be IllinoisBoy.
Oh, so his name is Brett?
Alright, Casey, here you go. Act normal. Act natural. This is no different than your usual chitchat.

```
KCbutterfly9: im sorry who?
```

CHAPTER 4

So much for playing it cool.
Pause.
Silence.
Yup. I've messed up already.

> **KCbutterfly9:** Oh Brett! jeez its been a
> while...what like 5 hours :P
> **itsyourboyybrett:** haha i almost forgot ur
> an hour ahead of me. could have missed ya
> **KCbutterfly9:** ah ur right. i could have
> gotten bored waiting and forgotten about u
> **itsyourboyybrett:** good u didnt
> **KCbutterfly9:** nah...ur stuck with me now

Pause.
Silence.
No response.
My brows pulled together tightly, my eyes narrowed, and my heart dropped. I was positive my face was squeezed into a grimace. I looked to the ceiling, attempting to recall our exchange from earlier today.
We had such great chemistry.
I looked back to the unmoving screen. No new messages, not even a notification of him typing.

Maybe I did make up that spark. It was only a half-hour conversation. I can't remember all we talked about while I was in class. The words were just pouring out of me. I didn't even have to—

I looked up suddenly at the new message notification.

> **itsyourboyybrett:** so Casey
> now that we've thoroughly failed at this
> second encounter
> y dont we start again shall we?
> **KCbutterfly9:** u read my mind
> i dont know whats gotten into me
> id like that
> **itsyourboyybrett:** so tell me what a girl
> like u is doing sitting in front of a
> computer on a friday nite?
> **KCbutterfly9:** well u see
> there was this guy i met today playing
> an online game and he really piqued my
> interest
> so much so that we didnt even finish
> playing
> we set up a time to chat again tonight
> and i've just been waiting for his grand
> entrance
> also slightly pissed that i lost our
> unfinished game and wouldnt mind a rematch
> ;)
> and you?

I slapped my palm flat on my desk, cursing myself. *Why am I so nervous? Play a little hard to get.*

itsyourboyybrett: and what game would that be?

KCbutterfly9: 8-ball pool

itsyourboyybrett: solid choice ;)

i like that one too

are u any good?

KCbutterfly9: i wouldnt say im a pro but i do alright

the site i play on makes it super easy. theres leader lines so ur basically guaranteed to sink the ball every shot unless of course u get out of hand on the power behind it

He already knows all of this.

itsyourboyybrett: what about in real life?

KCbutterfly9: my uncle has a pool table

itsyourboyybrett: so u dont need those leader lines after all

unless of course

he breaks out the bumpers for u

KCbutterfly9: haha he probably should

lets just say im still learning…

maybe i just havent found the

right teacher ;)

itsyourboyybrett: im pretty good on a table but ive probably had more practice than u :P

KCbutterfly9: aw come on now

that's not fair. just because you've been alive longer!

itsyourboyybrett: touché

well i hope ur mystery man hasnt kept u
waiting too long

KCbutterfly9: eh just long enough to be
fashionably late by any normal standards

im just exceptionally prompt

itsyourboyybrett: either way, lucky me

patience seems to be one of ur strong
suits

KCbutterfly9: depends on what im being
patient for

speaking of… u never answered my question

itsyourboyybrett: what question :)

KCbutterfly9: short term memory loss much?
it was like 30 seconds ago

itsyourboyybrett: i don't know what ur
talking about

KCbutterfly9: well i was telling u about
this boy I met that I seem to be wasting a
perfectly good friday night waiting for

itsyourboyybrett: right

now I remember

u asked me my own question

I deflated, settling back into my chair.
So much for originality.

itsyourboyybrett: its an interesting story
really

i met this fascinating girl today and shes
been on my mind ever since

```
i couldnt wait to get another chance to
talk to her
```

My stomach's doing somersaults. I perked up, leaning forward, letting my fingers dance across the keys.

```
KCbutterfly9: so u couldnt wait to talk to
me? :D
and what is it you were hoping to
talk about?
itsyourboyybrett: to be honest, i have no
interest in a rematch
KCbutterfly9: aw boo. then u have to give
me a shot at redemption somehow
itsyourboyybrett: okay lets play a
different game
KCbutterfly9: okay
what game did u have in mind?
wait a minute
no
i asked u another question
either u really do have a short memory or
ur very good at throwing me off track
itsyourboyybrett: maybe i just like it
when u catch me distracting u
KCbutterfly9: oh sweetheart, i'll call u
out every time
itsyourboyybrett: not what I meant but
fair point
KCbutterfly9: thank u
```

I winced.

What the hell am I thanking him for? He's right. I am distracted.

KCButterfly9: so back to my point...
we've covered that im an only child
itsyourboyybrett: and im from "the middle
of no-where"
KCbutterfly9: yeah we get it
the farm boy with the huge family thinks
im a big city girl :P
what are ur 8 brothers and sisters names
again? Joe Bob and Jamie Lynn have to be
in there somewhere ;)
itsyourboyybrett: easy...
if i remember correctly, u like to read
and want to learn French?
ya know, just checking cuz short term
memory and all...
KCbutterfly9: oui, j'adore le Français
and if i remember
u have no interest in school whatsoever
would prefer to play hockey
Oh... and u don't believe in Myspace :/
itsyourboyybrett: show off
KCbutterfly9: im a competitive dancer. dont
take it personally
its all about giving a good show
speaking of shows... u remember i love the
city right?
itsyourboyybrett: a point of contention

KCbutterfly9: the one and only city, is and always will be, New York

itsyourboyybrett: nope

KCbutterfly9: u can keep Chicago and ur Black Hawks
they'll never measure up

itsyourboyybrett: all im saying is ur selling urself short

KCButterfly9: oh yea? whys that?

itsyourboyybrett: u wanna be an accountant when u love to show off?
somethings wrong there

KCbutterfly9: clearly i was wrong about ur memory
u were paying attention

itsyourboyybrett: clearly

KCbutterfly9: so my pitfall isnt New York? u admit its the better city? just trying to clear that up…

A minute passed. He's typing. I brought the edge of my thumb to my teeth and bit down. He stopped typing. My knee bounced, and I clasped my hands, resting them in my lap to stop from fidgeting. Another minute. I curled my fingers into fists and scratched at the itch in the center of my palms. Still nothing. I brought my hands to the keys and flexed my fingers before pulling them away and replacing them in the exact same position.

KCButterfly9: im not selling myself short
im the total package

maybe someone just doesnt know what hes
got

AND

just because there's no such thing as
creative accounting doesn't mean I cant
invent it ;)

itsyourboyybrett: yea good luck with that…
cat lady

KCbutterfly9: alright

don't hate

i know u prefer dogs

itsyourboyybrett: they're just better

KCbutterfly9: agree to disagree?

itsyourboyybrett: sure

KCbutterfly9: at least we've got one thing
we agree on

itsyourboyybrett: what?

this town is boring as shit

KCbutterfly9: there's got to be more out
there

itsyourboyybrett: this just isn't enough

My heart erupted in a flurry of sparks.

CHAPTER 5

June passed by in a blur, as it usually did at the start of summer. Despite being the last one before college, not much was different from any other year. The days blended into nights, and weekdays were indistinguishable from weekends. Only slight parental supervision made the distinction of a weekday.

I spent my days lazily waking up whenever I wanted. Most mornings I'd grab a bowl of cinnamon-sugar cereal before heading across the field to Leila's house. We'd spend all day with the rest of the neighborhood kids at the pool, lounging in the grass, or in someone's basement playing Nintendo64. Some weekends there was the occasional house party, but mostly, every day was much of the same.

The only thing different this summer was Brett. I spent almost every night on the computer talking to him.

He made me feel like me. The me who was free of rules, obligations, and expectations. He wanted me to feel alive. He couldn't see me but he imagined that I lit up when I was talking to him, and he was right. I could feel the laces of my good-girl corset easing with each new night. My lips loosened at every conversation, my boldness spilling out like paint from a can that's been knocked over—*messy*. He saw me, and I wanted him to see all of me.

I hadn't yet worked up the courage to tell Leila, despite her incessant comments about my yawning every day. It wasn't like me to keep things from her. Come to think of it, I hadn't told anyone about my online life and especially not about this random guy I met. Something told me I wanted to keep it that way. I wanted him all to myself in our perfect little world. Apart from being tired, it seemed Leila couldn't tell anything else was going on in my life, and I decided not to open that can of judgment.

Sunday morning, July 3rd, I woke up particularly late after having a marathon of a conversation with Brett. We started on the topic of 4th of July plans and fireworks and ended up exploring the concept of pet names. I argued that it was a way for guys to cheat and not get caught. When you call every girl "honey," you never call them the wrong name. His philosophy was the opposite. Pet names were special, almost sacred, shared between two people. By the end of the night, he was calling me baby and I didn't object. I didn't make it to Leila's until after 1 p.m. Her brother answered the door and informed me she'd already gone down to the pool with Erin.

"To see if Tanner and Greg were there," he scoffed.

I flushed hotter than I should have in the heat of the afternoon.

I was slightly hurt that Leila had left without me but more jealous that she went with Erin. Erin had just moved to our condo complex during the middle of this school year and entered our scene as the "cool new girl." Of course, Leila was drawn to her immediately—a new challenge—and they became fast friends. Erin was almost a year older in age, several in experience. Boy crazy was an understatement. But she had the body for it, a perfect hourglass, combined with exotic blue eyes and thick wavy black hair. She basked in the attention she drew—especially Tanner and Greg's attention. Most of the time, I didn't mind. I knew my place. I wasn't that girl, at least not in everyone else's eyes. If she wanted to be, then good for her. I was just happy to be part of the group. Right now, I had all the attention I needed from Brett. It only got to me when I started to feel like Leila was slipping away. I found out a few nights they'd gone out with the boys without even asking me.

Or maybe they had asked.

I couldn't remember if I'd just turned them down.

I raced back to my house, threw on my plain black halter-top bikini, and glanced around my room for my beach bag. I caught a glimpse of Tanner's window through my own. From my bedroom window, I looked out across the brook stretching through my backyard. It was full of smooth stones, slick with moss where the tadpoles lived, and a bridge crossing to the backyards of the cul-de-sac homes.

Leila and I had known Tanner and Greg for years. They were part of the condo crew we grew up with, catching frogs in the shallow water every summer. I could see the light of Tanner's bedroom window when my curtains were open and I laid my head slightly more left on my pillow at night. He and I lived the closest, just across the bridge. We used to draw signs for each other before we reached the age where his older brother picked on him for it. Around the same time, Tanner decided he was the shit because that same older brother sometimes let him hang out with the older kids. Unfortunately, the cockiness stuck. I guessed he'd bulked up a bit this past year, the muscle complementing his olive skin and hazel eyes, but still, he wasn't the Greek god he thought himself for all these years. We'd all gotten over his narcissism quickly. It was more endearing at this point.

The three of us met Greg one summer at the clubhouse pool. He and his parents lived in the stretch of homes in the lower section of our complex. His house was the closest to the pool and the most frequently raided for midday snacks when we needed a break from the sun. His mom caught on and kept the pantry stocked with that giant variety box of chips, pretzel rods, and chocolate chip cookies. He was also the farthest away from the neighborhood action and spent most summer nights crashing on Tanner's couch.

Greg was an only child like me and started out just as shy, though he didn't need to be. He was tall and blond, with the most gorgeous blue eyes. He was kind, gentle, and smart too, but hid that from almost everyone in favor of imitating Tanner's ego.

I shook my head against the thought of our childhood, realizing my hand was pressed against my chest, and spotted my bag. I stuffed my towel and sunscreen through the opening. A familiar sensation flared through my body as I ran downstairs and out the door.

Not today, Erin.

Before I even got to the hill leading down to the clubhouse, I heard the high-pitched, flirty girl screams that were meant more to encourage than discourage the action going on. I had a quick thought to go home and wait for Leila to come find me later—*I can check online for Brett*—but pushed it aside when I heard everyone laughing. I rounded the corner of the clubhouse, passed through the chain-link fence into the pool area, and heard the screams again before I caught the ending glimpse of Greg whipping a towel at Leila's ass as she ran away into Erin's arms.

A couple of summers earlier, Greg and I had spent almost every day together. Leila had been busy. Greg had noticed that I wasn't around with the rest of the group without her bringing me along and knocked on my door. I had still been in my PJs with a pretzel between my teeth and embarrassment on my face when I swung it open. He just laughed and brushed passed me to come inside.

When school started that year, he'd joined the football team, become one of the jocks, and "forgot" he was one of my best friends. I fumbled with the memory, concentrating too hard on the resident sign-in sheet. Peeking through the gaps in my hair, I watched him now chasing after Leila and Erin and felt my chest squeeze. Something inside me stirred at the scene.

One of these days, I'll tell Leila that I'm not too fond of Erin. Maybe I'll even tell Erin to her face.

I almost turned around without even bothering to say hello when Greg noticed me.

"Hey! It's Case... Casey's here!"

I must have flushed bright red and looked away because he ran over as I was making my way to an empty chair where I saw Leila's bag and had the audacity to whip the towel at *my ass*. I squealed but caught the devious sparkle in his eye and started laughing as he jogged back to the group. When he got there, Leila enthusiastically waved me over after linking her arm through Greg's. The familiar sense of belonging warmed me, and I pushed aside any thoughts of going home.

We spent the day at the pool until they kicked us out to decorate and prepare for the 4th of July festivities the next night. When the streetlights came on, we headed back up the winding cement sidewalk that connected the pool to Tanner's house to sneak his parents' wine coolers and a few cans of beer they had stocked for their annual party. Our contraband hidden in our towels, we crossed the bridge to my house, not bothering to keep our chatter to a low volume and parked ourselves under my deck. I was the only one of us with a bi-level. The space on the ground floor under the steps was large enough to host a party on its own. My parents set it up with our summer furniture every year on Memorial Day. Like clockwork.

Everyone paired off, leaving me by myself in the lone single chair, as usual. Greg looked past Leila and caught my eye, his fingers expertly pulling the tab on his beer. The snap and fizz of popped cans echoed through the night. I nervously shushed everyone, pointing up in the air through the bottom of the deck to remind them it wasn't quite late enough for my parents to be sleeping with the holiday tomorrow.

"Oh, come on, good girl," Erin taunted. "What are they going to do… ground you?"

I simmered in my seat, trying to come up with the perfect retort but couldn't. I let out a breath and tried to relax, taking a sip of the too-sweet wine cooler. The cool drink eased down into my system, encouraging me to take another, larger swig.

As the booze kicked in, the laughter kicked up a notch. Tanner and Greg had no trouble making fools of themselves, and Erin was encouraging of their antics. Occasionally, I glanced up through the slats of the deck at the window to my room, thinking I'd seen the glow from my computer screen, but realized it was just the reflection of the moon. With an empty bottle by the leg of my chair and one half drunk in my hand, I caught myself trapped in my head.

I could be that girl.

I know these boys like the back of my hand. I could push their buttons, tickle their funny bones, stroke their egos just as well.

A wind rustled the willow tree that stood firmly in the middle of the yard, the branches scratching against one another. The breeze blew through our little circle, making me shiver.

It was late.

I sat in my single chair with my arms wrapped around myself, my towel tucked around my legs. The wine coolers had gotten to my head. Despite the wind, I was feeling warm and sleepy and couldn't fix my eyes to focus on the group around me. Someone was talking about something sexual, a scandalous escapade of some older girls from our town. Probably Tanner. I glanced at Leila, who was blatantly trying to keep Greg's attention, though he didn't exactly seem enthused. She'd thrown her legs over his and was attempting to cuddle up closer.

That was enough for me.

Swallowing the rotten taste in my mouth, I tried my best at convincing everyone I was just tired while insisting they stay and finish out their night. After slinking into the house and up the stairs quietly, I hopped online.

> **itsyourboyybrett:** hi beautiful
>
> **KCbutterfly9:** hey you
>
> **itsyourboyybrett:** i almost thought u forgot about me
>
> **KCbutterfly9:** never. just couldnt get away quick enough

A slow smile spread across my face.
Just a quick chat before bed.

CHAPTER 6

You'd think it would've gotten boring. The endless nights in front of a screen, the only sound the clicking of keys and a soft laugh cutting through the silence every once in a while. It didn't.

Talking to Brett consumed my focus.

I hadn't crossed that field to Leila's in weeks. I hadn't gone to the pool or to play video games. I didn't even hear the chatting and laughing outside of my open window anymore. I was oblivious.

I fixated on calculating how much time I'd be able to spend online after my parents went to bed and before I'd be too sleep-deprived to function the next day. I only needed enough energy to pick up around the house. Just enough to finish my chores before my mom and dad came home. All the while, thoughts of Brett absorbed every free moment of my waking life and occupied my dream world.

It was almost like a game.

What can I do to make him want to stay, to not want me to leave?

It didn't matter how tired I was. I needed more. More meant winning, and everyone liked to win.

We spent most of our time with me spilling my guts. He didn't volunteer much about himself, just his "brown eyes, brown hair, and trim body." Maybe I just wouldn't let him get a word in. I was usually excited and so distracted daydreaming about my new obsession that I couldn't stay on one train of thought long enough to push a level deeper. It didn't matter, though. I loved that he wanted to listen to me, and the words he did choose to share landed somewhere deep within me. It was the constant thrill of the chase. The next question, the next answer, the next minute, the next hour. He kept me coming back for more.

> **KCButterfly9:** *Gossip Girl* is what got me into reading
> **itsyourboyybrett:** whys that
> **KCButterfly9:** Nate Archibald is hot :P
> **itsyourboyybrett:** come on
> **KCButterfly9:** what? its true
> **itsyourboyybrett:** thats not the real reason is it

I don't know why, but I was still shocked he could see through me. He picked apart my answers the same as every other time I tried to cover the truth with my poorly constructed attempts at humor.

> **KCButterfly9:** idk i guess not
> **itsyourboyybrett:** so what is it
> **KCButterfly9:** it made me feel like i could be one of the popular girls
> ya know?
> Serena is so kind but shes pretty and everyone loves her

```
i guess i felt like… i can't have it in
the real world but i could pretend to be
the Serena in the books
```
itsyourboyybrett: `well if u were in my`
`high school i guarantee u would have been`
`popular`

I rolled my eyes almost involuntarily.

KCButterly9: `haha sure`
itsyourboyybrett: `im serious`
KCButterfly9: `if u say so`
itsyourboyybrett: `why couldnt i have met`
`you sooner`

My heart pounded and a giddiness rose from my stomach to my throat, splitting my face in a smile.

KCButterfly9: `that would have been nice`
itsyourboyybrett: `nice?`
`that's all i get?`

I typed out a salacious response detailing what else I'd like to give him, but slowly hit backspace until it was gone. I wasn't feeling bold enough.

KCButterfly9: `what would u have done if i`
`went to ur high school`
itsyourboyybrett: `i doubt we would have`
`known each other`
`id probably just have watched u walk by`
`wishing i could talk to u`

```
KCButterfly9: nah thats not true
id have seen u
itsyourboyybrett: and talked to me?
KCButterfly9: of course
itsyourboyybrett: would we have dated?
KCButterfly9: haha Brett!
itsyourboyybrett: what?
KCButterfly9: idk
itsyourboyybrett: u could have been my
girlfriend
```

Heat surged through my veins, coloring my cheeks.
His girlfriend.

Now I had a new daydream. What would it be like to belong to someone?

```
KCButterfly9: i would have liked that i
think
itsyourboyybrett: id have shown you off
KCButterfly9: is that all? ;)
itsyourboyybrett: no its not
KCButterfly9: tell me what else
```

He must have known what he was doing. Maybe he'd done this before with other girls. Thinking about the possibility that I was sharing him set fire to my jealousy.

Brett was just so different from anyone I'd ever met.

* * * * *

By the end of July, I was truly addicted and tired of waiting for the sun to set and the screen to glow through my darkened room to be able to talk to him. I had a cell phone but was still on the pay-per-text message plan with no long-distance calling. There was no easy way to use my cell without drawing unwanted attention to my newfound hobby when the bill came.

I threw a tantrum outside of the Verizon store trying to convince my mom to upgrade me to one of the shiny new Blackberry phones that had internet, unlimited messaging, and a camera. When she asked why I *needed* one so badly, I made up some excuse about everyone getting them for school. She didn't buy that. I quickly pivoted to boasting about its safety benefits. She could constantly check that I was okay while away at college—call, text, and email. If I was going to bend the truth, at least I'd try to be considerate of what mattered most to her. Eventually, she conceded.

We'd finally be able to talk whenever we wanted. More importantly, I'd *finally* get to hear his voice and see the face I'd been dreaming about.

The first time I called him from the comfort of my bed was around 11 p.m. on a warm Thursday night in early August. My dad would be getting up for work in a couple of hours, so I needed to be quiet. The room was so dark that late at night without the light of the computer screen. The moon wasn't bright enough to provide its usual spotlight through my window, splashing light on the floor. With my pillows surrounding me, I tucked myself into the corner of my bed, knees bent, leaning my head against the thin wall covering the bones of our house. I squeezed the phone between my hands, bringing the cuticle of my thumb to my teeth.

I was more nervous than the first time I logged in to chat with him. Nervous that my parents would hear me and walk in. Nervous for what Brett would think of my voice. Nervous

I wouldn't be able to keep up my same online persona without the ability to edit my responses. The backbone of my confidence, the screen, was going away.

He answered after three rings.

"Hello, Casey." His voice was smooth and low, wrapping around me like silk sheets.

"Hi," I whispered, and my voice went up an octave in an attempt to sound cute.

"Come on, Casey. It's me." He broke the ice.

I giggled, took a deep breath, and started over. "Hi, Brett. I knew I needed your voice in my life."

He laughed softly. "Really does it for you, huh?"

"Can't believe I've been missing it the last, what, two months?"

"Almost three," he corrected.

I smiled, warmth resonating across my skin. From then, everything just felt comfortable, easy. We talked long enough that I fell asleep, the phone still on my cheek when I woke up the next morning. For the first night in a long time, I slept deeply, not moving, and woke up feeling refreshed. I looked at the tiny screen and my first picture of him appeared in a message he'd sent at 3:17 a.m.

His face was slightly turned in profile, nose tilted up just barely. His dark brown, piercing eyes stared back at me, and a smirk played on his lips.

I think if he would have shown teeth, the smirk would have seemed dangerous.

His hair was long for a short haircut but didn't look intentional. Like he'd waited just a little too long for his next trim. The strength of his jaw was begging me to drag my fingers along it. I was partially disappointed that the photo showed only shoulders and above. I'd waited this long and wanted to see all of him. It looked like his shoulders were broad, but he didn't look bulky. I couldn't quite tell the rest of his build under the white hoodie with the signature moose splashed across the front.

Adrenaline rushed through my body like water through a hose that'd just been unkinked. I took a little more time getting myself together.

Putting on makeup for the first time in forever felt scandalous. I studied my face in the mirror, making sure to blend the purple eyeshadow just right to help my green eyes pop. I pinched my cheeks, looking for that bright pink color that could be confused as modest blushing and scrunched my long wavy hair with a touch of gel, making the curls more defined but not crunchy. I picked out my favorite black tank top that gave me the appearance of cleavage I didn't have. Then I arranged my best subtle duck-face pout, accentuating my already plump lips, sucked in my stomach tighter than I ever had before, and held the phone above my head, taking a downward shot that captured the length of my body. I signed the picture with "Xoxo" and hit send.

I couldn't wait for his response. All morning and into the afternoon, I checked for messages every couple of minutes.

Why isn't he texting me back?

I craved his response like a swimmer kicking for the surface as their breath ran out.

CHAPTER 7

Being the oldest of his siblings, he was on baby duty more often than I realized. His youngest brother was just two years old, and during the summer while he was home from college, his mother let go of the hired babysitter in favor of one that was built-in and free. He sent me a video of his brother as he came through the door earlier this summer, Max toddling into his arms, gabbing excitedly about Brett being home.

I had no idea this side of him existed.

This part of his life had never entered our conversations before. Late at night, it was just him and me.

We figured it out and quickly got into a back-and-forth rhythm, learning each other's schedules. No matter what was going on for either of us, he was my first good morning and my last goodnight. I couldn't get enough of him.

We still spent hours on the computer, as there wasn't always a good time for us to speak, and typing was easier and quicker on a computer than the compact cell phone keyboard. Sometimes the noise of his full house would be too much, or it would be too late, and I knew my dad would wake up and hear me.

Regardless of platform, our conversations became more frequent and intimate. I threw all caution to the wind and bared myself to him, sharing my deepest thoughts and darkest fears through late-night whispers and sultry images. He told me things he'd never told anyone, confiding in me, professing that our relationship was special, like nothing he'd ever felt before. He said I wore him down and stripped him bare.

I don't know why I wasn't more nervous when we crossed the line into sexual content. It wasn't like I had much to go off. The only experience I had was from the fourth grade when Tanner kissed me under his dining room table while playing hide and seek with Leila and Greg. That and the R-rated movies I watched at Leila's house. Her parents weren't as strict as mine and we watched whatever we wanted—*Dirty Dancing* and *Grease* among the favorites. I assumed nothing would ever happen for Brett and me in real life.

What's the harm in a little flirty conversation?

Late on August 18th, I was huddled under the covers, cradling the phone close. I remember the date because it was Leila's birthday, and I'd reluctantly been out with our neighborhood crew until after midnight—the first time I'd spent a night with them in a long time. It was one of those random crisp summer nights where the sky is crystal clear, full of stars, and the moon is almost as bright as the sun.

I heard a rasp in Brett's voice that I learned to mean he'd been thinking about me for a while. He could barely wait for me to finish telling him about my night before we dove straight into the deep end.

I listened to him describe the way he'd thread his fingers through my hair, holding the base of my skull tightly and massaging my lips with his. He'd graze my bottom lip with his tongue when he wanted me to open and let him in. I squeezed my legs tightly against the pulsing sensation his words drew from my body. In my t-shirt and too tiny underwear, I would press the length of my body against his, wanting every inch of skin contact. His hands would detangle from my hair and wander across the skin of my back and bottom, leaving tickling traces of him. I could almost feel his weight on top me, the thin fabric of my panties the only thing separating me from the swell of him.

I actually sighed into the darkness of my room, eliciting a low vibrating moan from the other side of the phone. I pictured falling asleep in his strong arms, his warmth keeping me comfortable and safe, before telling him I wanted nothing more than for him to be my first everything.

My eyelids were heavy, and I couldn't keep them open any longer. As we were about to end our night, a thought came to light in my mind.

"I have to tell you something."

"What's that, baby?" he asked, his voice low and sleepy.

I hesitated, not sure that I had the confidence to form the words. "I don't know how to say it."

"So just say it."

An unexpected tear formed at the crease of my eye and rolled down my cheek, dampening the pillow. "I think I love you, Brett."

The line was silent for so long I thought we might have gotten disconnected. After a minute of silence, I was about to attempt to recover.

"I love you too, Casey." I heard a tightness in his voice that was never there before and a hitch in his swallow.

"Are you crying?" I asked incredulously.

"Yes," he replied with an intake of breath and a small sigh. *Who is this guy?*

He'd never been this soft before. This was an entirely new side of him for me to learn.

And I fell harder.

* * * * *

A package arrived at my house one afternoon less than a week later from the return address B. Caviar in Illinois. Manila, a little bigger than the size of a standard piece of paper and padded. I felt a hard lump in the center, but the rest just felt cushiony. My body tingled in surprise as I bolted up the stairs, attempting to avoid my parents and any questions. Once behind the privacy of my bedroom door, I gingerly sank onto my bed, laying the package beside me and picking up my phone.

MESSAGE: BRETT

Casey: omg what is it?

Brett: open it baby

Gliding my index finger into the thick envelope, my heart thundered in my chest so loudly I could hear it. It was difficult to breathe, and my fingers trembled. I reached into the open envelope and realized it wasn't padded—I felt cloth. Bunching the material, I slid a navy-blue t-shirt out onto my lap and felt a hard, square box in the center. Unfolding the shirt, I pulled it to my face and breathed deeply, inhaling the scent of desire. The box was left resting on my thighs.

It was discreet, ordinary, black. Closing my eyes, I lifted off the top and let my fingers dip inside. My lids opened at the feeling of a smaller felt box.

Jewelry.

MESSAGE: BRETT

Casey: what is it? what is it? what is it?

Brett: just open it

Brett: ur gonna like it

I cradled the box in my lap and looked up to the ceiling, taking a shaky breath. On the exhale, I opened the box and glanced down at a solid gold ring. On the inside of the top was a handwritten note with two words: *Till Death?*

MESSAGE: BRETT

Casey: omg Brett

Brett: do u want to be mine?

Casey: yes!

Brett: forever baby?

Casey: forever and ever

Brett: then I'll keep you

Casey: promise?

Brett: i promise

Brett: i love you

Casey: i love you

Brett: computer later?

Casey: always

Brett: good girl

I slid the cool metal onto the ring finger of my left hand and stared at it, thinking about what excuse I'd tell my parents. My palms started to sweat while my mind raced into blank space. I pulled it off and stowed it safely back in its box, deciding I'd wear it at night and keep it hidden in its home during the day until I could figure out an answer to the inevitable questions.

That night, Brett and I promised we would be true to each other. There would be no one else… there *could* be no one else.

He was my twin flame, the other half of my soul. He challenged me, taught me, and loved me in a way I'd never experienced. Before falling asleep that night, I slipped inside his shirt, surrounding myself with his scent. It was different, not something I'd ever come across before. Somehow, it was still familiar and comforting, like the scent of my father's Old Spice on his pillow when I would sleep in my parents' bed after a nightmare as a child. I closed my eyes, feeling his warmth wrapped around me, my fingers gingerly twirling the ring.

This will not be easy to hide, nor explain if I'm caught with it on.

I didn't think there was any way for me to explain, to make anyone understand how I could have this intense connection with someone I'd never physically met before.

Within days, we started seriously discussing being together for real. My mind crawled with a sensation that told me I wasn't sure I wanted to actually meet him face-to-face. Maybe it would ruin what we had. Maybe I wouldn't be that same person I was behind my screens.

Is it too much too soon?

He said it would all be okay once we were together. People would see us, and it would make sense. It would be easier to explain that way.

My emotions trumped any logic when his voice swam through my mind. I didn't know how long it took, but I didn't think it was much time before he wore down my barriers and somewhat convinced me I needed to make this happen. I researched a few routes to drive to Chicago, looked into the cost of plane tickets, wrote down a few scripts to help me navigate telling my parents. The promise of his lips on mine was enough to push me to the edge of my comfort zone to find a way to make this happen. I felt like I needed him to breathe.

A broken record skipped over and over in my head.

If I could just have him for real.

CHAPTER 8

Mom tugged the shades open and let the blinding light spill into the room across my face. I squeezed my eyes tightly against the brightness, pulling the covers over my head, and groaned.

"*Mom...* What time is it?"

"Rise and shine, sweetheart! It's just after 11 a.m.," she cooed.

"Too early," I croaked and rolled over, taking the comforter with me.

I stuffed both hands under my pillow, propping my head, and pressed them together, getting comfortable. My eyelids flew open. I'd been wearing Brett's t-shirt and ring to bed every night this week. Mom and Dad were up and out every day before I rolled out of bed. Never once did I have to worry about waking up and stashing my new belongings, but yesterday was Friday.

"Now, young lady. You haven't gotten out of bed before noon any day this summer. What's gotten into you?"

"Nothing, Mom, I'm just tired!" I snapped.

I heard the floorboards whine against each other, muffled by the carpet just outside of my bedroom door and knew what was coming next.

"That's no way to speak to your mother," Dad boomed. I couldn't tell if he was angry or just throwing his weight behind Mom's accusing tone. "Apologize."

"Fine. Fine. Sorry, Mom."

"That's better. Now get up. We're going up to the lake."

My inner child perked up—we'd been going there for years—and I forgot myself, throwing back the edge of the blanket, putting my worn new t-shirt on display.

"To see the airplanes?" I asked.

Mom's almond-shaped brown eyes widened, and her eyebrows rose in surprise before she collected herself. I was impressed she was able to catch herself without a full reaction.

"It's a perfect clear day for them to be flying, just a little bit of wind. Come on, let's go," Dad exclaimed, as excited as a little boy, and continued down the stairs.

I looked away from Mom and pulled the covers up under my chin, exposing my fingers from the knuckles down.

Mistake number two.

Quickly pulling my left hand down, I shifted my focus to her face, waiting for her to say something... anything.

"New shirt?" A smile crept onto her face.

My mind raced, grasping for some semblance of an explanation. And then it clicked.

"I spilled on my dress the other night at Leila's birthday. Tanner lent it to me. I just grabbed the first thing I could find from the pile last night." I prayed my cheeks weren't blushing to give away my lie.

"Tanner, huh?" She winked with the entire left half of her face. I couldn't help but laugh.

"Please, Mom. You know it's not like that."

"Oh, no? I remember you two in fourth grade. Don't think Anette didn't tell me about you two under the dining room table."

Mortification took over my face and I was thankful. At least it covered my terrible attempt at a lie. She smiled and patted the end of the bed by my feet.

"I was beginning to wonder if you and Leila had a fight." She paused. A wrinkle formed between her brows and the edges of her lips tugged down almost imperceptibly. "You've barely been outside all summer."

Really? I haven't been that bad.

Leila checked in at first, when I didn't make it out for 4th of July or the rest of the month. For the first time in my life, I lied to Leila and made up excuses that I was busy with my parents. I didn't need anything other than Brett's near constant attention in my life. After I went out for her birthday, she stopped bothering to ask why I wouldn't come out. I wasn't surprised Mom thought we were in a fight. It'd happened before between us. Sometimes we fought like sisters.

"I've just been caught up," I whispered.

"College nerves?"

College. I'm going to college in less than a month. And orientation is... What day is it? That has to be happening soon.

I was thrilled when I received my Welcome Package earlier this summer. I wanted to register for the first available orientation weekend, eager to immerse myself with the people and places that would take me away. I tried to tell Brett about my acceptance to Drexel in Philadelphia and all the associated activities, but the timing was never right. Now, somehow months had gone by in our cozy bubble of just the two of us and we still hadn't broached the subject.

I sighed. "Exactly."

"Aren't you excited to go to orientation next weekend?"

Next weekend!

I tried to mask the shock and kept my face under control.

"Absolutely. I'm really looking forward to seeing the city again," I stated evenly.

"Oh! It'll be so much fun. Meeting all new people, being in a new place, new things to see, new food." She adjusted her tone lower, giving me the side eye. "Just don't be going out drinking all the time… or don't tell your father." Her eyes brightened, and she beamed at me.

I wanted to be excited. Somewhere deep down, I was still itching for the thrill of getting out. But doubt and fear clouded my excitement.

What will I tell Brett?

What will he say?

A thought, almost like the cartoon version of a lightbulb, dawned on me. He'd already started college. He had to understand. Relief spread through me slowly like the sun thawing thin ice, and my lips curled involuntarily.

"I won't tell if you don't." I winked, and we giggled conspiratorially.

"Why don't you see about patching things up with Leila tomorrow? I'm sure they'll all be out playing manhunt or something. They have every other weekend. You could use some fresh air and vitamin D while it lasts."

"Sure, Mom. I probably should…" A hint of worry laced my response.

"I'm sure she'll forgive you. You two always work these things out." She gave my foot a comforting squeeze through the thickness of my comforter. "Come on. Let's go. It's supposed to be a beautiful day."

Her eyes twinkled, and her short chestnut hair bounced as she turned to leave.

"I'll be down in a few."

Finally alone, I puffed out a breath of relief. She hadn't noticed the ring and had bought the story about Tanner. Either she was distracted, or I'd gotten that good at lying.

* * * * *

My legs were heavy marching up the stairs after the four hours spent hiking through the hilly terrain of the park. The extended outing was unexpected, but as the cool breeze from the lake hit my lungs, I suggested that we take the long path. Dad drew his face back in shock, mustering only an excited, "Okay!" while Mom pulled her shoelaces tighter. By then we were all a little sweatier and a lot hungrier than any of us anticipated, so we stopped for dinner on the way home.

I collapsed on my bed in an exhausted huff, my cheek pressed into the soft material, and inhaled deeply, holding my breath at the height of expansion. The air escaped through my lips as my eyes came to focus on the computer screen across the room. Still on my stomach, I reached to tug the phone free from my back pocket.

MESSAGE: BRETT

    Casey: hey babe can i give you a call?

Brett: always

Brett: well not always but u know what i mean

    Casey: haha okay

    Casey: give me a minute to change

Brett: oooo

Brett: any chance i can see?

I smiled, dropping the phone with the screen down and pushed back off my bed. I pulled the sweatshirt over my head and flung it toward my hamper before popping the button on my jeans and easing the zipper down, contemplating a shower.

It can wait.

I grabbed a t-shirt from my drawer and slid on the sweatpants I wore last night before relaxing back to lay my head on the pillow.

"Hey, baby." His voice vibrated through my body, my blood singing in response. I bit my lip reflexively.

"Hi." The one word was all I could manage.

"How was your day?" His voice was hushed.

I closed my eyes, picturing him on the other end of the phone and wondering what room of the house he was in, if he was alone. A sigh escaped my throat.

I miss him.

"It was good. I missed you," I purred.

"I missed you too." I could hear the smile on his face in his reply.

"We went to the lake for a hike," I continued.

"Oh, yeah. How far did you go?"

"No idea. We started on the long trail, but it was just so nice that we ended up taking another loop of one of the shorter ones. I'm going to be sore tomorrow."

He paused, and I wondered why he was taking so long to respond.

"So, when do I get to take you for a hike through Chicago?" he quipped playfully.

A flash of emotion cut through my center, some mix of anger and fear.

"Soon," I whispered.

"That's what you always say," he snapped.

That was quick.

His short fuse fueled my own. "I don't know what you expect me to say. It's not that easy."

"Why not?" he accused.

This is it. There will be no other time.

"Because I'm going to school in Philadelphia. Orientation is next weekend, and I move in two weeks later." It came out in a rush.

"You what? Wait, wait, wait… Orientation?"

"Yeah… didn't you ever go to Orientation?"

"Of course, I did." His tone was aggressive.

"So, what's the big deal?" I snapped back.

"It's just unnecessary."

I frowned at his tone, acid rising against my swallow. "Brett, where is this coming from?" I softened, attempting to calm him down.

"You won't come see me. You're going to school in Philadelphia, and now you tell me you're going there for an overnight?"

The last word came out as a yell, and I cringed at the number of people in his house who could overhear our fight. I bit my tongue to keep my tone level and assuring, despite the anger that brewed in the pit of my stomach.

"It's just one night," I mumbled.

"One night in a huge city with how many guys?" He spat out every word.

"You have nothing to worry about." I tried to sound reassuring.

"You'll probably forget about me."

"I could never." The shock on my face carried heavily through my voice.

"Sure," he chided and then went silent.

"Brett, come on. Don't be like this," I pleaded.

He didn't answer.

"Brett, seriously?"

I was talking to dead space.

"So, I'll just go then?" I asked sarcastically.

Nothing. And this time, I didn't have some algorithm telling me if he was typing. I fought to hold back tears that threatened to burst through my crumbling mask of defiance. I couldn't stand the sound of nothing and gathered every ounce of effort to hang up.

Silence could be deafening in the right setting.

CHAPTER 9

I woke up surprisingly early with zero messages and an uneasy feeling turning over in my stomach. Brett hadn't called me back after I hung up. He hadn't texted me goodnight and didn't bother to respond when I finally broke and sent him a goodnight message. Now, at 9 a.m., there was still nothing waiting for me.

Despair was my first feeling, followed by the itch to send him another message. I hadn't gone this long without him since the Blackberry hit the palm of my hand. By noon, I hadn't left my room and couldn't stop fidgeting. Like an addict looking for their next fix, I couldn't stop my fingers from tapping the tiny letters.

MESSAGE: BRETT
Casey 12:03PM: good morning

An hour later and still nothing. Despair warmed to impatience.

MESSAGE: BRETT
Casey 1:02PM: hey hope everythings okay
Casey 1:05PM: u never said goodnight

Three minutes had gone by. The screen still hadn't lit.

MESSAGE: BRETT

> **Casey 1:09PM:** come on talk to me
> **Casey 1:11PM:** u can't be mad at me
> **Casey 1:12PM:** i know u want me to come to Chicago
> **Casey 1:15PM:** i will soon, i promise

Thirty minutes and a grilled cheese later and not even bribery had worked. Impatience bled to annoyance.

MESSAGE: BRETT

> **Casey 1:48PM:** well fine, i dont want to talk to u either
> **Casey 1:52PM:** dont bother texting me tonight
> **Casey 1:53PM:** i wont answer

The edge of evening was quickly approaching, and I had no idea what to do.

MESSAGE: LEILA

> **Casey:** hey L what r u up to tonight?
> **Leila:** hanging out
> **Casey:** around here?
> **Leila:** yeah
> **Casey:** mind if i join?
> **Leila:** call you in an hour
> **Leila:** at the mall with Erin

Rage overtook annoyance without a fight.
Fine, Brett. Fuck me? No, fuck you.

* * * * *

That night, I joined Leila and the rest of the neighborhood in a game of Capture the Flag. She was shocked that I asked to come out. After some groveling at how sorry I was that I hadn't hung out with her all summer, she obliged.

Being outside in the crisp late-summer air was refreshing. I left my phone inside on purpose out of spite in case Brett bothered to text me back. I closed my eyes and took a deep breath, feeling my lungs expand and filling me completely with the scents of the nearing change of season. The leaves and grass danced in the golden tint of sunset.

In the wide-open field, Leila sat on the only rock, her head tossed back, laughing at something Tanner whispered in her ear. I flashed back to her and me, remembering when we drew with chalk all over that rock and realized I missed my friend. Erin wandered over with a guy I recognized but whose name I couldn't remember. Leila made space on the rock for her to sit. I looked around the field and saw mixed groups of boys and girls chatting. My eyes darted between them, searching for someone familiar to talk to.

The streetlights buzzed, stealing my focus with their soft glow. When I looked back, Leila was waving me over, standing side-by-side with the boy who came over with Erin.

The two team captains.

I took my time gliding through the grass, knowing I would be on Leila's team. I let myself have a moment to feel how different it was to be immersed in the outside world and stimulated by every sense, rather than watch the days pass from the inside of my four walls, in front of a screen, looking out.

Brett's an easy distraction from the types of summer nights I used to live for.

While I was preoccupied in my thoughts, the game kicked off. Everyone scattered in different directions. I hadn't paid much attention to any of the team choices, but knew I was always after the blue flag.

As I crept through the fading light to my secret hiding spot, I felt a twinge of regret in my heart and fear that I'd missed out on something. Memories of secret stolen kisses whispered in the wind, not one of them involving me.

My short-sleeved shirt was just thin enough that the breeze raised goose bumps along my skin when the sun fully went down. The cement foundation of the side of the house was cool and rough against my back. Beneath my feet, the dirt was loose, and my heels dug in when I crouched behind the thick brush that thrived all year round.

This spot was the best, and it was all mine. Easy to get to, well-covered, and close to the opponent's flag. All I had to do was wait out the other players, bide my time until I had an opening to bolt, and capture our victory. The team relied on my skills to outsmart everyone else and win. At least that's how it'd been every other summer.

There didn't seem to be much movement going on in this game, which usually was better for me. I thought of it as less competition. I wasn't the ace because I was fast. I was the stealthiest of the group. The fact that I was the quietest and didn't mind being alone had made me a hot commodity in the past. That had never struck me as odd, but now that I was huddled, waiting, left alone inside my head, it occurred to me.

Maybe being alone isn't a good thing.

I shut my eyes and thought back to the choosing of teams. Vaguely, I remembered boys' and girls' names called for the same team. My mind registered that as odd.

It's usually boys versus *girls.*

A flash of everyone dividing danced across my eyelids, recognizing couples pairing off.

What am I doing?

I miss Brett. I wish he was here. I wish I wasn't alone.

My thumb went to the place on my ring finger, reflexively searching to twist a ring that wasn't there. I lost my balance and stifled a yelp. My elbow scraped the rough edges of the cement, and my hair caught in the branches in front of me when I tried to catch myself. My eyes welled up, from more than just the slight pain of the scrape, and I tasted salt on the edge of my lips.

I changed my focus, self-assured that I was better alone, that I could do my job better by myself. My job right then was to win and that's what I would do.

I heard a rustle of leaves across the yard from me. The white brim of a baseball hat shone through the green bushes, and I knew who my opponent was. Something deep in my stomach clenched tight and warmth spread through my body.

At least one thing hadn't changed. Greg came to play, and he was alone.

Just like me.

In the cover of darkness, I pulled myself together and got my head back in the game. I pushed Brett out of my mind and ignored the sense of comfort I felt at seeing that familiar white hat. I crouched lower and slithered toward the edge of the house to peek around the corner. That was my winning tactic. I couldn't directly see the flag from my spot, which meant no one could see me and wouldn't see me coming right away. I had to be careful attempting a glimpse, but it was worth it for the seconds of extra time I'd have to make my move. Standing in the pit was a girl I didn't know doing a hell of a great job distracting a boy I did know from guarding the flag.

Perfect.

This would be an epic win. Not only was it the end of the season but also the only game I'd played this year. My reign would live on even if I had missed almost all the fun of the summer.

What reign? These people clearly don't care about your winning streak anymore. They're way past silly summer games. Look around—no one is paying attention, no one is competing against you, no one is even trying to defend the flag.

When did that happen? I didn't think I was missing much by staying inside. Why was this summer any different than the last?

I shook my head in an ineffective attempt to clear my thoughts. If I could just keep my mind focused and sneak past Greg, I had nothing to worry about. I turned back to where I'd seen the white of his hat and the trees moving. No sign of him despite my eyes playing tricks on me, showing shadows dancing on the sides of the houses. Peeking around the corner, I discovered the distracted couple guarding the other team's flag was missing. This was the window of opportunity I was familiar with. I inhaled deeply, exhaled quietly, and prepared to cross the yard to the finish line.

My nerves calmed. I could almost taste the sweetness of triumph.

Turns out there's not much skill involved in walking out of your hiding spot, nonchalantly, and picking up the undefended flag as you walk by. But that's what I did.

Epic?

Try anticlimactic. No shouting, fighting, or cheering. Only the quiet of the night. I had won the game, but no one was there to witness it, and no one cared. This was quickly turning into the worst night I'd had in forever. It was an extraordinarily uncomfortable feeling, considering the emotional turmoil I was already experiencing from not talking to Brett for the first night in forever.

I dropped the flag, turning to walk back to my house with my eyes on my now-muddy shoes. It had to be late, and the wind had picked up. To keep from shivering, I wrapped my arms tight to my body and shrank as far into myself as possible.

At that moment, I hated my parents for calling me out on my anti-social summer and forcing those feelings to the surface. And I hated myself. I'd done this on my own, ignoring my friends and losing touch. I'd missed a key new development that everyone else had gone through. It was entirely my fault.

Or maybe it's Brett's?

CHAPTER 10

My head was filled with all the things I wanted to say to Brett. Distracted, I'd gotten halfway through the yard when someone hooked strong arms around my waist from behind. The shadow his height cast over me showed the brim of a cap. He'd gotten a bit taller. His familiar scent that used to smell stale now smelled sweet.

Hi, Greg.

The length of his body was a welcome warmth against my back. Last year, I would have screamed and fought to get away. Now I was melting back into him before I knew what I was doing. I tried to shift in his arms and turn around, but he tightened his grip and dipped his head low enough to whisper in my ear.

"Gotcha," he said in a newly minted deep voice.

The sound resonated through my skull, down my body, and made my fingers tingle. The charge was electric but not shocking. A feeling like feathers fluttered across my skin.

"Game's over, Greg. I already got the flag. We won."

"I didn't say I got the flag. I said I got you." His arms loosened, and he nudged my side to turn me around.

I took a step back to look at his face and lifted my eyes to meet his. I opened my mouth to speak, but he beat me.

"I was wondering if you were ever going to leave your room," he began. "Been waiting all summer and you pick probably the last warm night before we all leave for school to come down from your tower."

"Tower? Who am I, Rapunzel?"

He reached out and flicked my hair between his index and middle finger. "You have the hair for it," he teased.

"Did you hit your head hiding under that tree tonight? Usually you can't wait to shout your latest insult in my direction and run off with the guys."

"Have you looked around tonight, Casey? There's no 'guys' to run off with."

I *had* looked around tonight, and I knew he was right. I stopped to listen. Behind the crickets were sounds of sighs, giggles, and the low hum of hushed conversation. A thought dawned on me. He had been right across from me just before I captured the flag. He must have seen me but didn't try to stop me.

"Did you let me win?" I blurted.

A wide grin spread across his face and reached his baby blue eyes. They danced in delight. "I said, gotcha."

"You're unbelievable." I rolled my eyes. "This is literally the worst night of my life. I'm going home." I turned and strode with purpose across the rest of the yard in the direction of the street leading to my house.

He easily caught up with my stride. "Wait up, Case. You've been busy all summer, I just thought you'd want to end with a win."

"Don't call me that, and why are you being so nice to me?" Everything he said was irritating and rubbing me the wrong way. He deflated and slowed. I felt a pang of guilt. "I'm sorry, Greg. I don't know what's going on."

"Talk to me. I'm a good listener."

I was quiet and kept walking. We were at the corner of my street and could see the soft glow of the porch light above my front door. Light from the TV streamed through the curtains in my parents' window. Either they were awake and waiting for me or had fallen asleep to the background noise of *Law and Order*. I thought about my room down the hall and the sleeping computer. Brett may have texted me. If I went in now, maybe he would be online waiting.

Or maybe not.

My stomach turned over and an awful taste rose in my throat. I couldn't handle another night of silence.

I decided I didn't want to walk through that door. Instead, I just stopped walking. Greg kept moving, not realizing that I had stopped until he was a few paces ahead of me. He turned to say something and noticed I wasn't there. I stood still as he came to stand right in front of me, blocking my view of the house—a welcome distraction.

"Seriously, Casey. What's going on? Why have you been hiding?" he asked.

I wanted to scream at him, "*Why do you care?*" Lowering my head, I lifted my gaze and peered through my lashes.

"I don't want to go inside. Will you stay a little while?" I pleaded.

He started walking toward my back deck while I stayed frozen, and he called to me with outstretched arms. "I have all the time in the world. The night is young."

I couldn't get my feet to move at first. A tremble spread through my body as I watched him walk away.

Why is he being so nice to me?

Why is now any different than when everyone else was around?

Then I felt a tug like an invisible thread willing me to follow.

He was headed for the familiar spot under the deck with the new table and chairs my parents had bought for a few bigger family BBQs—not that I had spent much time in attendance at them this year. It was a mix-and-match set of four chairs and a loveseat bench with ugly striped cushions. In a few weeks, it would go into storage until next season. Preservation at its finest. "Take care of your things and they'll never fail on you," as my dad would say.

How many times had Leila and I gone to this very spot when neither of us wanted to go home? How many nights had Greg, Tanner, and everyone joined us after our long days at the pool? Too many to count. Times when we chatted the night away, laughing until our sides hurt. We were in our own little world. A bubble of ignorance to time speeding by. I'd been pressing at the edges of that bubble, longing for it to burst and drag me away somewhere new. Now I felt like I wanted to wrap it around me and hold tightly like a warm blanket that had just come out of the dryer.

Greg sat in the loveseat and patted the spot next to him. I went to sit in a chair, and he frowned. Moving around the table toward him, I caught a glimpse of the night sky. I took a shaky breath and the cool air caught in my throat, letting me know just how cold I actually felt. It wouldn't be so bad to have some contact heat. I sat down close so our thighs were touching but far enough that I could still face him to speak. He relaxed into the corner and draped his arm across the backrest.

I had the odd desire to start a fight, but as soon as the thought crossed my mind, I knew it wasn't directed toward the boy sitting next to me. His usually smug face was soft, studying my eyes. It reminded me of the way he used to look at me before school's social boundaries were drawn, separating us.

Oh, what the hell.

"Remember a couple summers ago when Leila and I weren't speaking?"

"Best summer I can remember." He winked.

"Do you know why?"

He looked at me. Really looked at me. "I didn't really care."

"I told Leila that I was jealous you and she had hung out without me." I blushed, though I doubted he could tell through the darkness. "I told her that she was *my* best friend."

"Everyone knows that. She knows that. Why would you fight over that?"

"Because I also told her that I thought you were cute and that I wanted to hang out with you... without her. Turns out best friends can't like the same guy because she told me that you liked *her* and you'd never like me and to not even think about it. I didn't like that answer and I didn't believe her so I told her I'd hang out with you whenever I wanted and if she had a problem then we didn't need to hang out at all anymore."

He smirked. "Never had that much female attention in my life. Not even from my mom."

"Come on, Greg, I'm serious."

"Look, anyone can read Leila like a book." He paused to smile and leaned closer like he was about to let me in on the most important secret ever. "I don't like to read."

I let go of the breath I didn't know I was holding.

"Which is why I spent all summer with you," he said as he sat back, leaving the spot where his side was touching mine to chill.

On the inside, I was shaking with the same jittery sugar high I usually felt with Brett. This time it was the combination of heat radiating from Greg and my raw emotions. I reached for his hat and playfully snatched it from his head, putting it on with a tilt.

"What is it with you and this hat anyway? You know you stick out like a sore thumb in the dark with it on?"

He laughed and patted the brim over my eyes. "It's my lucky hat, my good luck charm. Usually when I wear it, I kick your ass."

"Not tonight apparently," I teased.

I pushed the brim back up so I could see, and then it happened. His hands were on either side of my face, his fingers laced through my hair. Before I knew it, his lips were on mine and I was instantly on fire. Feeling vulnerable, I was timid, but Greg knew exactly what he was doing. Strong fingers held my head in place while his jaw worked to manipulate mine. I remember having fleeting thoughts of excitement—I couldn't wait to tell Leila—mixed with split seconds of feeling ashamed like I was cheating on a test or lying to a teacher.

Somewhere in the middle, I tried to catch my breath. I opened my mouth a little farther and attempted to pull away, but instead felt the brush of tongue massage my own and murmured a sigh into his mouth. He broke away first, taking the hat off my head while I was still in a daze. My eyes focused on his, and I shook my head. I shifted in the seat, so I was almost sitting in his lap and pressed my lips to his.

This is too good to be over so fast.

I wrapped my hands around his neck and lifted myself farther out of the seat, pressing my chest against his, and dug my nails into his back lightly. Rewarded with a moan, I kept drinking him in.

Anything to hear that sound again.

His hands wandered to my hips. Hooking his thumbs into my belt loops, he pulled me solidly into his lap. My legs slid into a straddle and his arms wrapped around the small of my back. I was overcome with emotions: warm, safe, excited, content. I didn't know how long we stayed entwined in each other. I heard the lock click and window slide open before the call shortly followed.

"Casey Windsor, you get your butt in this house right now! Do you know what time it is?"

I popped up and banged my head on the deck. "Coming, Dad!"

Greg tried to hold back a laugh. After a playful slap on the arm, I kissed him again and stole the hat back while he was distracted. I turned quickly to go, but he grabbed my wrist, pulling me in close again.

Planting a kiss on the top of my head, he whispered, "Where have you been? I've been waiting for that."

"Distracted," I murmured into the space below his chin and breathed in his scent once more.

His grip loosened, and I bolted for the stairs of my deck, up to the back door. Just before slipping inside, I turned to see Greg ambling through the yard toward the path that would take him home.

"Hey!" I yelled softly. He turned in time to see me put the hat back on my head. "My lucky hat now!"

He winked. "All yours, Case. See ya around."

CHAPTER 11

Riding the high, I snuck through the living room, avoiding the creaking spots I'd come to learn, and reached the stairs leading to our bedrooms. Sprinting up the first few steps, I stopped short just before colliding with my dad, who sat in his pajamas, elbows on his knees and head resting on his hands.

"Oh! Dad, you scared me." I tried to regain my balance and composure, adrenaline still pumping through my veins. The kiss from moments ago replayed through my mind on a loop.

His reply was deadpan. "Nice hat. You get into the wine coolers again?"

It was more a statement than a question. I almost didn't hear what he said in my dreamy state and then it registered. My parents didn't care so much that I drank if they knew where I was getting it. Their home bar was the safest source. I tried to think of the best way to respond. Honesty was the best policy... most of the time. Boys were a different story. My dad was protective of his little girl. I had to be careful.

"Not tonight. Leila and I were out with the crew."

Is it a lie if I just don't tell the whole truth?

"Greg kick your ass at Capture the Flag again?" His face was blank, but his eyes sparkled with delight.

"Dad!" I squealed and then remembered I was wearing his hat and he probably had seen him leaving from my window. "Actually, no. I won for our team. Victory at last." I bragged sarcastically. I needed to shut this down before I word vomited what had happened in the last however many minutes with Greg.

"I'm pretty tired. Are we done with the inquisition? Can I head upstairs now?" I tried to move past him, but he didn't budge.

"Casey, I'm glad you were out tonight. It's not good to be staring at a screen all the time."

And there it was. The last twist of the knife on my roller coaster of an evening. My composure was crumbling, my fight or flight response activated to tell me to run. The high was gone. I was ashamed because I knew he was right, angry because I didn't want him to be, afraid of losing Brett's attention despite whatever just happened with Greg, and unsure of what to do next.

"Thanks, Dad. It felt good to be outside with my friends again. Maybe I'll take a break for a while."

My second lie tonight.

"I love you, bird." He opened his arms for me.

I fell into his big bear hug, taking every ounce of effort to not tense, or worse, start crying. "I love you more. Sorry I woke you up."

"It wasn't me. It was your mother. She was worried about you." He rubbed my back in comfort. "I figured you'd be in your spot. You know I trust you, but it's getting late to be outside and it's chilly. I told you to bring a jacket."

"I know. I didn't think I'd be out this late. Next time I'll listen." I meant it as I pulled back and kissed him on the cheek. "Goodnight, Daddy."

He patted my back gently. "Go on. But no screens tonight, Case. I mean it." His voice was stern and brought back memories of warnings from when I was about to do something wrong as a kid.

I promised and bounded up the rest of the steps as he descended for a midnight snack. Once inside my room, I closed the door softly and stared at the black screen of my computer. I turned to the phone resting on my nightstand and felt lost.

I couldn't break my promise, but the promises I made countered each other. I threw the hat on my bed without checking the phone and turned to get ready for bed. Reflexively, I pulled the solid gold band from its box and slipped it over my finger. While digging through my t-shirt drawer, I heard the muffled text chirp.

I all but dove for it, thinking it was Greg.

My phone doesn't really count as a screen. Does it?

It wasn't him.

MESSAGE: LEILA

Leila: thanks for the win!

    Casey: are u serious L

    Casey: what happened tonight?

Leila: well... since u must know...

Leila: Tanner found me first ;)

Not what I meant, but I'll bite.

I was torn about which direction to take my next text... Tanner? Greg? The game?

MESSAGE: LEILA

    Casey: what happened to greg?

Leila: oh come on

Leila: he's so last summer

Leila: plus I think he's into Erin now? Idk

That was definitely the wrong direction.

But also, I literally just kissed him so maybe that isn't true at all.

I knew Leila enough to know she was baiting me, but I was too distracted to let that bring me down.

MESSAGE: LEILA

Casey: sure

Casey: so when did we stop caring about winning

Leila: about the same time Tanner showed off his six pack at the pool this summer :p

Leila: and then solidified that the game is just an excuse to be alone with girls now...

Leila: he picked me to be on his team a few weeks ago ;) ;)

Casey: OMG! shut up

Casey: did you kiss him??

Leila: oh Case ur so prude

Leila: more than that...

Leila: what are we in middle school

Casey: no way! u didn't!?!?

Leila: ummmmm

Leila: yes I did! :p

This is huge.

Leila was the first of my friends to have sex, and I couldn't be more excited for her. I had so many questions. Half of me wanted to run over to her house right now and hear all the juicy details, but the other half was embarrassed that I didn't know moments after it happened. My best friend had had so many experiences this summer and I missed it all. Panic set in as I realized I was probably finding out after everyone else.

Some friend I'd become. Leila deserved better from me. We'd known each other since we were practically in diapers. She must have been itching to tell someone—to tell *me*—that she'd lost her virginity the minute it happened, and I wasn't there.

But if not me, then who?

I didn't want to think about that right now because I knew the answer and being replaced was too difficult to stomach. I felt an intense need to have my friend back and had a pretty good idea how to start piecing us back together. Now I had an excuse to keep avoiding a potential blowup with Brett and surprisingly, didn't feel entirely bad about it. And I forgot to be mad at Leila for not telling me that capturing the flag didn't really matter anymore. I guess I deserved it after being MIA all summer.

One last look at the computer screen and a scroll through my inbox with nothing from Brett helped me make up my mind. Guilt turned into anger and determination. He obviously would be fine without me for a little while longer, but I wouldn't be fine without my best friend. I settled back into my pillows for a long night.

Leila liked attention. She craved it. And I'd always been her biggest cheerleader—probably why she kept me around. Give the girl a podium and microphone and she'd talk for hours. All I had to do was listen.

> **Casey:** so what was it like?
> **Casey:** tell me EVERYTHING!
> **Casey:** EVERY! THING!

* * * * *

Leila wasn't one to spare details, and I now had a mental motion picture of her and Tanner's first tryst.

It sounded like it didn't ever happen like in the movies. There was no romantic stripping or mood lighting, no passionate rolling off the bed and hitting the floor gracefully while you kept at it. It was just a girl in a high school boy's dark bedroom, the two of them rushing to get each other's clothes off.

While Leila was not Tanner's first, the first round had still been quick. She'd stayed the night and Tanner had made up for it during round two. Since then, they'd kept at it like rabbits.

The full play-by-play had me picturing what my own first time would be like. My mom had always said that I should wait for someone I love, not necessarily marriage, but that there should be a strong emotional connection. For the last few months, I'd been thinking about it with Brett's face above mine. Hours would go by in our conversation where I'd catch myself fantasizing about taking a trip to see him. I'd plan my fictitious outfit and the first thing I'd say when I finally saw him. Some cliche line like, "Hey, stranger, fancy meeting you here."

Leila's story and Greg's kiss brought forward an entirely different first experience. I was no longer in a college dorm room in Chicago but in a high school boy's dark bedroom, in my same small town, with a white hat on the nightstand. I looked at that white hat now, sitting on the pillow next to my cell phone and thought about putting it on. I could almost feel his warm hands cupping my face. A replay of the flash of his eyes before our lips met danced through my mind. Picking it up, I smelled his scent, fresh and a little smoky like a bonfire in the middle of the woods. A shiver ran down my spine and my toes flexed against the sheets. I wanted to be consumed by his warmth again.

It was late, and my room was dark. The only light was the moon splashing through the crack in my curtains, the crickets chirping whimsically through my open window. If it were another night, the glow of the computer screen would have washed out the soft ray of light. That, or I would have been too absorbed by Brett's voice to notice the night's calming nature.

What am I going to tell Brett?

Tears prickled and promised to spill out. I held back hard. Shifting onto my side, I tucked my knees up into my chest as far as I could, bent my elbow under the pillow to cradle my head, and nestled into the comforter a little deeper. Most nights I'd be too warm this scrunched up, but tonight it was just what I needed.

With my phone in my hand and a new text message open, I started to type his name.

CHAPTER 12

The sound of a car door closing, and the front door squeaking woke me up. I lifted one eyelid to check the time: 7:03 a.m. That could mean only one thing. Throwing back the comforter and rolling out of bed, I was just about to pull the drawer open for a sweatshirt when I heard my dad's voice.

"Casey! Picnic time!"

I could already taste the salty sweet Taylor ham, egg, and cheese on a cinnamon raisin bagel—my favorite Saturday breakfast. It had been too long since Dad had indulged us with this treat.

"Coming! Be down in a minute," I replied, throwing the hoodie over my head and turning back to the bed to grab my phone. The mirror caught my attention, and I noticed the familiar bags under my eyes. This time I smiled, knowing I'd earned them from talking to Leila. I checked the phone as I was going down the stairs and nearly tripped on the cat and tumbled the rest of the way on my ass.

Twenty-seven unread messages. Twenty-seven messages before 7 a.m. on a Saturday.

Didn't I just go to sleep a few hours ago? It's only 6 a.m. in Illinois. I hope one of these is from Greg.

I shoved the phone in my pocket without opening any of them. They could say so many different things, and I didn't want to let anything ruin my morning. In the back of my mind, I was itching to at least check who they were from. My racing pulse let me know who I wanted it to be.

The blanket was already spread on the living room floor by the time I reached the last step. I made my way to the kitchen to grab the ketchup. *They always forget the ketchup.* My mom was pouring V8 into two small glasses for her and my dad.

She turned and gave me a knowing smile. "Rise and shine. How are we this morning?"

"Fine, thanks." I blushed.

Maybe it was her mother's intuition or, more likely, she must have talked with my dad. He probably told her he saw Greg leaving our backyard last night. She put two and two together and was waiting for the moment to ask me how it was.

Zero poker face.

"So…" she sang in crescendo.

"So what, Mom?" I snapped—probably a little too sharply.

I wasn't usually this tight-lipped. My mom and I had a fabulously open relationship. She was more like my best friend. I could tell her everything. Like when I wanted to go to a party last summer with Leila and knew there'd be drinking, all I had to do was tell her. That night, she gave me a glass of wine and said if I was going to drink, I'd do it with her first, so I knew what to expect. I never giggled so freely in my entire life. I woke up to a glass of water, two pain relievers, and a note on my nightstand, *XO Mom.* She made sure I had a ride there and back, and that if I needed *anything* to call her first no matter what, no matter when, always.

Why was I so hesitant now to tell her all the juicy details of my kiss with Greg?

I tried to think back to the last time we had one of our girls' talks and had trouble remembering. Apparently, Leila wasn't the only person I'd abandoned. But where I'd felt guilt for missing out with my friends, realizing that I'd disconnected from my parents just made me feel sad, unsure of who I was becoming.

I looked up at my mom and excitement sparkled in her eyes. I guessed she'd ignored my tone. She'd been waiting for this moment after years of watching us dance around each other and wanted me to spill my heart out.

"So..." Her voice was a bit more pleading this time.

I blushed again and smiled. "Greg and I stayed up talking last night. Sorry if we woke you up."

She gave me a suspicious look. "Talking?"

"Talking." I winked.

Moving toward me, she squealed and threw her arms open, getting ready to smother me with her hug.

"Oh! Honey!" She wrapped her arms around me despite my being stiff. After a few beats, she stepped back, extending her arms and rubbing her hands up and down my own. "Tell me all about it!" She looked at me appraisingly, searching for something different about me.

I softened slightly at her excitement but then remembered my dad was just in the other room. "Mommm, Dad is right in the living room. Later... *please*," I pleaded.

"Okay, okay, but you know your father and I talk about everything."

"Yeah, fine, but I'd just rather he not hear it from me," I said, turning the corner in the direction of my bagel.

I peeked into the pocket of my hoodie and saw thirty-two unread messages. My palm was sweaty gripping the keyboard. I wouldn't make it through breakfast without checking if this kept up. Ditching the phone on the stairs on my way to the living room, I took a deep breath and pressed my fingers into my eyes before entering the room and facing my dad. The stars were just clearing from my sight as I let out my breath.

Dad looked up at me seriously. "Sorry they didn't have no-pulp this morning. Can you manage with *some-pulp*?"

An unexpected laugh escaped my throat. I was expecting something way more threatening. Maybe like, "So did you use the computer last night?" or, "Did you keep our promise?"

Leave it to Dad.

A smile spread across his face, and his eyes danced the same as my mom's had, her feet carrying her down the short steps to the living room behind me.

"So how was last night?" Mom began.

I hesitated over how much I wanted to elaborate. The disappointment I felt earlier at how far disconnected I'd become flooded my system. Opening the top of my bagel to add a dab of ketchup and waste time, I thought about how many of these mornings I'd had with my parents and wondered how many more I would get now that I was heading to college. I looked up and smiled, preparing for a bite, but both their mouths were full, giving me the space to fill the silence.

This. This right here's real life.

Last night and this morning just felt right, like filling the void that was usually the place where Brett fit perfectly. Instead, I had inviting smiles and warm bodies I could reach out and touch at will.

Maybe I can find that "something else" out there without the screen.

I swallowed my first bite and started from the beginning, describing every detail of my night out as if I was writing a scene in a novel. When I reached the moment of climax, I left out a lot. I didn't need to make my parents squirm, or worse, glow with pride at my intimate foray. They both beamed with delight anyway at my apparent attitude adjustment after just one night with friends.

When we were finished, I pushed up my sleeves, intending to grab the trash and condiments in one shot. Spreading my fingers to grasp everything in the palm of my hand, the sun caught my gold band and I almost dropped the entire pile. With panic in my eyes, I glanced from Dad to Mom. She noticed my expression before searching for its source. I got up quickly and made for the kitchen, ignoring the lightheaded feeling of getting up too quickly.

Hoping she didn't see anything, I called to them, "I'll be down in a bit, just going up to change."

* * * * *

For the first time, it felt like I was marching up the stairs in punishment from someone other than my father. I scrolled through my inbox immediately after picking up my phone, proud of myself for holding it together at breakfast and dodging the bullet at the end.

There were now forty-one unread messages.

And I'm in trouble.

Five messages were from Leila left over from last night, and another three from this morning letting me know the group was going bowling tonight. A twenty-minute gap before the last one, asking if I wanted to come, made me wonder if she was deciding whether she wanted me there or asking someone else if she should invite me.

Two from Greg: *hey* and *what's up.*

The rest were from Brett, each increasing in level of panic.

What started out as curious of my whereabouts quickly turned to concern that something was wrong. The genuine fear in the earlier messages warmed my heart. But then, concern escalated to sheer terror and attention-grabbing threats of getting in his car to drive out and make sure nothing happened to me. Finally, rage. He was angry that I'd left him alone all night, that I hadn't bothered to keep my promise to be with him every day.

That's rich, considering he did the same to me the night before.

His rage came out in the form of jealousy, his last few messages assuming that I was "with some random guy" like the "attention whore" that I was.

He wasn't entirely wrong with that last bit, but it still hit hard. I was seething but underneath it sick to my stomach with genuine hurt.

I thought he loved me. How can you say something like that to someone you love?

I knew he was right. I had broken my promise to him, and it didn't matter that part of the reason was the quick promise I made to my dad after coming inside. The damage had already been done when I made the decision not to go in right after the game. My kiss with Greg had been the cherry on top.

The real shame stemmed from the deleted text I hadn't sent before falling asleep and my guilt was eating away at my resolve. I'd typed out a novel of a message, professing my love, apologizing for not trying harder to talk to him, and for being missing all night. I signed the message with our usual "I love you, goodnight, bye," but I just couldn't send it.

Now, I sat in my desk chair with my knees bent, head resting on my forearms, and stared at the blank screen for an indiscriminate amount of time. Scenario after scenario clicked through my mind like a slideshow, each ending worse than the prior.

I loved Brett, but after last night, I wasn't sure it was enough to live my life inside and online anymore. I wanted something real. Someone real. A few deep breaths and I worked up the courage to tell him the truth about last night.

This conversation will be too long to text.

I untucked my right foot, running my toes across the plush carpet under the desk, and leaned forward. With an exhale, I pressed the button on the tower and powered up. I zoned out listening to the fan kick in while the start programs ran. In a daze, I connected to the internet and opened Instant Messenger.

The sound of a door opening announced my arrival just as another message vibrated in the pocket of my hoodie.

PART II:

REINVENTION

CHAPTER 13

I have one night to taste freedom and indulge my desire for reinvention.

In the last six days, I've been twisted inside out. My best friend moved to Connecticut for college and the first boy I ever kissed flew clear across the country to play college football in California.

I'm still not convinced he didn't go just for the girls.

Fall Term at Drexel doesn't start until the end of September and I've been alone, walking on eggshells with Brett and itching to get out of this town. Waiting for my one night of escape.

It's the morning of orientation, and my parents are driving me the two hours to campus—despite my insistence that I would fare well on my own, taking the train from our small local station. Originally, they proposed a hotel room for the night. "A short vacation" was their excuse to avoid embarrassing me with questioning my comfort level at being alone in a new place for the first time. I visibly blanched at the mention, and they quickly backpedaled, rambling about future weekend visits once I was settled.

MESSAGE: BRETT

Brett: i miss you already baby

Casey: i miss you too

Casey: but its just one night

Brett: i know

Brett: but its one night i wont have you

Casey: you always have me

Brett: u have my shirt right?

Casey: of course. cant sleep without it

Brett: good. i'll be right there with you

Brett: try not to have too much fun

Casey: i'll do my best

Brett: u know I dont really mean that

Brett: i love you

Casey: i love you

It's just one night.

I throw my phone on the seat next to me and glance out the window. Drexel University, situated just between Philadelphia's 30th Street Station and the heart of West Philly, is somewhere between quaint and sprawling. The campus is an odd collection of buildings that span several blocks surrounding Market Street. Market is the main drag, the lifeblood that runs from the Waterfront to City Hall, clear through the campus, and out to the towns on the outskirts of the city.

Established in 1891, Drexel is seasoned. The Main Building shows its age with beautifully ornate architecture and winding corridors. Secluded classrooms, long since forgotten, sit unused in the attics at the top of staircases that students don't bother to notice as they blow past. To discover them you have to be lost or looking for someplace no one will find you.

The rest of campus is an uncurated collection, built at various points in time when expansion was necessary, with no obvious concern for matching architectural style. It draws a stark contrast to the prestigious University of Pennsylvania, all red brick and perfectly coordinated. For them, new buildings go up sparingly, their age indistinguishable from the first erected.

An imaginary line separates the two schools, though some streets are shared. Each side stays true to its own kind. Money and a touch of pretentiousness in the UPenn upturned noses and raw, clawing ambition resting on the shoulders of Drexel students. A slight rivalry exists, or more likely a bigger social divide that's never quite acknowledged publicly.

Drexel has a charm and brand of life all its own breathing through the streets that sets it apart from the rest of the city. It's what made me choose this place over any other school.

I'd always had my heart set on attending college in a city and was excited at the prospect of becoming a *real* city girl. The city holds a promise of new beginnings and endless possibilities. Over a million and a half new people and none of them will know, much less care, about my shy small-town persona. I can be someone different. I can be the real me.

Who even is the real me?

Brett gave me the confidence to take a baby step toward finding that answer. The real me is who I am with him, but this is my chance to see if I can be her without the glow of the screen. I can't contain my mix of nerves and giddiness at the idea of being able to reinvent myself.

My daydream dissolves as my phone vibrates through the seat, making me jump.

MESSAGE: BRETT

Brett: I hope u make some friends

His encouragement makes me smile and soften. The morning after Capture the Flag, he'd been so angry with me, and it was the first time I felt something from him other than adoration. But it came from a place of fear. After forty-eight hours, he realized his mistake when I stopped chasing him. My silence hit him just as his had hit me... only he didn't have the distractions that I did. He begged and apologized, pleading for me to never leave him again.

I'd felt that before.

To need someone.

I've needed him since the moment we met. Like an imaginary thread extending from my center through some uncontrolled airspace that connected us, he's made me who I am. He's made me whole, filling some void I didn't know was there.

Maybe tonight won't be like that night.

When I clicked that virtually imaginary button to end the chat connection and got up from my desk, he'd texted and called until I conceded and picked up. His first words, "I'll do anything," drew a smile to my lips and a thought to my mind. *I need boundaries.* He agreed to let out my leash, to be there for me when I was ready for him without the inquisition of where I'd been or who I'd been with.

MESSAGE: BRETT

Casey: thats the plan :)

Brett: well i'll be here waiting

I sigh contentedly, resting my hands in my lap and cradling the phone. My dad signals to the right, expertly navigating the several-lane highway and narrowly escaping a few aggressive drivers. A swell rises in my chest and draws a smile to my lips. I have a feeling of anticipation mixed with a pinch of unease at the newness of the passing windows. The combination forces my eyes closed and my breath quickens. Every mile closer, my heart skips a beat. My stomach is in my chest, my fingertips itch, and my palms are sweating. I shift in the backseat, turning toward the window, and let out a breath.

"Nervous?" my mom questions from the passenger seat.

"A little…" I'm unsure of what else to add.

"Well, you've got your whistle and the pepper spray that Dad got for you."

She doesn't realize that she's misinterpreted my nervousness. I'm not afraid of the city, I'm craving it. I'm nervous for the possibilities, for the choices. Those first interactions with new people, wearing my true face.

"Yes, I have everything, like we went over this morning," I snap at her.

She gives it right back to me. "Don't take it out on me. This school was all your decision."

"Sorry, you're right." I soften.

"Are you sure you don't want us to stay?"

"Absolutely positive," I say with confidence and remain quiet the rest of the short ride to campus.

MESSAGE: BRETT

Brett: so what does Philly look like?

He's trying.

I know he's trying to be okay with this, to give me the space we agreed on.

"We're here," Dad announces, pulling into the parking garage, distracting me from the text.

"Could you not have just dropped me in—"

He eyes me from the rearview mirror. The look steals away any further arguments resting on the tip of my tongue.

On the corner, I give my parents an awkward hug. With several "good lucks" and "be carefuls," and surprisingly no tears from my mom, they send me on my way. I hike up the duffel and readjust my backpack, attempting to look more put together than I feel on the inside. After rearranging my face to what hopefully looks like someone who knows where she's going, I walk toward the double doors leading me to check-in. After waiting in the long, snaking line of kids who look exactly like me, I finally arrive at the table marked W-Z. A tired-looking student in a bright blue t-shirt with a gold dragon sits behind it.

"Name and college." It's a bored statement, rather than a question, and he doesn't bother to look up.

"Casey Windsor, College of Business," I say sweetly.

Digging through the box in front of him, he hands me a white envelope, still not looking directly at me. "Name tag's inside—you'll want to wear that the entire time you're here. Map of campus—the dorm for tonight, Towers, is circled. Bunch of other forms for you to complete and turn in."

"Thanks." I turn to leave.

"Not finished." He stops me. I attempt to apologize, but he cuts me off. "There's a full afternoon of activities planned today. You'll want to head to the dorm to check in and drop your stuff, then make your way to the shuttle. It'll be on the corner of 33rd and Market. Departs at 1:30 p.m."

"Sounds great. Anything else?" I let my annoyance at his rudeness drip into my tone as I readjust my duffel once more.

He finally looks up, making eye contact, and then rakes his eyes down my body before dragging them back to meet mine. "All set." He smiles. His tone is noticeably more friendly. Placing his hand down on the table, he leans over just a bit like he has a secret. "There's a couple parties around campus tonight, maybe I'll see you there." He winks.

I can play this game.

I lift my eyebrows and give him big doe eyes, swallowing my nerves and excitement, before returning the smile.

"Sure," I purr and dip my head to look up at him through my eyelashes. I lick my lips and pull the bottom one between my teeth before releasing it slowly. "Maybe."

With my back a little straighter, I turn before his mouth catches up to his brain and pull out the map to find my way to this dorm called Towers.

CHAPTER 14

I don't know what I expected a dorm to look like, but Towers is nothing special. The floors are scuffed, and the elevators are rickety. I guess it'll be different with my fellow freshman spilling out of every room, but right now it just feels quiet. After an appropriate amount of time between settling in, getting changed, and pushing down the uncomfortable feeling of waiting in the empty room for my roommate to show up, I decide it'll be better to just go to the shuttle.

I push through the doors. The air is warm against my skin and the breeze blows my hair back. I close my eyes and let a gentle smile spread across my face in the warmth of the sun. My eyelids flutter open, and my gaze settles directly across from the dorms on a row of apartments, not shabby but not new.

A group of blond shaggy-haired guys in rugby shirts are lounging on the porch on the corner. I catch them pointing my direction and turn to look behind me, but no one's there. I burn under the weight of their gazes and quickly dash down the stairs, passing the dorm next to Towers. Admiring the big semi-circle building covered in neat rows of windows, I notice on the face of one edge reads *Calhoun Hall*.

Hmm. Like Noah in The Notebook.

Standing on the corner, I look down 33rd and see the back of the shuttle next to a mixed line of students leaning against the wall opposite. I find a comfortable pace, not wanting to appear slow like a tourist or overly excited in a rush. As I near the group of my peers, I laugh at the various style choices ranging from borderline pajamas to almost business casual. Suddenly I don't feel so bad for having changed outfits twice and am happy that I chose my trendy pair of bell-bottom jeans and a V-neck with a cami underneath.

A few students inch their way toward the bus. I hurry when the doors open, following my involuntary need to always be first.

I step up through the doors and hesitate.

In high school, where you sat on the bus defined your social standing. Everyone knew the popular seats were in the back. Everyone except the kids who didn't take the bus because they were close enough to walk to school. Unfortunately, I'm one of those kids. It took me a few class trips to make the discovery and another few to realize that cool was primarily a euphemism for easy after several particularly embarrassing mandatory "hand-checks" from the teachers on our way home from an overnight trip.

I walk up the three short steps and stare down the long aisle to the emergency exit door and the two double seaters that seem to flash "cool" in neon lights. I never got to sit in the popular seats then, but now is my chance.

This moment will seal my fate here.

Stifling the voice of doubt whispering in my ear, I walk with confidence and stop at the second to last row of seats. I want to be *that* girl, but something in me still doesn't feel worthy of the very last row.

Sliding across the vinyl, I press my side against the cool metal beneath the partially open window and feel my phone vibrate in the back pocket of my jeans. I decide to ignore it and notice the first few of my fellow students have taken the front row. I haven't been paying attention as they've come on, and I'm too far back to see their appearance and judge their stereotypes.

Shit. No one is walking to the back.

Wait. Did I mix that up? Is it the front of the bus where the cool seats are?

I internally kick myself for being a "walker" in high school and my stupid "always have to be first in line" OCD tendency. To quell the rising panic in my throat, I pull out my phone and see a waiting message from Brett.

MESSAGE: BRETT

Brett: hey baby did you make it okay
    Casey: all checked in
    Casey: got my room assignment... no roommate yet
    Casey: on the bus for activities

Immediately, new messages pop up in rapid succession. *He's been waiting for my response.*

MESSAGE: BRETT

Brett: ur going to text me the whole time right?
Brett: u won't ignore me? i hate it when u ignore me
Brett: please don't forget about me
Brett: I love u forever... u know that
Brett: remember baby
Brett: Till Death
Brett: you are mine

I look up and roll my eyes.

It's starting already.

I respond simply with a heart and bury the phone in my pocket.

After a quick scan of the bus, failure settles in. Most of the seats toward the front are full, with a handful of people sprinkled throughout the back rows. Where I'm eagerly monitoring the doors to watch my classmates choose their seats, the others in the back are staring out the window at the passing traffic.

Just as I'm about to hang my head, his eyes catch mine as he steps into the aisle.

You know in the movies when someone is cracking a safe and the screen pans in on the lock mechanism? Everything else is quiet as if time has slowed down to the space between heartbeats. You see the movement of the levers, and for what feels like forever the only sound is the click as each lock releases. The last one seats. The door opens. Everyone lets out a breath.

In this moment, I forget about the vibrating phone in my pocket. I forget the self-conscious feeling of sitting alone in the back of the bus, the fear that I'll be the same smart, but not intelligent enough, cute, but not beautiful enough, random girl that I was in high school. I forget the fear that my opportunity for reinvention is slipping away so quickly because of a stupid bus seat.

I exhale. He smiles. And time stops.

When time returns to a normal rhythm, the first thing I notice is his height.

All girls watch for height, but tall girls like me study it intensely. He's tall—"notice me," "bearhug" tall. The kind of height that would afford any girl the comfort of laying her head against his chest, wrapping her arms around his waist, and letting his arms settle over her shoulders enveloping her in warmth. It exudes a sense of protection and promise. I can't help but let my gaze travel over his casual athletic attire covering a lean body. Relaxed sweatpants with stripes down the side, plain white t-shirt, and expensive sneakers.

Maybe a soccer player?

I resist the urge to continue to let my stare wander over him as he makes his way to the back. I focus instead on his eyes coming toward me. They're green and brilliant and hold my attention with a self-confidence that could melt even the hardest of hearts. Mine is in a puddle on the floor.

Who. Are. You?

I draw my eyes away from his first, pulling my bottom lip closed to meet the top, unsure when exactly my jaw dropped. Shifting in the seat to cross my legs, I tuck an errant curl behind my ear and stare at my lap.

Please come sit next to me.

When I glance back up, he is standing in the aisle next to my row, face neutral.

"Mind if I sit here?" he asks with nonchalance, already bending to take a seat.

He's perfectly polite. Interesting... I was expecting arrogance.

I anticipate a small handshake and an introduction, but he takes his time retrieving his phone from the zippered pocket of his pants. My body itches with hidden impatience. Out of the corner of my eye, I see him thoroughly reading a text from someone named Cora. His thigh grazes mine, and a familiar burn blooms somewhere deep inside.

To distract myself from scanning his body again and show him just how important my time is, I pull out my phone.

See? I can do it too.

MESSAGE: GREG

Casey: hows california treating u?
Greg: not as good as u treat me ;)

I readjust my legs, squeezing them tighter. Next to me, I notice him type out a quick response with a smirk and stow his phone back in its place in his pocket. I'm aware of every inch of movement. My skin tingles where his knuckles graze my side as he pulls the zipper closed. It takes everything I have to continue to ignore him.

MESSAGE: GREG

Casey: coming home for Thanksgiving?? :P
Greg: Case i just got here
Casey: dont u miss me already?
Greg: always
Greg: hey i gotta get to class
Greg: see ya later

By the time I slide the phone back into my pocket and return to the present, I feel wonderfully warm and centered. The seat shifts beneath me, and my breath hitches. I see him canvassing my profile out of my peripheral vision. He returns the full weight of his attention to me, but I decide to refuse him the satisfaction of acknowledgment until he speaks to me directly.

"Hi, I'm Duke." I see his hand extend into view before I hear him.

That was quick.

This close, I can see the flecks of gold in his eyes that give them their radiance and a dark rim around the iris. I let my eyes trace the slight bump below the bridge of his nose down to his full lips and barely crooked smile. His face is long, his jaw not soft but not defined. His dirty blond hair is kept short and looks like it would be full of unruly curls if allowed to grow freely. I feel the need to sit on my hands to stop them from reaching out to run my fingers through it.

Just breathe.

I turn my head slowly to completely face him.

"Casey," I respond with a sweet smile, tapping the name tag fastened to the trim of lace on my tank top, and place my hand in his. I swallow against the sensation of his skin warming mine. Glancing below his face for the first time up close, I see the hard line of collarbone and the taut shape of his chest leading to lean biceps and long arms. I let myself feel his strong hand and the slight roughness of his fingertips grasping mine. No sign of a name tag.

"Are you in the College of Business or Arts and Sciences?" I ask.

"The College of Business," he says, giving me the answer I'm hoping for just as I feel the seat vibrate with another message. This time, I'm not sure if it's his or mine. He's watching me drag my attention back to his face after reflexively looking at the seat and doesn't say a word. I slowly pull my hand back to the safety of my lap.

"Are you going to get that?" I ask, pleading doe-eyed for him to keep his attention on me instead.

"I think that one was you." The disapproving tone sends a surge through my system like I've just been chastised.

I know who it is. I can guess what it says. He's not the attention I need.

All I need is Duke to keep staring right through me.

CHAPTER 15

"Oh," I say with my eyes downcast. "It's probably just my parents checking in."

I catch myself in my unhealthy tendency to shrink away from attention and the unconfirmed disappointment in his last statement.

No, Casey. Not this time.

I shove my insecurity to the side and lift my focus back to him.

"So, who's Cora?" I take a chance at boldness.

He's visibly taken aback at my brazen question, but I hold his focus.

What the hell. He's one person. If this doesn't go well, there will be more people, more chances.

After a space of time that clearly expresses I won't be backing down, he dips his head with a clipped laugh.

"Just a girl from my hometown," he says, reflexively reaching for his pocket again. Before he eases the zipper all the way, he thinks better of it and turns back to me.

"Where are you from?" he asks and responds without waiting for my answer, "I'm from Princeton, just outside, actually."

"Duke from Princeton." I narrow my eyes flirtatiously. "I'm from a small town in North Jersey. I won't bother with the name. I don't even think we're on the map."

"Try me," he teases. "I'm on the soccer team. I've probably played your team."

I giggle and shake my head.

That part of me is staying in that small town.

I reach for his hand, running my nails along the underside of his palm and each finger. I see his eyes widen and his eyebrows lift. A slight red tint colors his cheeks. My fingertips leave his, and he drops his gaze to where my hand was just touching him, his jaw hanging open slightly.

"I noticed your fingers are calloused..." I trail off.

He curls his lips, and his smile drips with charm. "I play guitar."

The statement doesn't need clarification. He's clearly used to this hobby drawing an instant swoon from his audience.

And it's working.

"I play piano," I say, surprising even myself for keeping calm and collected despite the quiver under my skin.

"Do you play the classics? I never took lessons or anything, so you have me there, but I can pick up on melodies pretty easy and play the popular stuff by ear."

I soften at the memory of my grandmother pulling out her beaten collection of sheet music from Beethoven and Bach and smile thinking about her yelling from the other room about my botched finger placement on that last note. I nod and let the nostalgia seep into my voice.

"My grandmother taught me. I've been sitting on the bench with her since I was three years old."

"Oh, really! That's awesome." He pauses, looking down at his empty hand again.

We both start our next question at the same time and are in the middle of insisting the other continues when two girls bound by toward the very last row, chased by a sporty-looking boy. The girls take a seat on either side of the aisle, claiming the two-seaters as their own. Across the aisle, I can see the girl has long, fiery red hair and a bohemian tank over an impossibly short jean skirt. Her face is pursed with attitude. Her name tag reads *Ava*. She's eyeing both the boy who chased her down the aisle and Duke, obviously familiar with sizing up her options.

Ugh, of course. Another Erin.

As she leans across toward Duke, the boy reaches for the typical male hand-clap introduction, cutting her off.

"Hey, man, I'm Ian."

Ava is visibly displeased with the interruption but composes herself quickly before she spots me in the seat next to Duke. Almost involuntarily, I shift, uncrossing my legs and angling my knees in Duke's direction. I lean over his lap, purposefully making contact with more of his body than necessary and reach my hand toward Ian while ignoring Ava. I hear Duke suck in a breath and slide his hand from where it's resting between my ribs and his thigh. He relaxes and rests it lightly on the curve of my back.

"I'm Casey. Where are you from, Ian? I see you're in the College of Business with Duke and me."

Before he can answer, a petite girl with shoulder-length, silky black hair and bright eyes pops over the seat. I sit up to see her, and Duke's hand slides back between his leg and mine.

"Same here! Nikki! Nice to meet you, Casey, Duke." She turns her head from me to him. "Ian's from Connecticut, I'm from Florida, and Ava's from Jersey." She gestures and everyone turns their gazes to Ava.

She smirks, clearly happier with the attention on her.

"Cherry Hill, and you?" Ava directs the question squarely to Duke as if I don't exist.

Ava is the definition of cool girl, and I feel slightly intimidated and out of my league. I'm unsure if I can win this battle but decide there's no way to find out but to try. The gentleman that he is, Duke responds for both of us.

"Casey and I are from Jersey." He glances my direction, a glimmer of heat in his eyes that only I can see.

I smile venomously.

"Oh, are you two together?" Ava asks with a hint of sarcasm.

I pause just short enough to let the question linger. "Oh, no. We were just getting to know each other."

Duke looks back at Ava encouragingly.

I'd give anything for him to keep looking at me.

"So anyway," Ian interjects before she can respond, "My buddy was here last weekend, and he has an upperclassmen friend who lives in U-Cross. Apparently, they have orientation parties every weekend for the freshies. You in?"

"How are we supposed to get into that?" I ask without thinking.

Fuck.

Everyone laughs.

Ian smiles wickedly. "Don't worry your pretty little head, girl. Let me take care of that. Just meet me at the entrance of U-Cross at ten p.m. What rooms are you all in?"

I return the smile, looking him over while figuring out how to suggest we should exchange phone numbers. Obvious jock, part of the popular crowd with sandy blond hair, cloudy blue eyes, and a stud in his left ear that's a bit bigger than it needs to be.

I wonder if that's real.

He could be my type if not for that hunk of rock and his obvious penchant for interruption.

He's probably a better match for Ava.

Nikki yanks me back to reality, clapping with an outward excitement that I'm keeping bottled inside with a mix of nerves, insisting the girls get ready together. We exchange room assignments and plan to meet in Ava's room at 9 p.m. The last of the seats fill, and the bus doors close.

Coincidentally, Ava and I are rooming on the same floor.

* * * * *

Somewhere in the middle of the day, I hastily promise Brett that I'll call him before bed just to calm him down. I lie that I'll be going to sleep early, feigning fatigue from being in the sun.

When I get to my dorm room, I see the other bed made and a purple duffle on the desk. My roommate is nowhere to be found. I smile at the bag.

If I ever meet this girl, we could probably be friends.

Standing in front of the extra-tall dorm bed in nothing but a jean skirt and bra, I hear my phone start buzzing on the empty desk at exactly 8:30 p.m. I ignore the first call, digging in my bag for the tiny black vest I've never worn but threw in at the last minute in case there was an occasion to dress up. A second call comes in, threatening to shake the phone over the edge to its demise on the hard porcelain floor.

I feel the smooth surface of the buttons on the vest and tug it free.

I miss the second call.

Pulling a white lace tank top out of my bag, I throw it over my head, scrunching the bottom to reveal a sliver of abdomen just above the waistline of the skirt. I slip the arms of the vest over my shoulders and fasten the buttons quickly down the front. A surge of adrenaline courses through my system at the outfit that I would've never been caught dead in before. Grabbing the worn navy-blue t-shirt, I quickly slide it on and jump into bed, pulling the comforter up to cover the skirt, and snap a picture before pressing send on Brett's missed call.

By now it's 8:45 p.m.

Fifteen minutes to act convincingly tired enough and make it out the door to Ava's.

He picks up on the first ring.

"Hey."

The one-word response is all I get.

CHAPTER 16

"Hey, you," I smolder, hoping my sleepy seductive voice will suppress his frustration. "Hang on a minute." I pull the phone from my ear and send the photo through, hearing the ping indicating his receipt.

"That's my girl." His tone softens. "So how was it?"

"Nothing special," I say, forcing the elation and anticipation from my voice. "It was a bunch of team-building and trust activities with our respective colleges. Just something to get to know people before classes start." I carefully choose my next statement. "I met a few girls on the bus. We ended up on the same team all day and had dinner."

"Any guys?"

I stifle an audible intake of breath. "A few, but I tried to keep my distance," I say and yawn for effect.

"Sorry." *He almost sounds like he means it.* "I was worried about you all day."

"No need to worry. Like I said, it's only one night away. I'll be home tomorrow."

I check my phone again to keep track of the time, 8:54 p.m., and swing my legs over the side, bouncing my feet with nerves. I need to be walking over to Ava's in a minute.

"I know. I just want you all to myself," he teases.

"You have me," I purr.

"But how long will I have you?"

I peek at the clock again.

I don't have time for this.

I can't afford to spend the time giving him the comfort he needs tonight. I put as much emotion into my voice as I can muster.

"Forever, my love. You know I love you."

He sighs. "I love you so much."

"Listen, I'm pretty tired. Would you mind if I get some sleep and text you in the morning?"

"Do I get a good morning picture?" he teases.

"Of course. Always."

"Alright. Sleep good, baby."

He's waiting for me to say it. The way we always end our call. The line we started using after several nights of "No, you hang up... no, you."

All I have to do is say it, and he'll let me go.

"I love you, goodnight, bye."

"Love you too, goodnight—"

I hang up before I hear him finish and check the time again.

9:05 p.m.

Grabbing my tiny black clutch, I throw my phone and license inside with my lip gloss and cash and yank the door open, almost smacking into the blond hair, blue-eyed girl who I presume is my roommate.

"Hey!" she sings. "I'm Jessica! You can call me Jess, though. Either or. I don't mind. *So* nice to finally meet you. Sorry I wasn't here to settle in before the bus left. We got stuck in traffic, and I had to run from registration to here and back to the bus. It was a nightmare," she prattles on.

I'm not listening.

"Casey," I respond the first time she pauses for breath, dismissing her welcoming introduction. "I'm so sorry but I'm about to go meet some friends. Catch up with you later?"

"Oh, sure. A bunch of us on the floor were about to head to the common area anyway." She looks a little deflated as I whirl past her and am part way down the hall looking for Ava's room number.

"We'll do breakfast," I call, hoping that makes up for my abrupt rudeness.

Rounding the corner, I make my way to Ava's door and knock a few times. 9:18 p.m. There's no answer. I'm not sure where U-Cross is, how to get there, or how long the walk is. *Surely forty minutes is overkill.*

I wait a few more beats, listening through the door for the sound of talking or music but hear nothing. I knock again and still no answer. Digging in my bag for my phone, I remember only exchanging numbers with Nikki during a break in our group's water balloon toss this afternoon. Ava was nearby, but if she heard us, she pretended not to.

MESSAGE: NIKKI

Casey: hey! just at Avas... so sorry I'm late
Casey: my parents called
Casey: where are u guys?

The door opens, and I look up, expecting to see Ava, at the same time my phone pings with a response from Nikki.

MESSAGE: NIKKI

Nikki: hey! we went downstairs to find Duke and Ian
Nikki: come meet us!

"Um, hi?" A tall, overweight girl with wiry hair stands in the dark doorway with a sleepy look on her face and a scowl.

"Oh! I'm so sorry. I didn't mean to wake you. I was looking for Ava?"

She makes an annoyed, almost disgusted face. "Yeah, she left with some girl twenty minutes ago."

Anger simmers in my blood. They left at exactly 9 p.m.

Fuck Brett for making me late. And Ava for... everything.

"Thanks so much…" I pause, waiting for her name.

"Amy."

"Thanks so much, Amy. Again, I'm so sorry to bother you." I turn in the direction of the elevators and look down at my phone to type a response.

MESSAGE: NIKKI

Casey: coming! wait for me?

"Have a great night!" I call and hear the door shut heavily.

I hurry back down the hall, passing the common area, and make eye contact with Jess as I walk by. Her face brightens with surprise. After giving a small wave, I continue my path. I tap my foot waiting for the elevator to rise to the eleventh floor.

In my old life, I'd have been more likely to fit in with Jess… or Amy.

My ears ring at the exhilarating fact that I've successfully made it into a group with Duke, Ian, and Ava instead. I step inside the elevator with a satisfied smile and press *Lobby*. Seconds later, the doors open and the first thing I see is Duke's smiling face. My heart skips a beat, and my composure slips. Pulling myself together, I stride through the gate and to the group.

"We ready to go?" I smile sweetly in Ava's direction, calm and collected.

"Now that you're here," Duke responds with a wink and slight blush.

I lean into his side as we pass through the double doors. Ava and Ian are ahead of us and Nikki is at my side. Nikki links her arm through mine and pulls me out of earshot of Duke.

"I'm so sorry. Ava didn't want to wait," she squeaks.

"Totally fine." I fake passivity.

"But Duke said we shouldn't leave without you."

I smile at her, and her eyes twinkle. She lets go of my arm and runs ahead to Ava. I melt back into Duke's side, falling in line with his stride.

"What was that about?" he questions, oblivious to Ava's obvious cat and mouse game.

"Just girl talk, ya know."

I grab his hand, suppressing a shiver at how comfortably his palm fits against mine. He laughs, a short nervous sound, as I turn to walk backward, pulling him along to the rest of the group. Ian has his arm slung around Ava's shoulders and Nikki is chattering away. I'm not paying attention to the streets or directions, just following our leader.

We arrive at a short double staircase in front of automatic sliding doors. Tilting my head all the way back, I see a lighted sign at the top of the building, *University Crossing*. I look to the right and see Market Street buzzing with cars and people.

Ian takes out his phone and fires off a quick text. A second later, he's ushering us through the doors, bowing ostensibly. "M'Ladies."

Nikki and I giggle as we walk by. Ava acts like she owns the place.

"Get your IDs out, gents," Ian instructs in a low voice. I pull mine easily from the front pocket of my tiny bag and notice Nikki rifling through her clutch.

She looks up with panic in her eyes and whines, "Guys…"

"What?" Ava snaps.

I flinch. All our heads turn to focus on Nikki.

"I think I left my ID in my room."

"You're not actually serious?" Ava asks, dumbfounded. "Duke, Ian, come on, let's go. Nikki, go back and get it and call us when you get here."

I roll my eyes.

She's such a bitch.

"No, wait. I don't want to go back alone." She looks at me, pleading. "Casey? Go with me?"

Three pairs of eyes weigh on me, waiting for my answer.

* * * * *

The walk back to U-Cross is awkward. I'm quiet, unsure what to say to Nikki. It's been almost an hour, and no one is answering our messages.

It took us a solid twenty minutes to find our way from U-Cross back to Towers without Ian leading the way. We had trouble with security getting back up to our rooms since Nikki didn't have her ID. They actually escorted us. Once there, she couldn't find it anywhere. We both tore through everything she brought. Finally, she checked the back pocket of her jean shorts and there it was, all along. She apologized profusely the entire elevator ride down.

This must be karma for how I treated Jess. Maybe it'll make up for it if I have breakfast with her tomorrow? Yeah, I'll do that.

Arriving at U-Cross for a second time, we didn't know whether to go inside. Without Ian or his friend to sign us in, we didn't have a chance of getting past the security. We decide to sit outside, even in the slightly chilly night air, and wait a while. I sink into my frustration while Nikki asks a few students walking by if they'll sign us in. Each refuses wholeheartedly. After another thirty minutes of waiting, I've had enough.

"Well, that's it," I state, standing up and turning to go back the way we came.

She runs up to me. "No, you can't go! We'll figure this out. Come on, I need to go to this party."

I whip around, causing her to take a step back.

"You? *You* need to go to this party? Yeah, duh, we all *needed* to go to this party!" I stalk off down the path, intent on getting back to the dorm to go to sleep and get this night over with.

"I'm sorry, okay. How many times can I say it? I know I messed up. I always mess up."

That stops me. It strikes a chord.

It's okay, Nikki. I'm trying to be someone different too.

I slow my stride, letting her catch up.

"It happens. I'm sorry, I just can't sit outside and wait any longer. It's not worth it at this point." I shake my head. "I'm going back. You should come. I don't think you should be out alone."

She looks like she's close to tears but follows me back to Towers. At the elevators, I turn to her. "I'm just going to go back to my room. Maybe I'll see you at breakfast?"

"Sure," she mutters, keeping her eyes down.

It's an excruciatingly quiet elevator ride despite the whizzing sound of the gears pulling the cables. My floor is first. I step off quietly and turn before the doors close.

"Have a goodnight, see you tomorrow," I say and catch a glimpse of her sad eyes.

"Bye," she says as the doors close.

The common area is empty when I walk by. My room is empty when I come through the door.

"Is everyone having a better night than me?" I yell into the dark room.

I take my phone from my clutch and throw it on the bed. It bounces and lights up displaying a message.

MESSAGE: BRETT

Brett: hope ur sleeping well... i miss you

I tear my clothes off and leave them in a heap on the floor under the bed. Tossing Brett's t-shirt over my head, I crawl onto the thin, crunchy mattress and curl into a ball.

Tomorrow will be better.

I close my eyes and force sleep to take over.

CHAPTER 17

I wake to the obnoxious sound of my roommate's alarm at 6:00 a.m.

What the actual fuck.

I turn to look across the room, lifting my heavy eyelids in her direction and making awkward eye contact. She's already dressed in running tights and a long-sleeved thermal.

Who doesn't turn off their alarm when they're already awake?

"Sorry! I thought I turned it off. Guess I had it on just in case from last night. I was thinking about a quick run before breakfast and the welcome session. Want to come?"

A quick run?

I can't think of anything I want to do less.

"Sure." The word is out of my mouth, surprising me for the second time in the last twenty-four hours. "I have to warn you. I'm not much of a runner. I was a dancer all throughout middle and high school, but the long-distance thing was never my style."

"No worries, I didn't used to be either. Started this summer with a guy I liked for *forever* back home. We'll go slow and not very far so we can be back in time to shower and have breakfast."

I sit up in the bed, letting the comforter fall to my waist, realizing I never put shorts on last night.

"Hey, neat shirt," she says. "Boyfriend back home missing you?"

I shake my head, buying time to decide whether to lie or tell the truth.

One weekend… a little fib can't hurt.

"Not anymore. We broke up because I'm going here. Would you mind turning so I can just grab my bag? Sorry."

She turns to pick up her phone, checks, and immediately puts it back down before lifting her foot to the edge of the frame to tie her laces. When her back is turned, I quickly hop down off the bed and rifle through my bag again for my gym clothes. I probably should have worn these yesterday but wasn't sure what people would be wearing and went for fashion over function. I'm thankful to have them now and dress hurriedly. With a coy smile on my face, I put my index finger between my teeth and snap a selfie. I'm still looking at my phone, concentrating on sending the photo to Brett when she turns back around.

"Ready?" she asks.

I bend to tie my own laces and look up with a hesitant smile. "Are you sure you want me to come along?"

She laughs. "If you're bad, we'll just walk. I just want the fresh air."

We end up in a light jog most of the way as I follow her through the streets of West Philadelphia and Fairmount, past the art museum and back. I'm glad she knows where she's going because I'd be lost in a heartbeat. Not to mention how much concentration it's taking for me to keep up with her *and* try to contribute a modicum to the conversation. It's a good thing she's the chatty-type and I don't have to volunteer much.

By the time we get back, I'm a sweaty mess, but my muscles are deliciously fatigued and I'm going to be the good kind of sore tomorrow. We're laughing as we make our way through security and into the elevator to our floor to clean up. The silence between us and the rattling of the elevator jogs my memory of last night. A flash of remorse hits me.

"Hey, Jess, mind if I invite a friend to breakfast?" I ask, readying a message for Nikki.

"No worries. The more the merrier. Just tell them to meet us in the lobby at 8 a.m. We'll meet the rest of the guys from the floor that I was with last night and head down."

MESSAGE: NIKKI

> **Casey:** hey! hope u slept well
> **Casey:** my roommate and i are going to grab breakfast
> **Casey:** before the welcome session
> **Casey:** want to join?
> **Nikki:** Hi!
> **Nikki:** Yes!
> **Nikki:** Perfect!
> **Nikki:** Lobby?
> **Casey:** yep. meet us there at 8

I throw the phone on my bed with a satisfied smile.

So what if I missed the party last night? I bet it was nothing special anyway. I'll just have to find Duke at the welcome thing.

I'm pulled back to reality by the sound of a text.

MESSAGE: BRETT

Brett: good morning beautiful
> **Casey:** morning handsome

Casey: i just went for a run

Brett: no way

Brett: u?

Casey: i know right? who'd have thought

Casey: my roommate asked

Brett: she single

Casey: WHAT?!

Brett: just kidding

Brett: relax

Casey: better be

I'm standing by the door, creepy smile-texting when Jess catches me.

"You sure about that breakup?" She winks, eyes glittering, and grabs her shower bag on the way out the door.

* * * * *

The Welcome Session is held in the largest classroom auditorium in the College of Business building. The room could easily fit three hundred students, but when we arrive, it's nearly empty. Jess is the early type, and so is the rest of our little group apparently. I was hoping to come a little later so I could scout out where Duke was sitting and cozy up next to him.

Jess insists on a row in the middle and quite near the front. I convince her that a few rows back would be better so we'll be at eye level with the speakers. I pick a row that's easy enough to glance back at the doors as people walk in and let everyone file into the row ahead of me, leaving two open seats at the end of the aisle. It's a gamble, but I cross my fingers that some loner won't try to slide into the end.

A middle-aged professor in a full suit and tie and broad-rimmed glasses is at the front talking to what looks like a group of upperclassmen. They're definitely students but not fresh like all of us patiently sitting in the audience.

Who wears a suit on Saturday?

I wonder if that'll be me some day?

The room is filling quickly as we near our 9 a.m. start time. So far, no one has dared take a seat next to me. I don't know if I just seem unapproachable, pulling my phone out every two minutes, or if I'm unconsciously shooting daggers at anyone who looks interested.

Also, so far, no Duke, Ian, or Ava.

Start time rolls around and Mr. Suit announces that we'll just give everyone a couple more minutes. He cracks a joke about not being so nice on the first day of class. The upperclassmen laugh while everyone else looks nervous. I smirk, thinking that's sort of funny but also the least threatening thing I've ever heard.

I'm lost in thought, wondering if my absent new friends are alright, when the session gets started.

Mr. Suit is actually Mr. Finneghan, and he wears a suit to these because, "First impressions are everything." He oozes confidence while adjusting his cuff links.

Thankfully, my two seats are still empty. One of the upperclassmen is loading up a welcome video when I hear the doors in the back squeak open. A female voice laughs and shushes her accomplices. My stomach drops. Everyone turns to look.

I turn my head and see Ava in giant dark aviator sunglasses that cover more than half her face. Behind her, Duke and Ian are sporting baseball hats pulled down low. All three look sloppily put together.

"So nice of you three to finally grace us with your presence," Mr. Finneghan booms.

"Anytime." Ava is entirely unfazed.

My jaw drops. Ian snorts, trying to hold back a laugh. Duke looks like he's going to be sick. Chatter spreads across the audience.

I'm not the only one who can't believe her audacity.

"Quiet down, everyone. Hasn't anyone seen the circus before?" Mr. Finneghan jokes.

It's Ava's turn to flush red.

"Take a seat, you three. The rest of us would like to get on with our day if you'll allow it."

She glides across the auditorium, looking for a group of empty seats. I sit up a little straighter and catch Ian's eye with a slight wave at shoulder height. Luckily, he notices just in time to make a quick right and turns down the aisle to my row, Duke in tow, leaving Ava oblivious to her lone wandering. She spots a few seats and turns to motion the boys. When they're not behind her, her eyes dart anxiously. She recovers, quickly sinking into a seat and leans low on the armrest. She pulls the glasses from her face, collapsing them, and rests her forehead on her fingertips. Ian clunks into the seat next to me, leaving Duke on the end and me simmering in irritation.

He nods toward me and attempts at a whisper.

"Thanks, pretty girl." It comes out a little loud and a little slurred together.

If I wasn't so turned off by the stale smell of beer coming off him, I might be thrilled at the new nickname. I tilt my head toward him without looking away from the PowerPoint screen.

"Anytime."

From the corner of my eye, I see Duke smirk at my response, and bite my lip to hide my smile.

Take that, Ava.

CHAPTER 18

My eyes glaze over after the third student testimonial in the welcome video. They're inspiring, but at the moment, my brain is calculating the best approach to leave this session with Duke's phone number.

An idea sparks, and I pull out my phone and open a new contact. In the first name field, I type *Ian* and stealthily pass my phone to him. His gaze shifts down to my hand and back up to my profile. I smile and wink without turning my head, doing my best to ostensibly flirt while not being obvious to the presenters at the front of the room. He grins devilishly and licks his lips, brushing my hand as he grabs the phone. I suppress the desire to wipe my hand against my jeans. He adds his last name and phone number.

As he's about to pass the phone back to me, Duke lifts his palm in front of Ian. Ian glances down and back up at Duke. I turn my head and see a confused look on Ian's face. Duke's fingers flex, motioning Ian to pass the phone to him, and I hold my face neutral, not wanting to give away my euphoria that my plan worked.

Thank God.

An accomplished, satisfying flutter shakes my breath, raising goosebumps along my arms. Duke leans slightly in his seat and places the phone directly into my upturned palm. It takes every ounce of effort not to look, but I close my fingers and tuck the phone in my pocket without checking the contact he added.

We spend the rest of the session in companionable silence until Mr. Finneghan thanks us all for our attention. He motions to the teaching assistants with him along the front, explaining that everyone will be available for questions during the subsequent luncheon. Duke stands first, stepping out into the aisle toward the front of the room and the presenters. He ushers Ian past him and extends his hand for me to step out in front of him and my heart races. I thank him, taking a step toward the exit before remembering who I came with and pivoting back to the small group still congregating in the row.

"Duke, Ian, you remember Nikki?" She beams at my reintroduction before I motion to Jess. "This is my roommate Jess and some of the people from our floor... Sorry, guys, I'm bad with names."

Each nods and extends the customary name and hometown that I'd learned this morning is the appropriate introduction when meeting new people at college. When it's Jess's turn, her eyes seem unimpressed, almost disappointed.

"Hi, nice to meet you," she says, not granting them any more of her time. It dawns on me that she must disapprove of their earlier interruption. Or perhaps she, like everyone else, can tell they had an unsanctioned, particularly late night.

"Well, shall we?" I state to no one in particular, turning my eyes to focus on the line of students at the exit and hoping someone will follow me.

While waiting for the crowd to organize itself enough to shuffle through the double doors, I check my phone.

No new messages.

Where is Brett?

I find it odd to have nothing from him, given our earlier exchange that I left dangling unanswered once Ian and Duke arrived. Shifting against the tightly packed crowd, I grip the phone with both hands and navigate to my inbox, thumbs poised, ready to type out a lengthy message apologizing for the delay. I see a message from Brett marked *Read* that I surely didn't read.

Oh, shit, which one of them read it?

I'm beginning to read the message when Duke walks up next to me, bumping my shoulder.

"So, who's Brett?" he asks, a hint of a joke hanging on his tone.

A moment of panic, not knowing how to answer, is quickly overcome by an idea.

I don't have to tell him any more than he's told me.

"Just some guy." I breeze by the question, suppressing the slight twinge of guilt I feel at reducing Brett to nothing.

I imagine the different directions this conversation can take.

I could pry about last night... But probably classier if I don't come off as the jealous type.

I turn to face him, carefully walking sideways, and ask, "How long have you been playing guitar?"

We're stopped by the slow-moving group of students in front of us, and I tuck my hair behind my ears nervously.

He speaks over the top of my head, looking for something over everyone surrounding us. "I was probably ten or so when I started taking lessons."

Look at me... Please, look at me.

I feel my cheeks heat, and my feet involuntarily step closer to Duke, closing some space between us. A short, stocky guy in ripped jeans and a stoner hoodie seizes the opportunity

I've created to squeeze behind me, making a beeline toward the coffee table. I steady myself and place my hand on Duke's bicep, feeling the warmth of his skin before focusing on the length of muscle flexing under my touch.

"Sorry. Do you ever give lessons?" I ask, hopefully.

"I haven't." He places a hand on the small of my back, pulling me slightly closer and saving me from being bumped by the expanding group of people filling the space I left open behind us.

"Would you?" I ask, stepping into him and peering into his face.

He looks down as the length of my body meets his. His eyes fix on mine as if we aren't in the middle of a packed hallway.

"Are you asking me to teach you?" he asks slowly, his eyebrows spike before settling.

"Maybe… after we move in… you could show me?" I blush.

I try to ignore the glimpse of red hair I see behind Duke, weaving through the crowd in our direction, and pray he'll answer before she interrupts.

Say yes, say yes, say yes.

"After we move in then." His tone is a hint unsure, but his lips curl into a small smile.

I feel a text vibrate in my pocket.

Shit.

He removes his hand from my back as if he'd been resting it on a hot stove and only just realized it was burning.

"You'll have to let me know which dorm you end up in when you find out." His voice is flat as he nods in the direction of the phone in my pocket.

As close to a "text me" affirmation as I'm going to get, I guess.

I frown and look down before replying to him.

"Of course," I murmur.

I'm about to tell him to do the same when both Ava and Jess appear. Jess links her arm in mine, stealing me away to rejoin the other group. Before we break into the circle, she looks at me with a serious face.

"How do you know them?" Her voice is low and suspicious.

I look at her with my head tilted in question and then realize she has no idea that these were the "friends" I was meeting last night.

"Oh! I met them on the bus yesterday. They were part of the group of people I was meeting up with last night," I respond with renewed clarity and pause, waiting to gauge her reaction. Then I think to clarify for good measure, "Including Nikki!"

She looks at me, her eyes narrow, and barely and gives me an, "Mhmm," before officially bringing us back into the group.

What's so wrong with Duke?

I shake my head and scan the crowd. My eyes connect with his longingly. He holds my gaze for a second before breaking away, half-heartedly replying to whatever question Ava's just asked. I watch him as he follows her away toward a larger group of what must be the popular people from their respective hometowns. My heart tugs wistfully at the fact that I'm not currently standing in their group before I turn to look over the group of people I am standing with.

It's just one weekend. The first of many.

Plastering a half-fake smile on my face, I insert myself into the conversation on latest market trends.

Absolutely scintillating.

CHAPTER 19

The two weeks at home after orientation fly by in a blur and move-in day is here already. It's Friday and we're on our way to my 12 p.m. move-in time slot. This time, my mom and I are in one car, following my dad in his pickup truck packed with most of my life, for the now familiar two-hour drive. I let my thoughts wander.

Jess and I were somehow lucky enough to successfully request a roommate reassignment and are living together in the two-room, suite-style dorm called Race. She has an actual roommate named Hope. I've been lucky enough to end up roommate-less after a string of girls were assigned and then reassigned due to Jess and my last-minute request. I'm excited to have my own room but also that I'll have a friend to live with instead of complete strangers.

As the days leading up to room assignments passed, the disappointment that Duke still hadn't texted me ate at me more and more. I finally couldn't take it any longer and sent him a message once our room assignment was official. The "I'm sorry, who is this?" response suddenly made sense of why I hadn't heard from him. When I told him it was me, he sent back a flurry of apologies about never asking for my number.

Unfortunately, he isn't in Race but just across the small one-way street in Calhoun. We've texted every day since then.

Each day closer to being on campus, we flirted with the line of intimacy but never quite crossed it.

There's something here, though. I can feel it.

After orientation, Brett and I had a long talk about what life is like starting college. I was pleasantly surprised that he was happy with how he thought the night of orientation panned out.

Maybe I can have my cake and eat it too.

I told him I wasn't entirely sure what to expect but anticipated it wouldn't be much different than the one night away. He promised we could make it work this way so long as I promised to text him like I did and try to call him at least on the weeknights. He said we could make it through this term, maybe even this year, and then I could transfer to Chicago. I think I've known all along—a sentiment I kept buried deep down—that I don't have it in me to move halfway across the country for him, despite how infatuated I may have once felt.

My mom pulls me back to reality. "Did you remember the bathroom box?"

"I'm sure Dad grabbed it." I pull out my phone to check for messages.

"Well, could you just call him and make sure?"

I look at her, my jaw hanging open. "Are you serious? Is it really that important? I'm sure I can get a shower curtain *somewhere* in Philadelphia." I scoff and turn my attention back to my phone.

"Can you just do it, Casey?" she snaps.

"Whoa, Mom."

I'm about to rag on her and then it dawns on me that she must also be experiencing a lot of feelings right now. Her baby girl is about to leave the nest. After seventeen years of constant attention, she'll have to find something else to focus on. I'm having trouble thinking about life without someone I just met a couple months ago. I can't imagine what she's going through thinking about me not being home anymore.

I change my tone. "Of course, Mom." I look at her and see her face is tight. "You know I'll be back. Right?" I tease.

"No, I know." She lets out a nervous laugh, holding back tears.

A wide smile spreads across my face. "Well, listen, can you just get it out now? I don't really want you crying in front of everyone."

"Oh, just wait until you have kids one day, missy," she chides with a hint of laughter in her voice.

"Yikes. Not there yet, Mom," I joke and bring the phone to my ear, calling the truck in front of us.

* * * * *

The street in front of my dorm is blocked off for move-in day. My mom and I pull in behind my dad and get out as a girl in a "New Student Move-in Day" t-shirt approaches.

"Name and room number?" she sings, overly cheery.

"Casey Windsor, 11-113."

Pulling a green highlighter from her ear, she yanks the cap with her teeth and highlights a row on the spreadsheet attached to her clipboard.

"Perfect. Here, please keep this on your dashboards. There's a two-hour limit." She turns and motions behind her. "Those orange bins are for your use, but they're first-come, first-serve. Best of luck and welcome!"

She bounces on to the next group of parents and students behind us. I turn to my parents, feeling slightly overwhelmed, and look up at my dorm.

The students who are already moved in have wasted no time decorating. Everything from signs and flags to messages and pictures can be seen on almost every window. I'm mesmerized, trying to take everything in when Dad breaks my trance and gives me direction.

"Bird, why don't you go get one of those bins? Mom and I will start getting things off the back. Piece of cake."

In a daze, I make my way to the row of bins and pass a boy and girl fighting.

He's my height and lanky, with a mop of curly dark hair flopping over his forehead. He's wearing cargo shorts and a t-shirt with an Xbox controller on the front. I think he must be just the slightest bit chilly in the brisk, late-September air. The girl is about his size, maybe a little overweight, in low-rise, flare-leg jeans and a simple black V-neck. A small line of pudge peeks out between the hem of her shirt and top of her jeans. I cringe internally and readjust my own shirt reflexively.

"I told Mom we should've brought our own cart!" the boy complains.

"If you didn't have so much *stuff!*" the girl yells back.

"This is going to take *forever!*" he huffs.

"Everyone's doing the same thing. Look!" She swings her arm out in gesture and wails me in the back. I spin and see his face. He looks visibly distraught.

"Abby! Look what you've done. God, would you just go back to the car, please?" He steps toward me. "I'm so sorry. My sister has zero spatial awareness."

"Oh, it's okay," I reply, grabbing the edge of one bin. "I'm Casey," I say, slowly pushing off in the direction of our mutual parked cars.

He does the same and catches up. "I'm Elias."

He sticks out his hand in front of me while I'm still moving forward. It knocks into my chest. I laugh and stop pushing as he launches into another apology about personal space.

"Nice to meet you Elias. Where are you from?"

"Portland," he states, matter of fact.

I wait, but after several seconds realize he doesn't intend to clarify.

"Oregon or Maine?" I ask.

"Oh, right! Maine," he says and then continues as an afterthought, "What about you?"

"New Jersey, just outside of New York."

"Oh, awesome, that must be cool. I've never been there." He must see the shock on my face and stops to wholeheartedly laugh before continuing. "What room are you in?" He points up at the building.

"11-113, you?"

"I'm on nine… Nine-something. It's on my paper in the car… Hey! Why don't we exchange numbers?" he asks as if the thought is genius.

"Sure, okay." I smile and pull out my phone, opening a new contact.

I like Elias.

He's all over the place, but it's funny and endearing. We exchange numbers, agree to message each other once we've moved in, and head in the direction of our separate cars. My parents are wearing cat-that-got-the-mouse grins when I arrive back at the truck.

"So, who was that?" My mom draws out the question.

"Elias from Maine," I state.

She turns to conspire with my dad, repeating, "Elias from Maine."

He raises his eyebrows and whistles.

"You two are the worst! Come on. This is going to take forever as it is. Let's get going," I suggest and roll my eyes.

They both start loading perfectly stacked boxes into the bin while I turn and glance at Elias. He's arguing animatedly with a woman who looks exactly like an older version of his sister Abby. I shake my head, getting back to unloading the truck. Suddenly my nerves are calmed and a flood of excitement washes over me.

I wonder who I'll meet next.

CHAPTER 20

Two hours later, I'm standing in my room alone. I stare at the piles of boxes, shelves, and suitcases wondering where to start.

Not wanting to draw out the goodbyes any longer than necessary, my parents stayed just long enough to help me unload everything into my room and feel slightly like I belong here. With tears in all our eyes, we shared tight hugs and "I love yous" before they left me to start unpacking for my new life.

I start on the boxes. My mind wanders involuntarily to my class schedule as the innate straight-A student in me takes over. When I'm sure I've run through the week, early classes and all, the thought of first-weekend parties creeps in. My skin tingles with excitement at first, flushing to nerves quickly after realizing I might not have anyone to go with. Jess doesn't exactly strike me as the party type, and I haven't kept in contact with Nikki. I'm not sure I trust Ian enough to go with just him and my status with Duke is unclear.

I shake my head, casting away the nerves, and reassure myself that I'll meet plenty of people before that becomes a problem. This is college and everyone's in the same position on their first night, looking to find their group of friends. Glancing around my mostly put-together room, I'm surprised that Jess hasn't arrived yet. I throw the purple silk robe that

I'm holding over the back of the stiff standard-issued metal desk chair and reach for my phone when a loud knock on the door startles me. Unsure of who'd be knocking, I hesitate and continue to check for messages.

MESSAGE: BRETT

Brett: hey

Brett: how'd move in go?

MESSAGE: MOM

Mom: miss you already xoxo

I'm disappointed and dying to send a message to Duke but promise myself I won't look desperate for attention and text him so soon after moving in. Oddly, there's nothing new from Jess, either.

MESSAGE: JESS

Casey: are u here yet?

Another knock and a "Hello" is called through the heavy wooden door—a guy's voice.

I pick my way through the cardboard carnage and into the empty hallway leading to the emptier living room and the main door. Glancing through the peephole, I see the shaggy hair from this morning, and it clicks.

Elias!

I slip the latch to unlock the door and press the handle down, swinging it inward with a smile on my face.

"Elias! What are you doing here? You remembered my room number?" I ask, incredulously.

He taps his head in a "this thing is a vault" motion. "I'm more of a set up as you go kinda guy but figured you might need some help?" He sounds hopeful.

"Absolutely. I'm just waiting for my suite-mate Jess to get here with her parents. Come in! What about your roommate? I figured you'd be meeting people on your floor," I ramble.

He moves through my doorway and starts to answer. Just then, I hear another "Hello" from the main hallway and recognize the sound of Jess's voice. Elias steps in, and I trade places with him in the hall.

"Ah, Jess! You made it!" I squeal in delight.

"Ugh you have no idea," she huffs. "We left the house late, Mom *had* to stop for coffee, one of the throw pillows for the couch came loose on the highway, and then when we got here..." She pauses, frustrated, waving a perfectly manicured hand. "Did you know those orange bins are first-come, first-serve? I've been standing down there for practically half an hour waiting for someone to bring one back—oh... hello!" She beams at Elias.

"Hey, I'm Elias."

She extends her hand politely. "Jessica. You can call me Jess, or either really. Either is fine. I don't mind."

He takes her hand gingerly, a twinkle in his eye. "Hi, Either. Where are you from?"

She giggles. "You're funny. I'm from The Main Line."

When there's no look of understanding in his eyes, she continues, "Malvern. Pennsylvania. You must not be from around here."

"Nope, Portland." His tone is matter of fact again. He glances at me, and then as if something on my face jogs his memory, he clarifies, "Maine, not Oregon."

"Oh! Very nice. Makes total sense then. Of course, you wouldn't know The Main Line. I guess it's really just a PA thing. I have to remember that for when we start meeting more people. At orientation, there were a bunch of people from this area and—"

"Jess, where are your parents?" I cut her off.

"Oh, right! Let me just drop my bag. They're downstairs waiting for me to help unpack. I should probably go get them. You'll be here when I get back?" she asks, looking between me and Elias.

"Of course. Elias was just about to help me finish unpacking my room. We can help you once everything is up here," I assure her.

He nods in agreement.

She walks into the living room and literally drops her bag in the center of the floor. "Perfect. I'll just be right back!"

I stride back through the doorway and pass Elias on the way to my room.

He follows and comments, "She seems nice."

I laugh and continue toward the rest of the boxes.

Walking into the room, he notices my purple silk robe. Without asking, he picks it up and slips it over his shoulders, turning to admire himself in the mirror on the inside of the closet door. Twisting back to face me, he pulls the sides out like a dress and jokes, "Do I look pretty?" With a goofy grin, he dips into a curtsy and then grabs one of the long ends of the tie, twirling it in circles through the air.

"Oh, my God!" I fake mortification. "Take that off!"

"No way, this is awesome!" He picks up the closest box and opens it, pulling out my favorite coffee mug. He holds it up and asks, "Kitchen?"

"Bathroom actually," I joke.

He pouts at me.

"Oh, come on, seriously? Joke… duh," I tease.

He sticks his tongue out at me and leaves the room, still wearing the robe. I hear the door squeak open and Jess chatting with her parents. The chatter stops.

"Oh, my God!" she shouts in a rush and erupts in more giggles. "*What are you wearing?*"

"Oh, this old thing?" I picture him pinching the fabric between his fingers, lifting it off his chest.

I quickly rush into the kitchen area. "Sorry! That's mine." I flush, embarrassed.

An average-height older gentleman with salt and pepper hair wearing khakis and a light blue polo stands behind a trim, well-manicured woman with a perfect light brown bob, tailored blue jeans and a Lilly Pulitzer blouse. His hands rest on her shoulders.

"Well, I think it's stylish," the man comments.

"See!" Elias turns to me. "He thinks I look good."

Jess giggles again. "Casey, these are my parents. Mom, Dad, this is my suite-mate Casey and her friend Elias."

"Walter." The man extends his hand toward me and then Elias.

The woman follows suit. "Karen, so nice to meet you both. Well, Jess, we'd better get started."

"Elias, why don't you help Jess and her parents? I can take care of the rest of my room." I don't need him discovering any of my bras or panties.

God knows where they would end up.

"Sure. See you in a few." He slides the robe off his shoulders and lets the fabric slip through his fingers into my waiting hand.

With the four of them gone, I pull out my phone, dragging my feet back to my room.

MESSAGE: MOM

    Casey: miss u both too!

    Casey: let me know when u make it home <3

MESSAGE: BRETT

    Casey: it wasn't bad

    Casey: i'm working on unpacking

    Casey: made a few friends

Brett: thats great

Brett: good luck

Brett: i'm jealous

    Casey: why?

Brett: wish I was getting to meet u

I don't know how to respond, so I just don't. I scroll through my inbox to the last message from Duke and reread the last few exchanges with a smile. My fingers itch to send a message, fighting with the logical side of my brain that says he'll text me when he wants to talk to me.

Screw it.

MESSAGE: DUKE

    Casey: hey! hope move in's going well!

I wait, leaning against the doorway to my room with the phone cradled in my fingers, hoping for an answer.

CHAPTER 21

After we've helped Jess settle and said goodbye to her parents, the three of us venture into the halls in search of new friends. We spill out onto the eleventh floor in a heap of laughs. Elias has been keeping us entertained for the last several hours.

As we walk down the hall, Elias knocks on every single door that's closed and barges into the ones that are open. Jess talks to *every single person*, getting their entire life's story in the first five minutes. I just concentrate on remembering their names. The three of us collect and lose people along the way, eventually making it to Elias's floor and all the way to his room at the other end of the building.

Having worked up an appetite, we descend the double-wide, metal steps into the dining hall. I tip my head back, looking up through the glass structure encasing the stairwell and into the darkening evening sky. I've been lost in thought the entire walk over. At first, it was strange to be entering the private spaces of people I don't know, but after the first few rooms, I was energized by the thrill of meeting new people. Now, looking up, the smooth bleed of light to dark is calming and quiets my mind. Every person we've met has been so welcoming. I've felt more and more like a new person with each interaction, and it's intoxicating.

I almost walk into Elias in my inattentive state. He waves his arm in front of my chest and cracks a joke about "mom-barring" me. We're nearing the bottom of the steps when I notice him motioning to a guy standing by a sort-of hostess station. A short, older woman in white kitchen livery guards what looks like a credit card scanner. The first thing that strikes me about the guy is his shoes. They're a cross between dressy oxfords and loafers.

They're an odd choice for a college freshman.

He somehow makes them look casual.

He's paired them with dark wash, tapered jeans, a crisp white t-shirt, and a slim-fit, black, zip-up hoodie. A thin, dark cord hangs low on his chest. His golden hair is long in the front and lightly styled to look messily un-styled. He's artfully put together.

I internally take stock of my own outfit and instantly feel underdressed in my low-rise bell-bottom jeans and navy blue fitted hoodie, a large white moose plastered prominently over the left side of my chest.

I guess I'll have to make another upgrade.

At first glance, I can't see how this person and Elias are friends. They couldn't be more opposites. He looks up from his phone and greets Elias with a smirk and the familiar male handshake and then shifts his gaze to both Jess and me while Elias makes the introduction.

"Ryan, this is Jess from *The Main Line.*" He emphasizes using air quotes. "And Casey, from somewhere in New Jersey just outside of New York."

"Nice to meet you both. I'm *actually* from New York." He looks at me expectantly.

I blush, unsure of what to say, but Elias rescues me, cutting in.

"Ryan's dad and my dad are sailing buddies. He has a summer house next to my family's on one of the islands just off the coast of Portland."

Jess chimes into the next empty space. "Wow, sailing! Ryan, do you sail? Drexel has a team although I think practices are probably super early in the morning and there's a lot of traveling, obviously. But it could be fun!"

I'm constantly amazed at the amount of knowledge Jess has stored up for use in small talk.

Ryan's response is casual. "I do sail, but I hadn't considered joining the team. I'll have to look into that."

There's no way he is going to look into that.

It's finally no longer acceptable for me to not contribute to the conversation. I choose my response carefully. "Very impressive. I don't know much about sailing, but my grandfather has a boat down in Florida. We go to visit every summer."

"I didn't know that!" Jess beams at me. "So cool, where in Florida?"

"Just north of Palm Beach."

"Just outside of New York. Just north of Palm Beach. Well, Casey, you are a girl shrouded in mystery."

He's challenging me. My knee-jerk reaction to shrink away is creeping through my system. I swallow against it, shoving it down deep.

One day this'll come naturally.

"Stick around. Maybe I'll let my mask slip." I look him squarely in the eyes, daring him to come at me again.

Ryan breaks into a wicked grin, raising one eyebrow. "Maybe I'll do that." The words drip off his tongue in a purr.

"Okay, you two." Elias inserts himself between us. "Shall we?"

He hands the woman his student ID and gestures toward the entrance to the food stations. She swipes it, hands it back, and robotically replies, "Thank you. Next."

"After you." Ryan steps to the side to let Jess and me lead the way. She follows me forward but twists her head to continue the conversation.

"So what dorm are you in, Ryan?" Jess asks.

"Calhoun," he replies with a hint of disgust in his voice.

A sharp flash of emotion splits through me at the mention of his dorm assignment. I can't place whether it is jealousy, excitement, or something else.

Duke.

"Ah! Right across from us. We're in Race. Which side are you on? Maybe we can see your room from ours?" Jess bounces along next to him.

We're picking our way through the choices. Ryan and Elias break away when we stop at the salad bar, but we meet back up at the "Dinner Special" station for chicken, mashed potatoes, and green beans. All of us agree the gravy looks a tad suspicious.

"I'm facing Arch Street." I overhear him answering Jess, picking back up where they left off, while heading toward the dessert.

Elias and I are both walking toward the drinks. I bump his shoulder.

"Sailing? Summer home on an island?" I look at him dumbfounded. "What are you some kind of Maine royalty?"

He laughs. "Just outside of New York must be a really small place."

"Really small." I admit.

"Don't get your panties in a twist." He eyes me. "By the way, Ryan's gay."

"He's gay?" I repeat. "Oh!"

My shoulders relax, some of the tension melting away.

* * * * *

Ryan invites us back to Calhoun after dinner. Just before we reach the few steps toward the entrance, Jess gets a call from someone back home. She frowns, covers the mouthpiece, and mouths, "It's urgent." I make eye contact with her, telepathically asking if everything is okay. She just smiles in my direction and promises to let us know when she's headed over to meet us before turning toward the dirt path that will bring her back to Race.

We hand over our IDs to the public safety guard at the desk. He looks miserable, and I can't really blame him. I try for a smile and some small talk while he takes down our info and get nothing but a grunt in response. I shrug and look at Ryan. He rolls his eyes and pushes through the turnstiles.

While standing at the elevator, I notice a piano down the hall in the common space.

"Can anyone play that?" I ask, pointing in its direction, keeping up the small talk.

"I believe so." Ryan shifts his gaze for just a moment. "I saw a guy there earlier today when everyone was moving in."

I nod without responding.

The elevator dings, announcing its arrival. The three of us step inside, and Ryan presses the button for floor seven. We've arranged ourselves into separate corners, each looking at the other person. I lean back against the front corner, looking back toward Elias in the back corner, before realizing I may be accidentally pressing buttons. I push off the wall and readjust my sweatshirt, allowing a thin line of my abdomen to peek out above the top of my jeans. Ryan glances at my movement before dropping his head to a text he's just received. Elias's eyes flash from the hemline to my face and back. I wrap my arm across my stomach, resting my elbow on my wrist, and drop my hand across my lips to cover a smile. I sigh and shift to rest my back on the doors.

"Do you play?" Ryan asks, several beats after the initial jolt of lifting off the ground floor.

I'm already enjoying the extra attention when the warm confidence washes over me. "Yes. My grandmother taught me," I say with pride.

"You'll have to play for us sometime," Ryan challenges.

Elias wiggles his eyebrows. "Yeah, you'll have to play for us sometime." His voice lilts flirtatiously.

"Yeah, I don't think so," I scoff.

"Then why'd you ask?" Elias teases. Ryan rolls his eyes at our exchange.

I'm trying to hide the blush spreading across my cheeks and find the best response when the number seven lights up. The doors clang and slide open. I turn to step out of the elevator, realizing I probably should have let Ryan out first, and run face-first into some guy's chest. Stumbling backward, I repeat my apology while trying to recover. I get my bearings and finally look up to see who I collided with.

A cool rush runs down my spine, like someone dropped an ice cube down the back of my shirt. I can't stop the shiver that racks through me.

CHAPTER 22

It's Duke.

"Ca-Casey! Hey…" he stammers, a little color coming to his cheeks.

"Hi." I dip my head low and look up through my eyelashes.

Ryan and Elias file out of the elevator and fan out on either side behind me.

"You don't live in Calhoun?" Duke asks, confused, despite knowing the answer.

"No. But I do," Ryan responds, stepping around and in front of me.

I find his posture oddly possessive but can't figure out whether it's toward me or Duke.

"Hey, I'm Elias." He jumps in, extending his hand, and nods. "This is Ryan and you clearly know Casey."

"Duke," he responds more evenly, shaking Elias's hand before Ryan's. Ryan lingers a bit longer than I'm happy about. "You live here, too?" Duke asks Elias.

"Nah. I'm in Race with Casey. Met her at move-in." Elias smiles back at me. "Where are you from?"

I'm quiet during the initial exchange of pleasantries, observing from behind the wall of Elias and Ryan, who have both stepped in front of me to interact with Duke. Duke's gaze darts between them and me despite my lack of contribution to the conversation. Everything they're talking about we've already discussed over text the last few weeks.

And more.

God, he looks just as good as at Orientation.

Why didn't he text me back?

I'm alone in my head wondering why he appears nervous and almost uninterested to have run into me when I see a glimpse of the red hair. Ava enters the triangle of space we are occupying in front of the elevator before I hear her familiar voice.

"Duke, you coming?"

My blood boils and I turn toward the sound. Plastering a giant smile on my face, I muster the sweetest voice possible.

"Avaaa." I draw out her name as if I'm excited to see her. "So *great* to see you again. I didn't know you live in Calhoun."

"Oh, hey. Cassie, right?" She looks unfazed, not ruffled in the slightest to see me.

"Casey," I correct her.

"Right," she says dismissively. "Yeah, I'm on this floor."

Out of the corner of my eye, I see Ian enter through the opposite doorway.

"Hey, Ryan, thought I heard you. Do you mind if I use your speaker system?" Ian stops short, spotting me standing in the cluster of people. "Hey!" He grins. "How's it going, pretty girl? You live here too?"

His eyes rake down my body, stopping at the skin peeking out above the button of my jeans. He doesn't bother to try to hide his gaze. I'm torn between the heat of the attention and distaste at the way he's looking at me but make a point of answering for myself this time.

"No, I'm across the street in Race," I say, returning his smile. "We just ran into Duke coming back from dinner. Ryan signed us in. This is Elias."

Ian comes forward for the bro handshake, back-slap combo with Elias, but his eyes never leave mine. I can tell Ryan and Duke are looking at me and feel a slight twinge of tension fill the air.

"You all have already met?" Ryan questions.

I refuse to break eye contact with Ian first. Something about Duke and Ava boosts my confidence.

"We were at the same orientation," I answer, still without taking my eyes off Ian.

"Ah…" Ryan's voice fades dramatically.

Duke steps toward me, and Ian shifts his gaze from me to Duke. I suck in my bottom lip and squeeze my stomach muscles when Duke brushes my shoulder before stepping past me.

"We were just headed down to the dorm meeting," Duke says, checking his phone. "I think it's at 9 p.m. Right, Ava?"

I slouch slightly, my confidence slipping as I realize he wasn't stepping toward me but toward the elevator to press the call button again. Elias shifts to stand by my side, and I feel a buzz coming off him but can't place the emotion.

Jealousy or protection?

"Oh, right, that's tonight," Ryan adds, sounding bored.

"There's a party on Powelton," Ian chimes in. "We should go!" he says to no one in particular.

"We are," Ava responds.

Ryan looks at Elias and me. "I should probably go to this. Sorry you have to leave so soon after getting here."

I ignore his statement, instead focusing on Ian.

"When and where?" I fake nonchalance.

"I'll text you the address. The theme tonight is Dress to Impress."

His face lights up in anticipation while his fingers fly over the small keys of his Blackberry. A second later, I feel my pocket vibrate and pull my phone out to see a text from him with the address. Elias moves slowly from my side toward the elevator.

"Come on, Case, we should head back for our own floor meetings anyway."

"Aw, my friends back home call me Case." I smile nostalgically.

"Aww," Ava mocks. "Isn't that sweet."

I shoot her a glare, about to deliver a comeback when the elevator sounds again, announcing its arrival. We all pile in, and Ava presses the lobby button. Everyone stares straight forward, barely making a sound. The silence is awkward.

At the third floor, Duke subtly turns his head toward his shoulder, as if to look back at me. The ding announcing our arrival at the lobby pulls his head forward again. Elias and Ryan exit first to the right for Ryan to sign us out, followed by Duke and Ian to the left toward the common room. I hang back, letting Ava step out before me. A string of curse words run through my mind watching the back of her head as she walks away.

I shouldn't have let her go first.

She turns slightly with a waggle of fingers and calls, "Buh-bye." I see the smirk on her face as she, Ian, and Duke continue down the hallway.

I turn to catch up with Ryan and Elias, adding a little run to my steps before coming up behind them.

"So, can we go to the party?" I clasp my hands in front of my chest, playing off my pleading tone in an overly dramatic begging motion.

"We can. After the meeting," Ryan replies at the same time that Elias says quietly, "I have to call my girlfriend." Disappointment tugs at the corners of his lips.

"What! You have a girlfriend?" I ask, not hiding the shock in my voice.

I did not see that one coming.

"Yeah, back in Maine," Elias explains.

"Seriously, Elias?" Ryan prods. "I thought you would have broken things off with her by now."

I'm even more shocked that Ryan already knows this interesting fact.

"We're seeing how long distance works until she's finished with high school."

I soften.

Long distance. I know what that's like.

"Aw, that's sweet, Elias. What's her name?" I ask.

"Maggie. She's a year younger than me," he clarifies although I sort of figured from his statement about finishing high school.

Ryan is filling out the time next to our names and handing the sheet back to the guard. He looks up at me. "Elias and Maggie have been dating for three years. He's absolutely smitten, though I told him he needed some space coming to college."

I imagine what it would be like not to have the familiar unread message from Brett waiting for me every time I check my phone and understand entirely why Elias has trouble agreeing that he needs space coming here. For a moment, I consider sharing this with my new friends, a show of camaraderie that I'm sure would be welcomed, when a message vibrates in my pocket.

MESSAGE: DUKE

Duke: sorry about that

Duke: catch up later?

    Casey: anytime

    Casey: just let me know

I return to the waiting faces of Elias and Ryan. A darkness fills my mind, clouding my honesty with fear and something else.

Better not.

CHAPTER 23

Thank God Syllabus week is a real thing.

After a weekend full of parties, drinking, and so many new faces, I'm exhausted before classes even begin. All I want to do on this fresh fall Monday morning is wrap myself in a blanket and stay in bed, replaying the way Duke looked in those dark jeans and plain black t-shirt Friday night. My stomach turns over at the memory of Ava hugging him around the waist after sinking the winning shot at beer pong. They were on the same team. He saw me with Ryan, Elias, and Jess and waved.

Just waved.

Maybe I was more drunk than I thought, but was he also looking at me the entire night? Why didn't he just come talk to me? And why didn't he answer my text the next morning? It was just breakfast.

I mindlessly pull on my favorite pair of jeans and the biggest, chunkiest, sweatshirt I can find before rushing out the door to my first class.

Thankfully, each class is cut short after introductions, disbursing the syllabus, and maybe an awkward icebreaker designed to help students get to know their classmates. I can't imagine the professors are ignorant enough to think we need an icebreaker to meet people on campus. By the first day of class, most people have already established some semblance of a friend group. I'm only slightly upset that I'm back with the same group of people I would have been with in high school.

Okay, maybe more than slightly. And they're really not too bad.

Duke is in a few of my classes, though the only attention he's given me in person so far is a slight nod in passing. He's always sitting in a group with Ian and Ava. Occasionally, he answers my text messages, but the flirty innuendos are gone. I think back to the last text exchange before we moved in. He told me I'm exactly his type, though he didn't think he was exactly boyfriend material. I assured him that I was in no way looking for a boyfriend, but that didn't mean he couldn't be my type either. I signed it with a wink, and he responded with a tongue out smiley face.

What went wrong?

Thursday after class, I run into him in Starbucks. I smile at the fact that we're both alone. A devious plan races to the front of my mind and I place my hand on his bicep before letting it drag down his arm as I come up to stand next to him in line. He startles but doesn't flinch away from my touch and finally looks into my eyes with the same confidence from the first time I saw him.

He responds wholeheartedly to my initial questions on class schedules and dinner plans before his face drops and he reaches into his pocket for his phone. I stop trying to continue the conversation after getting distracted one-word responses for the next five minutes. He's concentrating so hard on his phone, dropping a smirk, before looking up at me at the last second almost missing me say goodbye. I thought I caught something in his eyes as I turned to walk away, but I was too busy trying to hide my own disappointment with my nose buried in my own phone.

By the end of our first week, Jess and I have planned our next few weeks ensuring that we'll stay on track with classes while also finding time to participate in extracurricular activities. Unfortunately, she's not really interested in the party scene, but Ian has helped me make sure I don't lose out on that activity. It's a perfect coincidence that Ryan lives with Ian, and they both live on the same floor as Duke.

After the first few weeks, in my attempt to catch Duke's attention another way, I've convinced Jess and Elias to hang out at Ryan's more often than at Race. My success rate at persuading them to go out, however, is fifty-fifty. Elias has a strict schedule with Maggie, and Jess has told me multiple times she needs to keep a balance between social and academic. It's almost anal.

And I thought I was OCD.

We learn quickly that Powelton Ave is the spot for freshman parties. The row of houses across from Drexel Park, just before Powelton turns into 31st Street, are a guaranteed good time. Especially Thursday through Saturday with their basement kegs and jugs of jungle juice. Those looking for something a bit harder venture farther off campus.

Liquor and beer are enough for me.

Fridays are the best. The last one on the end, the Party House as it is so lovingly called, has a new theme every Friday: Anything but Clothes, Toga, Graffiti. It's five dollars at the door for guys, unless they bring five girls—each—with them.

Girls are always free.

And there's never a shortage of girls.

Ian is usually at the door, welcoming the ladies.

Once I saw Nikki standing at the flip cup table, giggling and gabbing with a group of girls who looked just as excited to be there as she was. I smiled warmly, happy that she found her place, but didn't bother to go say anything, and she never recognized me anyway.

A few nights I passed Ava picking her way through the minefield of trashed red cups and packed bodies to sit at the door with Ian and the guys who live in the house. She looks right passed me every time, like I'm invisible.

Twice I found Duke tucked in the corner of the dark basement next to the keg with a group of guys I don't know. Every so often I steal a glance in his direction from the center of the sweaty dance floor. The light of his cell phone reflects off his glassy eyes. If he notices me, he never does anything about it.

Elias has only joined us once in the two weeks we've gone out. Every other night he's been on the phone. I'm torn between encouraging him to join us and supporting his long-distance relationship. I've been able to maintain my own long-distance relationship, messaging Brett during class and calling him at night when I feel the loneliest. There isn't an easy way for me to convince Elias that there can be a balance between his two lives without explaining my own history. And I won't do that.

The four of us—Elias, Jess, Ryan, and I—have formed a happy little group, despite having different interests. It's comforting to feel like I have somewhere I belong, where what I have to say is taken without judgment, and people want to be in my company.

The familiarity is something I didn't know I'd been craving.

During the third week of class, after too many nights in a row of binge drinking, Jess drags me to a business fraternity rush event. Apart from it being on a Friday, at this point I also have no desire to join a business frat. I want to join a real sorority, a social sorority. With their passwords and rituals, promises of instant best friends and lifelong friendships, I'm sold on going through recruitment next week.

Jess insists that we diversify our interests to ensure we appear well rounded at graduation, so here I am. I'm not entirely happy about it, but I know she's right. I spend an hour following her around and can barely get a word in during any of the chitchat. After one more drawn-out conversation, I get fed up with my fake smile and wander over to the coffee station.

When I pick up one of the Styrofoam cups, a girl asks from across the table, "Is this as lame as it feels?"

I smirk, eyes concentrating on pouring the scalding liquid into the thin cup.

"I thought it was just me," I say, finally lifting my focus to her face.

She's striking, tall and lean, great bone structure unobstructed by makeup, long flowing dark hair, unstyled. Her natural beauty comes from taking care of yourself from an early age. Too pretty to be here in this fluorescent basement snooze-fest.

A smile tugs at the corners of her lips at my comment. "My roommate dragged me to this thing. I didn't even want to come."

"Same," I mutter in solidarity.

"And on a Friday night..." She sighs.

There are certain people you meet and have an unexplained instant connection. The kind where you know without question you'll be close friends. You can tell this is a person that you can be yourself with. You might even be able to trust each other with secrets. I look intently at her face again, searching for some veil of dishonesty that might hold me back. I don't see anything there. Her eyes are genuine.

I brighten at a thought. "Hey, I know a party we can go to if you're interested?"

Ian invited me to come to the Party House for School Girl night. I regrettably declined because of this event, but he pressed that I'd be more than welcome to join if I changed my mind. Ryan and Elias had already made plans to go see a movie off campus and play Xbox all night, anyway. I wasn't sure I wanted to go with just Ian. But now—

"Yes," she answers, a little too quickly.

I laugh at her eagerness that mirrors my own. Shifting the steaming cup of coffee to my left hand from my right, I extend my free hand in her direction.

"I'm Casey."

She takes it, shaking firmly. "Stella."

"Where are you from?" I look down, idly stirring my black coffee for no reason other than to fidget.

"Here. Just outside of Philly."

"Very cool. So, this is home for you?"

"Pretty much. I just love it so much I didn't want to leave. Now I'm getting to explore a side of it that I never really have before."

Her honesty is refreshing. It's crisp, concise, real.

"Don't have to leave anything behind," I murmur low. I have to stop myself from slapping my hand over my mouth after that comment.

She matches my regretful tone. "Or can't get away from anything."

I look up, surprised at her statement, and ask, "Something you're trying to run away from?"

"Story for another time." She forces a nervous laugh. "What about you?"

"How much time do you have?" The question falls out of my mouth before I have the chance to make up my mind again about how much I want to share.

"However long it takes to get from here to that party." She laughs, coming to stand next to me. I know in this instant that I'll tell her everything.

I can't stop the grin covering my face, reaching all the way up to my eyes. "Let me introduce you to my roommate, and then we'll get out of here."

"Which one is yours?" Her eyes glimmer at her own humor.

"Ha! The blonde one at the table over there not letting anyone else get a word in edgewise."

"Ah, one of those." She catches herself before fully rolling her eyes.

"Jess is great. Super organized and ambitious, the kindest person I've met here so far, but she has *so much* to say."

"That's better than my roommate. She's great one-on-one, but in group settings like this she's super quiet. She asked me to come so she would have someone to talk to. I didn't have the heart to say no."

"Which one is she?" I ask, leaning into her conspiratorially.

She lifts a finger off her coffee cup, pointing subtly. "The quiet girl with the glasses right there."

I see the girl's shy smile, her lips buttoned despite the conversation flowing around her.

"I'd love to meet her."

She bumps my shoulder. "It's a plan. Jess first, then Michelle, then your long story."

* * * * *

Stella and I leave the basement of the Student Center and the "rush event," our sides burning with laughter. She learned exactly how much Jess has to say, and I learned how sweet but painfully shy Michelle is. We decide to stop at Towers for Stella to change and then Race for me to change, and finally Calhoun to meet Ian. I told her about Ryan and Elias on the way out, expertly ignoring the topic of Duke. She promised to do her best to convince them to drop the controllers and join us. I can't help but try my own luck with the task.

MESSAGE: ELIAS

Casey: come to school girl night with us?

Elias: Ryan n i are going to play xbox

Elias: and then im calling Maggie

Casey: i made a friend

Elias: good for you kiddo

Casey: u'll like her

Casey: think about it?

No response.

MESSAGE: RYAN

Casey: convince Elias to come to school girl night?

Ryan: im not even going to school girl night

Casey: come on! im bringing a friend

Casey: u'll like her

I hold onto the phone willing him to respond. He can't resist a good theme.

MESSAGE: RYAN

Ryan: what time?

    Casey: YES!

    Casey: we'll be at Calhoun around 10?

Ryan: okay

Ryan: call me when ur here

I return the phone to my pocket, and we descend the short steps onto the wide sidewalk.

Stella's face turns dubiously serious. "Okay, spill it."

We have plenty of time, but I'm not sure how to start or where to begin. Talking about my relationship with Brett shouldn't be this difficult.

There's no better way than to just say it.

"So, I sort of have a boyfriend. He goes to the University of Chicago. We're sort of on a break. Well, I'd been trying to break up with him, but I somehow just couldn't. And then he suddenly suggested that I take some time moving here to figure out what I want, which actually made me not want to lose him. Then I met this guy at Orientation, Duke. Oh god, I'm obsessed. I thought he was into me too, but then I ran into him in Calhoun—he's on the same floor as Ryan and Ian—and he was completely uninterested. So now I'm sort of just feeling like I want to—"

Stella cuts me off. "Wait, slow down. You have a boyfriend in Chicago. That doesn't sound like such a long story."

"Well…" I falter, looking for some excuse to take the place of the truth.

"Oh, just tell me already. It's not like you killed anybody."

"How do you know?" I tease.

"I don't, but you don't look like the type." She winks.

"Well, I met him… sort of… in an unusual way…"

She's quiet, waiting for me to elaborate. We're just about to cross Market Street, and I pause, waiting to respond until we are on our way up the next block.

"We met online." I leave it at that and look away.

She stops walking. I can't see her beside me anymore and turn back to face her. Her hands are down by her sides, palms forward, fingers spread.

"*That's it?*" she asks, unconvinced.

I don't respond.

She stalks toward me. "That's your big secret? You met someone online?"

"I'm *dating* someone online. We've never met." I feel the need to clarify.

"So what?" Her tone makes my cheeks heat.

I guess I've made a big deal out of nothing.

"So... I don't know. People don't really do that."

"Sure they do! It's like almost what Myspace was built for."

"Well, not where I'm from. No one knows, and now that I'm here I sort of want to keep it that way."

"So, what are you going to do about it?"

I shrug. "Got any suggestions?"

"Oh, I don't know, how about tell him the truth about what's going on with you?"

"That would crush him... and probably me."

"Probably best not to keep crushing on this guy Duke, then." She smirks. "No pun intended."

I pout. "It's so hard..."

"Do you love this guy?"

I don't have to think about the answer.

"Yes, I do. He's the only person who ever made me feel like the real me is worth anything. Like other than my parents. Until I came here... and now I feel like I can be who I want to be. There's not much judgment when you're meeting people and they don't know your history."

"Fairness and truth are the basis of any healthy relationship in my opinion. Be honest with yourself and be honest with him."

She's right, but I don't want to admit it.

"Sounds to me like you're maybe not finished with Mr. Chicago," she continues.

"Brett," I correct her. "His name is Brett."

CHAPTER 24

After a short time in Towers, Stella is the perfect schoolgirl. Turns out she actually went to private school, making her outfit authentic. A few modifications—rolling the waistband and dropping a few buttons on the top—and she's ready.

She's casually sexy, and I try to contain the taste of envy coating my tongue and gush, "Oh, my God, you're perfect!"

"Thanks, doll." She winks. "Let's go. It's your turn." A wicked grin spreads across her lips.

In my room, Stella wanders around the tiny space admiring the photos I have of friends and family from back home tacked up on my wall while I rifle through my closet in search of something that could be considered "school girl." In a moment of panic, I realize the only items remotely close to the theme are my business casual clothes reserved for formal campus events and interviews.

Stella pulls me from my distress. "Hey, who are these people in all your pictures?"

"Hmm?" I respond, at first distracted. "Oh! The blond one is my friend Greg, the other is Tanner, and the girl is my best friend Leila. We all grew up together," I explain without turning away from the closet.

I yank my best, knee-length pleated skirt from its hanger and swipe through the rest until I arrive at a crisp white button down.

"He's pretty cute!" she says, devilishly.

"Which one?" I ask, wondering if her tastes align more with Greg's boy-next-door charm or Tanner's arrogance.

Elias and Greg are pretty similar underneath it all. Kind, teasingly funny, loyal.

Her tone drops a level seductively. "The blond one."

Of course.

I turn toward her, holding up the skirt and shirt. "Can we work with this?"

"We can absolutely work with this. Do you have scissors?"

I run out of the room and into Jess's and grab the scissors out of the tray with her ruler, highlighters, and erasers. I hold them up deviously coming back through my doorway and extend them toward Stella. She has the skirt laid out on the empty bed across from mine. I see Brett's t-shirt peeking out from under the covers and nonchalantly walk over to straighten out my bed, tucking the shirt under my pillow. But the sight of it has already sparked a reminder.

"Perfect!" Stella breaks out into a devilish grin.

MESSAGE: BRETT

    Casey: school girl night ;)

    Casey: wanna see?

  Brett: of course

She hacks off the bottom with the scissors and asks if I have a tie. I don't, but I bet that Ryan or Ian have one that I can borrow. Her work finished, she hands me the skirt, instructing me not to button the shirt but to tie the tails in a knot exposing a provocative line of skin, and glides out of the room.

"There's vodka in the freezer," I call out to her while undressing.

I pull the skirt over my hips, expecting to feel the hem graze my knees. The short fabric feels unfamiliar. Thinking about the rest of my wardrobe, I remember the tall socks I usually reserve for my boots. They'll be a nice complement to the shortness of the skirt. I look down at my plain black bra and wrap my arms around my stomach self-consciously. Sliding the shirt up over my shoulders, I reflexively begin buttoning from the top down. I'm just about to reach the last button when Stella re-enters, toting the vodka bottle.

"Shot glasses?" she asks.

I point at the desk next to the unmade bed and the short stack of shot glasses I bought at the gift store after my first weekend here.

"Hey, leave that unbuttoned." She points to my shirt.

"Oh, right!" I undo the top two, the skin of my chest peeking out, and then the bottom and tie the tails in a tiny knot just below my navel. "What about these?" I hold up the knee-high socks.

"Perfect!" She points at them and then at my feet. "Shoes?"

"I was thinking Chucks?" I am not wearing my sensible high heels, and I don't have anything sexier.

"Edgy… I like it." She smiles while pouring out two shots. "Oh, also, do you have red lipstick?"

"I think so." I roll the socks over my knee and pad through the hall to my bathroom and my small makeup bag.

She calls from my room, "Have anything to chase this with?"

I dig through the lightly filled bag for the red lipstick I used to wear for dance competitions. Lying right next to it is the black felt box. I flip the top and see Brett's tiny gold band. I'd almost completely forgotten about the dainty piece of jewelry until right this second. I rub my thumb and index finger across my forehead, squeezing at my temples before dropping the box back into the bag and zipping it closed.

Making a mental note to pick up a few more makeup options from CVS the next time I'm there, I grab a can of Red Bull from the fridge for Stella. It's left over from the four-pack I bought to get me through the night last week writing a paper for my Creative Writing class. Handing her the can, I lean over the small mirror on my desk and pucker my lips. The deep red makes the green of my eyes pop. I pull back, looking over my whole face, and smile, internally encouraging myself.

I look fucking hot.

I stand up straight and step into the center of the room, reaching for the full shot glass.

She whistles. "So, who are we trying to impress tonight?"

"Better question… who are we *not* trying to impress? Cheers!"

We clink the glasses together, vodka sloshing over the side of mine and trickling over my fingers. I trade hands, tip the shot into my mouth, and swallow, wiping my wet hand along the side of my skirt. With my face squeezed into a wince, I shake my hand, motioning for the Red Bull. She hands it to me after a sip. I take a big swallow and let out a relieved sigh.

"Next time, you should get flavored vodka," she instructs.

"I'll keep that in mind. Ready?" I ask.

Twisting and turning in the hanging mirror on the back of my door, I admire my work.

"Where to?" she asks, crossing behind me to return the vodka to the freezer.

I know I shouldn't, but I can't help being a tease. Turning sideways, I pop my hip, accentuating the curve of my ass, bend my arm up to bite my finger playfully, and finally, once the angle is perfect, snap a picture. I smile, hitting the send button that will carry the image away to Brett.

"Calhoun!" I call out to Stella and look back down at the phone.

MESSAGE: RYAN
Casey: on our way
Ryan: okay. Ian's already there

MESSAGE: BRETT
Brett: WOW
Casey: thanks :)
Brett: button up that shirt tho
Casey: what u don't like it?
Brett: i do
Brett: but so will everyone else
Casey: thats the point
Brett: tease
Casey: exactly

First the ring and now he's trying to tell me how to dress? Forget it.

I don't wait for his response, knowing I'll only be more annoyed, and throw the phone in my clutch before meeting Stella at the door. She looks me up and down appraisingly. I do the same to her, lingering on her flat stomach and perfect chest.

If only I looked like her.

"You're going to love Elias and Ryan," I gush.

The vodka has warmed me already and the ugly blue hallway carpet wobbles in my vision. I shake my head and turn to lock the door.

"I'm sure I will… Duke going to be at this party by any chance?" I hear the smile in her voice at the question.

"I don't know." I hide my own smile, keeping my face turned and concentrating on my keys.

CHAPTER 25

Stepping through the door, my skin warms after being out in the brisk October night without a jacket. My eyes widen at the scene.

A wave of shirtless guys wearing only neckties pull and paw over a bunch of girls in devilishly short skirts, and shirts that should be considered bras. I take a steadying breath and adjust the knot of my button-down, lifting it up a bit higher.

I need a drink.

Ryan takes my hand and I clasp Stella's before he leads us deeper into the house toward the kitchen. I pick my way through the bodies pressed together against the wall of the hallway and try not to stare at their locked lips. The three of us step over several dropped red cups and finally arrive at the stack that sits next to the jug of jungle juice. Lifting three off the top, Ryan fills them to the brim before turning toward the stairs to the basement.

Elias left to call Maggie before we even got to Calhoun. I didn't hide my disappointment when I called to beg him one last time to join us. The thought of my friend sitting at home on the phone vanishes as we enter the dark basement.

As soon as our eyes adjust to the darkness, Ryan spots a skinny guy wearing only a vest and a bowtie from across the room. He pulls us close and informs us he'll see us later before stalking off directly toward him. Stella shrugs and pulls me into the middle of the crowded dance floor. I don't know how long we spend dancing in the crowd before I realize my cup is empty and I'm thirsty for another. Ryan is still off to the side talking up his new friend.

Stella opens her eyes and notices I've stopped dancing. Before I can tell her I need a refill, she leans into my ear and yells over the music, "I need some air!" and points her thumb up toward the ceiling.

"Okay. Let me just tell Ryan," I yell back.

Slithering through the throng of couples grinding on each other, I find Ryan. When I get to him, I slide my hand down his arm and squeeze his hand. He says something to the guy and then leans in my direction.

"What's up?" he asks with a hint of concern.

"Stella and I are going to get some air," I say, my lips pressed against his ear.

He nods and motions that he's going to stay down here before squeezing my hand back to send me off. I turn, looking up over the heads of everyone between me and the stairs, searching for Stella through the mix of dirt and steam I didn't realize has been hanging in the air. She's standing at the bottom of the steps, partially hidden by a guy her height blocking my view. I can see her smile at whatever he's saying, but it looks fake.

Finding my way toward them, I reach for Stella and slip between her and the faceless guy hitting on her.

I pull her hand up the stairs and call over my shoulder, "Sorry! I need her!"

At the top, I stop short, my jaw hanging open slightly. Stella knocks into my back, pushing me farther into the hall and away from the stairs. I turn to apologize and quickly glance back to the corner of the kitchen where I see Ian, his arm snugged around Ava's neck, holding her face to his. I shake my head, laughing under my breath, and roll my eyes.

I guess she got tired of also chasing Duke.

I knew they were more right for each other, anyway.

"Thanks for that." Stella grabs my arm, stealing my attention away from Ian and Ava, and pulls me down the hall in the direction of the front door.

At the front, the now somewhat familiar housemates stop us.

"Ladies, great outfits." One of them lifts his solo cup to his lips as we try to sneak by. Stella steps out onto the porch, edging along the railing past the group of guys who live here and girls who don', before we hear one of them call out.

"You can't hang out here. If you want to smoke, you have to go out back."

I follow her, focusing on the line of people waiting to pay and enter, before calling back to him, "Oh, we just need some air."

He shakes his head. "Still need to go out back."

"Fine." Stella stares at him, agitated. She slinks back and passes me, grabbing my hand again. "Come on, Casey."

How tipsy is she? It's not really that big of a deal to go out back.

"Let's stop for a refill?" I squeeze her hand. She turns and nods.

Before I sneak back through the door to follow her, my eyes meet Duke's familiar gaze. I look away quickly.

Stella and I squeeze our way toward the kitchen and the back door, passing girls huddled over their cell phones and a few couples still making out. I glance behind me toward the front door before stopping behind Stella at the jug. I tuck my clutch under my arm and pull the tap, letting the bright pink liquid pour into my cup, and feel the familiar vibration. I consider ignoring the message, but the image of Ian and Ava face deep in each other pops into my head and changes my mind.

Maybe it's not Brett.

Once outside, we find space in a corner away from everyone smoking. Stella takes a deep breath of the fresh night air. I notice her shift uneasily and reach out to grab her arm, but she steadies herself against the fence.

"You okay?" I ask, taking out my phone. Whatever she says, I don't hear.

MESSAGE: DUKE

Duke: was that u?

    Casey: where?

Duke: are u at a party?

    Casey: yeah

Duke: i think i just saw u

Duke: outside on the porch?

    Casey: oh sorry

    Casey: i didn't see u

"Hello," she sings, waving in front of my face. When I still don't look up, she puts her hand over my screen and pushes my phone down. "I feel better. Do you want to go back inside? Find Ryan?"

"Everything okay?" I repeat, noticing the color returning to her cheeks.

"Yeah, I think the heat just got to me. Ya know what? I have to pee. Let's go to the bathroom first?"

"Okay. Maybe find some water too." I look back down at the screen.

MESSAGE: DUKE

Duke: where are u now?
   Casey: heading back inside
Duke: i'll come find u

I suck my bottom lip between my teeth, hiding a smile, and tuck the phone away.

Now he wants to find me?

The sweetness hits me when I take a swallow of my drink, sending a twinge through my teeth. I trail Stella past the open living room, toward the second-floor bathroom, and catch Duke standing by the keg. He sees me and falters. The tap misses the edge of his cup, and he looks down as the liquid splashes his pants. I don't stop moving.

Upstairs, we're surprised to find the line for the bathroom is short, though not short enough. Stella dances in place waiting for the three girls who went in before us to come out.

I check my phone again.

MESSAGE: DUKE

Duke: come back downstairs

I press my lips together and chew the inside of my cheek, deciding not to answer. I keep scrolling through my messages.

MESSAGE: BRETT

Brett 9:47PM: that skirt looks familiar

Brett 9:52PM: wish i was there to take u to that party
Brett 9:55PM: and take u home
Brett 11:37PM: hows the party?

The alcohol surges through my veins, and my fingers flex over the small keys.

MESSAGE: BRETT

    Casey: take me home huh?
    Casey: to do what? ;)
Brett: u know what
    Casey: tell me
Brett: i'll tell u when u call me
    Casey: boo ur no fun

The bathroom door swings open and the girls laugh, pushing past us.

"Oh, thank God!" Stella shouts.

She rushes in, pulling me by the hand. I throw the door closed behind me and lean my back against it for a second, trying to keep the messages from Brett and Duke in separate boxes of my mind. Pushing off, I check myself in the mirror. My cheeks are warm and pink, and my nose is slightly red from the chill of outside after the sauna-like temperatures of the basement. I wipe a smudge of mascara from below my lashes and fix my lipstick. The clutch on the counter vibrates with my phone inside.

"Who's that?" she asks.

"Probably Brett," I respond easily, forgetting myself for a minute but then remembering I'm with Stella.

"Ooooo." She eyes my reflection in the mirror. "Mr. Chicago."

I smirk at the nickname thinking about the first time he called me *Jersey*.

"He likes my outfit," I tease.

"Of course, he does. You should tell him to thank me for the skirt."

I laugh at her confidence and consider taking my phone out to do just that. She finishes and we switch places. After washing her hands, she fixes her own face and leans on the countertop. Her head bows, and her hair falls toward the sink.

She murmurs through the curtain of hair without looking up, "Thanks for the rescue earlier. That guy was a total douche. He was so trashed."

I turn my head toward her and joke, "Sorry I wasn't there to rescue you sooner."

"Me too." I barely hear the whisper.

"Did you know the guy?" I ask tentatively.

She still doesn't look up.

"Stella?" I coax.

There's a knock at the door.

"Just a minute!" she calls, lifting her head, and leans back against the door. I stand, flush, and quickly wash my own hands.

"I just didn't think I would run into him," she says with her eyes closed.

I raise an eyebrow at her. "And who is him?"

"The guy I should have been trying to run away from. Instead, I came here."

"Boyfriend or something?"

"Used to be. We dated junior-senior year, but then he cheated on me." She looks directly into my eyes. "I never thought he would follow me here. That plan was over in my mind after I slapped him."

"Oh, God, Stella! I'm so sorry." I hold my jaw closed, trying not to let my emotions slip and make it worse for her.

"Don't be. I just want it to be over. Like actually over."

"And I'm assuming he doesn't?" I ask.

"I don't know what he wants. I don't really care. It's unforgivable." Her tone is disgusted.

I see her face and decide not to press the issue. After one last adjustment to my outfit, I squeeze her arm.

"Let's go." I drop my hand to hold hers.

Stella walks out first, passing a longer line of girls, and turns to go down the stairs. I follow her slowly, careful not to knock any of the cups on the floor along the hall.

"Casey." The familiar voice makes my heart flutter.

I turn my head in the direction my name came from and see a tall figure leaning against the corner in shadow.

"Stella." She looks back up the stairs at hearing my voice. "Give me a minute?"

She nods and calls up to me, "I'll meet you at the jungle juice." I nod in return and turn to walk toward the figure.

"Duke?" I ask, already knowing the answer.

"Hey," he drawls, his tongue sounding thick in his mouth.

"Hi." I smile sweetly.

He eyes the collar of my shirt, his gaze drifting lower to the skin of my abdomen and the shortness of my skirt. It takes forever for him to drag his eyes back up to my face, his stare settling somewhere near my lips.

"Nice outfit," he murmurs.

I scan the dark jeans and zip-up hoodie he's wearing. "I don't think you dressed the part," I tease.

He laughs, still glancing over me without responding.

"Now you want to talk to me?" I continue, to fill the silence.

He pushes off the wall, coming to stand right in front of me. I smell beer, what I think is weed, and something sweet underneath.

"What do you mean?" Sweetness drips from his tone. His smile is lopsided, and he bites his lip.

I suck in a breath at the sight of him in the dim light and feel his energy roll off him as he towers over me. "I mean, you haven't given me the time of day."

He wraps his hand around my arm, stepping to the side and pulling me with him as a group of girls come up the stairs to get in line. I glance down at his hand, feeling the strength of his fingers and the warmth of his skin, before glancing back into his eyes.

"When was that?" he asks innocently.

"When has it not been?" *Does that even make sense?*

He laughs again and runs his hand down my arm, dropping it before it reaches my wrist.

"Well, I'm here now." He flashes his best charming grin.

"And how do I know you won't get distracted again by that phone of yours?" I narrow my eyes at him.

"No one on there deserves my attention like you do."

Oh. I like hearing that.

"Oh, really? What happened to Cora?" I tease, placing my palm flat on his chest, and inhale, holding my breath.

"Cora who?" He places his hand over mine.

I slowly loosen my breath and slide my hand out from under his.

Okay, Duke. Let's play.

"Well, I have to get back to my friend, Stella." I smile and scrunch my nose. Without waiting for a response, I pivot toward the stairs.

"Wait. Casey," he calls after me.

To my surprise, he follows me through the crowd of people. When I reach Stella, she's talking to Ryan in the bright kitchen, refilling her cup with her back to me. Ryan looks up and sees Duke behind me. His eyebrows shoot up, alerting Stella there's something to look at. She turns and glances from me to Duke and back to me. With one last step toward them, I hold my cup out to her.

"Who's this?" she asks, taking my cup.

"Duke!" Ryan shouts, surprised, answering her question. "Fancy seeing you here."

Her head falls forward slightly. She stares at me, wide-eyed. I smile.

"Well, Duke. Nice to meet you. I'm Stella." She tilts her head slightly.

"Nice to meet you too." He extends his hand toward her.

She raises her cup to take a sip before handing me mine and leaving him hanging for a space of time.

Is she just testing his patience? What's going on here?

He's about to drop his hand when she finally reaches out.

"Where you from, Stella?" he asks as they shake.

"Here. And you?"

"Princeton." He shifts his eyes in my direction.

"Duke from Princeton," she teases.

I giggle at her response—the same as mine when I first met him.

"That's right." He laughs, not taking his eyes off me.

"Well, Duke from Princeton, we were just about to go back downstairs."

"We were?" Ryan sounds equally surprised at this.

She whirls on him. "Yes. We were."

I have no idea what look crosses her face, but Ryan rolls his eyes and replies, "Well, come on then."

He pushes past us toward the stairs leading back down into the packed basement. We file behind him. Duke places his hand on the small of my back, guiding me down the dark steps. We descend into the enveloping warmth and darkness, the bass pounding through our chests with each beat.

At the last step, I lose sight of where Ryan and Stella have disappeared into the crowd. I see only darkness and flashing lights, and I'm not sure I even care where they've gone. All I can feel is the heat of Duke's hand directly on my skin. He slides his hand from my back to grip my waist and pulls me tighter into his side before he ushers us into the mess of people grinding on each other. My cheeks burn watching the way the girls are pressing back into the waiting hips of the boys they're dancing with. I close my eyes against the flashing lights and hear my heartbeat in my ears.

I can do this. And I can absolutely do this with him.

Duke curls his hand around my waist and splays his fingers across my stomach. I suck in reflexively at his touch and feel the line of his body press against my back. His fingers snake through the belt loops of my skirt, pulling me closer. I melt back into him, keeping my eyes closed. His hips press into me, forcing me to start moving against him to the beat of the drums pulsing through the speakers. My head is heavy from the heat and the alcohol. I hinge at the waist, wanting to lean forward, but Duke holds me tightly against him. He slides his hand up my stomach and across the knot of my shirt, gently grazing the skin where the buttons are open before lightly resting his hand around my neck. My breath hitches in my throat and quickens. I lean my head back against his chest, still moving my hips in time with his.

Yes. Oh, my God, yes.

I don't care that other people are rubbing up against me or bumping into us, I'm just trying to remember to keep my grip on my cup. All I can concentrate on is Duke's finger dipping below the seam of my skirt, tickling the sensitive skin just above my hip bone. I exhale a sigh, and he dips his head, pressing his lips against my ear.

"Turn around," he demands in a whisper, despite the volume.

He loosens his grip on my neck and nudges my side, giving me just enough space to swivel in his arms. I keep my head down as the front of my body lands firmly against his. His hands come to rest at the small of my back and I lean my forehead on his chest. I smell his scent more than the mix of everything else in this basement. I feel his hands flex and grip my ass as his knee parts my legs and my hips shift just enough to seat us closer together.

I didn't think it was possible to get closer.

I feel a familiar ache between my legs and crush my hips against his. A low moan vibrates through his chest. He drags one hand up my side and grips my chin, tilting my head back. I only now open my eyes and meet his gaze. His eyes are glassy and hooded. His lips are slightly parted. I see his jaw clench and relax as he sucks in a breath.

Just kiss me.

I pull my chin away from his grasp and tilt my head farther back, exposing my neck and letting my eyes close again. My hair tumbles over my shoulder and down my back, tickling my skin, before I feel his fingers lace through it. I lick my lips and bite the bottom one just before he firmly pushes my head back up. Our lips crash together, and I can barely breathe. My hand opens, dropping the cup on the floor. I reach up to cup the back of his neck.

His lips are soft. Just as soft as I imagined they would be as they massage mine. I'm surprised when I feel his teeth nip at my bottom lip. I gasp and try to pull away. He holds the back of my head tightly and his tongue slides between my parted lips, swirling around mine. My hands trace down the front of his body, stopping at the top of his jeans to grab at his waist. Balling the hem of his shirt in my fists, I attempt to pull him tighter to me.

The song changes, and he loosens his grip on my hair. He gently tugs it to pull my head back to look at him. I tuck my hands into his back pockets, distracted for an instant when my fingertips graze the edge of his phone. Our eyes meet, heat burning in his gaze, and I'm lost in him again. He doesn't say a word before dipping his head and bringing his lips back to mine.

Is that me vibrating or him?

CHAPTER 26

I open my eyes knowing I'm in my room but unsure if someone else is in the bed opposite me. Vague snippets of memory flood in, of the four of us laughing our way to the dorms.

Duke has his arm around my shoulders. Ryan has his around Stella's. I remember approaching Race, the first one to be home, not wanting to break away from the group. Stella hugs me around the neck, sloppily kissing my cheek and proclaiming she loves me before Ryan pulls her back to him and tells me he'll get her home.

My lips tingle and the memory of Duke kissing me rushes to the front of my mind. Lifting my hand from beneath the covers, I lightly touch my swollen bottom lip and turn my head to the right.

No one is there.

A sigh of relief escapes my throat. I wanted Duke to kiss me. I didn't even mind how drunk I was, or he was. I just didn't want to go farther without being able to remember every second. Every touch, every sound, every feeling. I want to be able to memorize every detail of my first time.

Detail. Every detail. Why is that familiar?

A pang of guilt hits me like a punch to the gut.

I technically just cheated on Brett. Wait. Can you cheat on someone you've never met? Oh, God. This isn't even the first time. Greg...

I squeeze my eyes shut and swallow hard, groaning out loud.

It's fine. It might not even happen again. I just won't mention it.

There's a tentative knock at my door. Dread surges through my system.

"Casey?" Jess asks and exhales a gush of air.

"Come in, Jess!"

There's a creak, and the door swings inward.

"Hi," she greets me in her usual chipper tone. "What time did you get in last night?"

"I honestly couldn't tell you." I laugh and then ask in alarm, "Did I wake you?"

"No! No. You just weren't here when I got home from the event. I was worried when you didn't answer my text."

I wonder if I woke her roommate. I probably should've asked if she said anything to Jess.

"I'm so sorry. I must have missed it!" I lie, thinking I probably didn't even bother to read it at that point.

I sit up, scooting my back to the wall, and pat the space next to me. She bounces farther into the room but chooses to sit on the other bed. I scrunch my face to wake myself up.

"What's up? You're awfully cheery for a Saturday morning at... What time is it?"

"8:30 a.m. I met someone last night!"

I glance down and realize I'm wearing the familiar blue shirt I tucked away last night and search for my phone under my pillow. Tugging the comforter up a little higher, I hit the lock button to check for messages.

"What about runner boy?" I ask, remembering the instigation for her hobby and the guy she'd been talking my ear off about for the first few weeks of class.

"Oh! We ended things last week. I mean, we both just realized it wasn't going to work. He's in Texas, I'm here. Neither of us really wanted to do the long-distance thing. That never works anyway, right?"

I try to hide my involuntary flinch.

That was fast. Two weeks? Maybe three?

This is not what I needed this morning. If Jess can't make a long-distance relationship work, how the hell am I supposed to?

She continues unfazed, "Anyway, I stayed late after the rush event to help the members clean up. I figured the best way to get an in with them was to stick around, help them out, get some one-on-one when no other prospective members were around. I ended up chatting with this guy Bear. That's a nickname. He's from Lancaster and on the crew team. That has to be crazy with the morning practices. I can't even imagine although I guess I've been getting up kinda early to run."

She pauses, noticing I haven't acknowledged anything she's said while scrolling through my messages and remembering last night. The quiet grabs my attention and I look up.

"Sorry, Jess. Lancaster, crew team, yes, go."

I toss the phone onto my pillow and focus on my friend.

"Oh, Casey, he's super cute. He reads all the same things I do, we like the same music, he has a younger sister he dotes on. I really like him." She beams at me.

"So, what's the problem?" I return her smile warmly.

"Well, how do I know if he likes me too?" she whines.

"Did you exchange numbers?" I ask, as if this is obvious.

"Yes!" She can barely contain her excitement.

"So text him and ask him to get lunch or something?"

"Oh, my God, why didn't I think of that?"

I laugh as she bounces off the bed and practically runs to her room calling behind her, "Thanks, Casey!"

My attention returns to my own problems, and I let myself feel the disappointment that flashes through my system just now at not having any messages from Duke. I resolve to give him the morning to message me, thinking he's probably still asleep. Brett's *Good morning, beautiful* text draws a smile, but more than that, his explanation of what he would do to me last night makes my stomach flutter and the space between my legs ache.

Just like it did when I was kissing Duke.

I shake my head, clearing Duke from my mind, and send Brett a reciprocating good morning message, accompanied by a cozy picture wrapped up in his shirt and my blankets before rolling out of bed.

I take a second to confirm lunch plans with Stella, Elias, and Ryan, grab my towel, and cross to my shower. The hot water pelts my skin, washing away the film covering me from last night. With the steam curling around me, I think I should have showered last night and can't remember why I didn't.

* * * * *

Stella and I enter the dining terrace attached to her dorm together and spot Ryan and Elias sitting at a table in the corner. Elias has his head buried in his arms. I catch Ryan's eye and motion to Elias, mouthing, "What's wrong?" A frown pinches my face waiting for his response.

He mouths back, "Maggie," and my good mood crumbles.

After waiting in the short line for burrito bowls, Stella follows me to the table and sits down opposite Ryan. We pull our coats off and settle in. Elias doesn't move a muscle.

"Elias, what happened?" I ask in a soothing tone.

He doesn't look up, his voice muffled through his sweatshirt. I can just make out the words. "Maggie broke up with me."

"Oh, no." I groan and reach a hand across the table and lay it on his shoulder.

My mind races with excitement, thinking maybe now Elias will come out with us, but it hits me instantly how awful that is.

My friend is in pain.

Guilt takes over and worry washes over me as it registers this is the second long-distance relationship that has ended in the same day.

First Jess, now Elias.

While I'm lost in my thoughts, Stella offers some comfort, despite not knowing Elias.

"I'm so sorry," she says, her voice dropping at the end.

He looks up at the unfamiliar voice and studies her, cocking his head a little to the side. "Who are you?" His voice brightens.

"Stella." She extends her hand across the table toward him.

"Hi, Stella." He grasps her hand, holding her attention.

"I don't know who Maggie is, but… her loss." She smiles.

Pain still paints his face, but he straightens. "You're right. I'm a catch."

I can tell he's faking, but I see a glimmer of my jokester friend coming back to life. I sit back and listen to the exchange between Stella, Ryan, and Elias as they get to know one another and decide I'll wait to fill them in on my moment with Duke last night.

CHAPTER 27

The next two weeks before midterms, my focus is absorbed by class and sorority recruitment. I don't have the time to obsess over why Duke is ignoring me—again. I thought after the night he kissed me, he would at least acknowledge my existence when passing me in the hall of Calhoun almost every day. He barely even responds to my text messages.

Whatever. I don't need him anyway.

I don't even have the energy to pick apart my pendulum of a relationship with Brett. I know it's wrong of me to keep stringing him along, but I can't help it.

I can't put into words what it is about him that I can't let go. He's a part of me. The part that gives me confidence.

It's easy enough to keep up. When I'm busy, I respond to every text on autopilot. Late at night when I'm not, I call him to hear his voice. It still does things to me that no one else can.

No one else? Is that really true?

When I do get a moment to see my friends, I feel left out. During the days I've been busy, Ryan, Elias, Jess, and Stella have all been spending time together. The sharp jealousy conflicts with the sense of belonging I have at finding the perfect sorority. My friends know all each other's stories and even have a few inside jokes. I have to consciously drown out the burning in the pit of my stomach.

My fear of missing out is slightly quelled one Saturday night at dinner. Elias seems to be coping well with his separation from Maggie, at least on the surface. I'm a little intrigued at the looks that keep passing between him and Stella, though. Peering a little harder at her face, something seems off about her. There's a slight crease between her brows and the edges of her mouth tug down almost imperceptibly. She looks at Jess, and her cheeks pull tightly into a smile that doesn't reach her eyes.

Her head jerks as Ryan slides into the booth next to her and slings his arm across her back. I don't notice the tension in her shoulders until I see it melt away as recognition floods her face that Ryan is sitting next to her.

"So..." Ryan begins with a wicked grin. "Ian has a connection to get us fake IDs."

"You're joking?" Jess asks incredulously.

"Not at all. You want to get into the bars. Don't you?"

"Sign me up, Coach!" Elias slaps the table. "I'm ready for it."

"Mine could use an upgrade." Stella looks up from her wallet and throws a poorly made California license on the table.

My jaw drops. "You already have one?" I ask, staring at Stella.

She shrugs. "What? I grew up in the city. Everyone has one." Her tone is so nonchalant.

"I'm in. What's it cost?" I ask, looking at Ryan.

"A hundred dollars and a picture against a blue background. I need both by tomorrow."

"Let's go take pictures now!" Jess shouts and claps with excitement.

I check my phone. It's 5 p.m. Two hours until the Ritual Night round officially begins.

"I have a few hours before my recruitment event. Let's go!"
I stand and start piling up everyone's trays.

Jess and Stella name places they think they've seen a blue background while Ryan and Elias are buried in their phones. The girls link arms and bounce up the steps, Ryan trailing behind them. Elias slows to walk by my side.

"Missed you, Case!" He leans into my shoulder.

"I know. I'm so sorry I've been busy. How are you holding up?" I ask, genuinely concerned.

"Holding up what?" he jokes with a wink.

Another joke. He can't ever just give me a serious answer?

I give him a suspicious look and half a smile without saying a word. He flings his arm around my neck and snugs me in tightly.

"I'm good, Casey." His smile widens, baring his teeth. "Just peachy."

"Hey, you two!" Jess calls from the top of the stairs. "Casey has to get ready soon. Let's go so she's not late. We need her to be in perfect form to get into that sorority she wants!"

Warmth blooms in my cheeks, spreading to my chest and down my arms.

They really do care about me.

"Coming, Jess!" I punch Elias in the ribs lightly. "Come on. You don't want to be the reason I don't have any friends for the next four years. Do you?" I tease.

"Don't have any friends?" He contorts his face in mock shock. "What are we, chopped liver?"

"More like mushy peas." I giggle and run up the stairs. "Last one up's a rotten egg," I yell over my shoulder.

"Oh, no, you didn't! I'm coming for you, Casey!"

The five of us spend the next hour dashing between locations until we find a bulletin board on the third floor of the Main Building. We wandered up and down random staircases, getting lost in corridors we didn't know existed, passing classrooms that looked coated in dust until we came upon a board covered in faded blue paper. And it was perfect. We got what we needed just as I remembered to check the time.

7:15 p.m.

Shit. I'm going to be late.

At ten of eight, my lungs burn, my sides are tight, and my feet pound the concrete in the only pair of black high heels I own. They're too sensible for the black bandage dress I bought especially for this event. My long legs make the length look shorter than it is, but the three-inch heels tone it down in comparison to the girls surrounding me.

Grabbing the now-familiar name tag at the door, I attempt to calm my breathing while fastening it to the strap of my dress.

"All right, ladies! Follow the stickers on your name tag for the two houses you'll be visiting tonight."

Close to two hundred girls collectively bow their heads to scan their name tags. I have a carnation and a rose.

"Carnations, this way, please!" A tall blonde in a billowing black swing dress with bell sleeves holds up a sign covered in pink carnations.

A shorter girl to my left puffs out a breath and catches my eye.

"Here we go." She giggles.

"We got this." I smile at her encouragingly.

* * * * *

A short ten days later, I'm the owner of a shiny new Pennsylvania license that has my same name but says my birthday is four years earlier than my real one. I'm also the proud pledge of my top choice sorority, wearing my new pink pin over my heart with pride. On Wednesday of midterms, the five of us plan to venture to Caverns—the notorious college bar—to test out the IDs and celebrate all the things.

It takes some coaxing to get Jess to agree to go out the night before our math midterm, but I'm able to convince her that we can both pass the exam with our eyes closed. She folds and asks if she can invite Bear. They've been hanging out more but haven't gotten any closer to crossing the line between friends and a hookup.

Elias decides to host the pregame. Since Jess and I live in Race with him, it's just easier logistically to only sign in Ryan and Stella. Turns out it doesn't matter anyway. Over the last two weeks, Elias has made friends with the students who work the front desk and they let him skirt the sign-in rule for his friends. Before Jess and I turn the corner, we hear the music blaring down the hall—something Jay-Z— and look at each other in surprise. This is a change from the usual quiet of his previous every-night phone call with Maggie.

I lift my closed hand to knock but notice the lock has been flipped and the door is cracked. Inside, Elias and Stella are cozy on the couch, his arm resting across the back behind her. Ryan is in the bean bag opposite them. Each of them is clutching a red cup and talking animatedly over the music.

I thought there'd be more people with all the noise.

"Heyyy!" Elias greets us when the door swings open and we step into the small kitchen area. Ryan jumps up, coming over to wrap us in hugs, and gestures to the counter before opening his mouth to speak.

"Help yourself," Elias says from the couch, cutting Ryan off.

Ryan grabs the tequila and refills his cup. "Can I make you something?"

I see sweating bottles of vodka, rum, and tequila. A can of Four Loko is crushed in the small sink. Splashes of spilled booze dot the counter between shot glasses stamped with designs of Spain, France, and Italy.

Jess was slightly upset that Bear declined. He's twenty-one and would've had no trouble getting into the bar but holds himself to a strict policy of no drinking until he's finished with all his exams. She moves closer to the counter and picks up the glass with the Eiffel Tower on it.

"Can I use this?" she asks, looking at Elias.

"What's mine is yours!" He winks.

I look at the couch and at Stella. Her face is scrunched, eyes looking down into her cup.

"Hey, Stella!" I yell over, hoping she'll look up.

She doesn't but responds, "Hey, Casey, what's up?"

I return my attention to Jess just in time to see her barely flinch as the cold vodka hits her tongue. I've never seen the girl take a shot before tonight.

"Whoa, girl." My eyes widen.

She lifts her hands in question. "What? I know *how* to drink. I just usually don't." She lets out a short laugh and wanders over to the couch next to Stella.

Ryan hands me a cup. "Vodka and club soda." He winks. "Your usual."

The first sip is bitter and takes me a moment to swallow. Then a warmth spreads through me, reaching my fingers and toes. The second sip goes down easier, and I drag a chair closer to the group.

Elias leans forward, slamming a cup down on the center of the coffee table. "Kings anyone?" he asks, shuffling a deck of cards.

"I'm in," Stella replies immediately.

"Let's do it!" Jess claps.

"Yes, but only one game. I want to go to the bar by 11 p.m.," I chime in.

Elias nods. "You got it, kiddo!"

* * * * *

Elias tips the mixed contents of the king's cup into his mouth with a gulp while Jess and Ryan cheer for him to chug it down.

Of course, Elias lost.

He stops to wince at the combination of vodka, tequila, and Four Loko before guzzling the rest of the cup. I check the time, commenting that we all must be warm and feeling it enough to head to the bar.

I try to grab Stella on the way to ask what's wrong, but she and Elias are glued at the hip with his arm perpetually slung over her shoulder. Both laugh the entire way, chatting about Maine Lobster versus Philly Cheese Steaks. It feels wrong to break her happy mood now, considering how down she looked when I walked in. I make a mental note to ask her if everything is okay tomorrow.

Ryan stands with me and Jess, the three of us in line ahead of Elias and Stella. We're a little less drunk than the two of them and figured we'd have the composed confidence to convince the bouncer that our IDs are real if it comes to that.

I'm a little surprised when we get in without any issues.

Once inside, my eyes dart in wonder. I've been to a bar before but only during dining hours when the tables and chairs are spread out. This is another scene entirely, the space cleared of any indication that this establishment also serves food. Bodies are everywhere, tightly packed together on both the dancefloor and near the bar. The wet, sticky floor is littered with cups and napkins. Several girls huddle together, giggling around a cell phone, while another group has their arm around a girl with smeared mascara and tears streaming down her face.

I pick my way nicely through the crowd to the bar, holding Jess's hand and pulling her along with me. It's loud, a mix of Top 40 music and groups of people competing to hear each other. I put my cheek to hers and ask into her ear what she wants to drink. She responds with two of whatever I'm having. I lean across the bar, attempting to catch the bartender's attention.

"What the fuck, man?" I hear a couple of angry voices behind me.

A second later, Elias pushes through the last couple standing next to me and bumps my shoulder.

"Let's do shots!" His yell is loud enough that I can hear him perfectly over the noise.

I blanch at his unusual inconsiderate attitude.

"We have a midterm in the morning. Let's not go crazy," I respond, a touch of warning in my voice.

"Midterm shmid-term! We're here! Let's do it!" he cheers.

"You go for it!" I put my hands up defensively and shake my head.

The bartender approaches us. Elias has at least remembered his manners enough to let me order first. I ask for two vodka sodas with lime for Jess and me, and Elias orders two shots of tequila.

One for him and one for Stella?

I knit my brows together and turn to look for her and Ryan, spotting them standing at a high-top table near the makeshift dance floor. I notice the space where everyone is dancing is actually a section of wooden floor that I assume belongs to the dining tables in the daylight.

When I turn back, Elias has already drunk the first shot and is tipping the second into his mouth. He finishes with a "Woo!" and asks for two cans of Pabst, slapping a $50 on the edge of the bar and yelling, "Keep it!" after the cans slide across.

I've never seen Elias in this atmosphere. He's the usual jokester but on steroids. His energy is intoxicating in itself, but fueled by alcohol, he's the life of the party.

Also kind of obnoxious.

Making a beeline for Stella, he hands her one of the cans. He takes her other hand and spins her around before she can take a sip, causing her to stumble into the crowd. Their faces come dangerously close together as he catches her around the waist.

Uh oh. That look at dinner the other night. The coziness on the couch. And now this. What's going on?

Both laugh. He leads her deeper into the crowd on the dance floor. I lose sight of them and turn back to Ryan and Jess, letting out a puff of air. The two are still scanning the throng of bodies. I'm not sure if they're doing the same as me and looking for Elias and Stella, or someone else.

"Do you want to dance?" I ask Jess and Ryan.

Jess shakes her head.

Ryan leans toward us to speak over the music. "I'm going to go get a drink." He lifts an eyebrow in the direction of the bar.

I turn my attention to where his gaze is focused and recognize the guy he's locked eyes with. I'm not sure where I recognize him from, but he is definitely familiar. When I return to Ryan, he winks at me and slinks away.

"Come on, Jess, let's dance!" I poke and prod at her sides until she's laughing.

"Okay, okay, let's go!" she concedes.

"Yesss!"

After a gulp of drink, I take her free hand and plunge through the initial wall of dancing bodies in search of Elias and Stella. We find them in the center. A circle of people has formed around them, Elias hooting and leading Stella in a mess of spins, twirls, and arms. Jess and I laugh and join the crowd clapping until the music changes and the circle breaks, flooding with people. We push toward them, and the four of us end up dancing and drinking until several beats into a new song, I see Elias and Stella with their foreheads pressed together, swaying slowly despite the high tempo.

Do I really have to play mom tonight? Yes... yes, I do.

Pressing my lips to Jess's ear, I tell her to stay with Stella, and slide my hand around Elias's bicep to tug him to the side. He doesn't stop dancing while he follows me.

"Elias, do you know what you're doing?" A firmness seeps into my voice that reminds me of my own mother.

He laughs at my concern. "I'm great, Casey. Stop being my mom! I can't believe I've been missing this."

"I'm not trying to be your mom. I mean with Stella." I nod my head in her direction where she and Jess have their hands on each other's sides dancing slightly off the beat.

"We're fine. We're having fun!" he yells over the music, waving his arms and wiggling his hips. He's so uncoordinated and I can't help but laugh.

"I just don't want you to regret anything tomorrow." My voice is a little lighter.

He stops moving and looks into my eyes. "Case, it's okay. I won't let anything bad happen."

I pause. His response makes me question if he knows more than I do. Before I can ask, we're interrupted by Jess and Stella.

"Bathroom break," Jess yells, looping her arm around Stella's waist.

"Go!" Elias pats my, Stella, and Jess's asses as we make our way off the dance floor.

The three of us cross the bar to the stairwell leading down to a second, secluded bar and the bathrooms. I see Ian leaning over yelling an order for a round of shots. He catches my eye and smiles with a thumbs up. I get a glimpse of red hair behind him, thankfully facing away from me. When we finally make it to the bathroom, there's a line, but I let out a relieved sigh.

"What's got you smiling?" Jess asks me.

Stella leans her head against the wall, her eyelids drooping heavily.

"Nothing, I'm just happy we're all here tonight," I respond.

A stall opens and I encourage Stella forward, but she moves slowly. "Stella, you okay?" I ask.

"Yeah, yeah," she calls back from behind the closed door. *We need to get that girl a water when we get back to the bar.*

Jess checks the time on her phone and looks up, distraught.

"What time is it?" I ask.

"1:27 a.m. We should go." She looks at me, her brows pinched together and a small frown forming on her face.

"You're probably right. I think Stella needs to go home anyway." I laugh. "We might have to leave Ryan and Elias, though."

"Oh, my God! I know right? What has gotten into him? I've never seen him this crazy."

"He and Maggie broke up," I remind her.

"Ah, right. But that was like weeks ago. I wasn't that beat up when I broke up with my Texas boy," she says on her way to the next empty stall.

"You weren't dating for three years…" I feel the need to justify Elias's reaction as I step into my own stall, letting my thoughts linger.

I'd feel the same about Brett, I think, and that's only been a few months. Elias gets a pass.

On the way back up to find the boys, I ask Stella if she wants to come back with Jess and me. Before she can answer, Elias runs up behind her, wrapping his arms around her waist, and picks her up with a growl. She squeals in delight.

I've lost them both.

With a slight pout, I scan the crowd, but Ryan is nowhere to be found. Elias's promise to not let anything happen repeats in my head, and I press against the uneasy feeling in my stomach. I find the nearest opening at the bar and ask for water, no ice. The bartender is surprisingly quick at delivering this time. Walking toward my group, I see Stella and Elias have their lips locked on each other. Jess is staring on in shock.

"What the hell happened?" I ask Jess.

"They just started making out." Her eyes are wide.

I tap Stella on the shoulder. She breaks away and shifts to look at me.

"Listen, you should really come back with us," I plead with her.

"*No way.*" She stares at me, eyes glazing over.

I know it's a bad idea to let her stay, but I don't want to make a scene on our first night at this place.

"Fine." I take her hand and force the water into it, closing her fingers around the plastic cup. "At least drink this."

I lean around her while she sips and grab Elias by the shirt, pulling him toward me so I know he can hear. "You take care of her tonight. You got me?"

He stares into my eyes again. "Of course." Despite sounding drunk, his tone is convincing, and my nerves calm slightly.

"Good. Our final is at 8 a.m. tomorrow. I'm calling you at 7:30 a.m. Okay?"

"Okay." He kisses my cheek.

Oh, boy, Drunk Elias.

He will most definitely regret something he does tonight.

CHAPTER 28

My voice is as tired as I am as I yell through Elias's suite door for the millionth time. I've been knocking for a solid ten minutes and still haven't heard any movement inside. My knuckles hurt, and I'm about to give up when his roommate swings the door inward in a huff, sleep still in his eyes.

"I'm so sorry, Elias and I have a midterm in thirty minutes—" I try to explain.

He raises a hand to cut me off. "He brought a girl home last night. You're welcome to come in and wake them up."

My jaw hangs open. I can't make up my mind whether I hope it's Stella or not. I settle for hoping it is and that he was just taking care of her after being drunk. I step past him and notice the bottles and shot glasses still on the counter.

Classy.

"Sorry for the mess." I feel the need to cover for Elias. "I'll make sure it gets cleaned up."

"No sweat," he calls over his shoulder, shuffling down the hall back to his room.

I stand in front of Elias's bedroom door and let out an audible breath. I can't believe this is happening. I knock lightly, but there's no response. I try again with a little more force and wince as the wood bites against my knuckles.

"What!" Elias yells through the door.

"Elias, our math midterm is in twenty minutes!"

"Oh, shit!"

I hear shuffling and a cup hits the floor followed by a splash.

"What's going on in there?" I ask.

I smile devilishly despite the fact he can't see. There's hushed whispering and drawers opening before Elias slips through the crack in the door, forcing me back down his hallway.

"Who ya got in there?" I wink at him.

"Come on, come on, let's go do this." He ignores the question, pulling the door back and walking toward the elevator banks.

"Hey, did Stella get home okay last night?" I try a different angle.

He looks over his shoulder at me. Now he knows I know.

"I brought her home." He doesn't elaborate.

"To *her* home or to *your* home?" I tease.

"She's sleeping in my bed."

I run up and punch him in the arm. "Elias!"

"I know. I know!" he groans.

"She better not just be some rebound. Don't screw this up for our group," I chide.

"I know, okay! We both agreed it was a mistake. It'll be fine. Promise."

"Oh, yeah… when did you have time to agree to that?" I press while we wait for the elevator.

"After it happened." He shrugs.

"You had a serious conversation like that when you were both three sheets to the wind last night at the bar? Like I believe that," I retort sarcastically.

The doors open, and we step into the empty carriage. He takes a corner in the front and faces the doors, leaving me to lean against the side and stare at him. My face pinches waiting for his response. I lift a brow at him when he glances my direction and clear my throat.

"I'm waiting," I state, expecting an explanation.

"Well, it happened this morning actually. She woke up needing water at like 5 a.m. so I got it for her. When I slid back under the covers, she started rubbing my side and it just sort of... happened."

I look away, blushing.

I did not think it went that far. I guess it makes sense, though. Something has definitely been off about Stella. Maybe they both needed it.

"So yeah, we were a little more coherent when we had the conversation. She said it first if it makes you feel any better," he continues.

"I gotta talk to Stella." My voice is coated in worry.

He looks at me, searching my eyes before answering, "She'll be here when we get back. I have to sign her out."

The bell sounds, announcing our arrival at the lobby. We spill out, practically running toward our exam.

An hour later, Jess, Elias, and I trudge our way back to Race in a sleepy haze despite having plans to grab Stella and get something to eat. I want to tell Jess about the two of them before we do but don't think Elias will want to deal with the barrage of questions that come along with Jess's personality. I settle on a quick text as we approach the dirt path between Calhoun and Race.

MESSAGE: JESS

Casey: Elias and Stella slept together last night
Casey: she was in his room this morning

Casey: im going to go check on her when we get back

I watch her feel the phone vibrate and hesitate before reaching to pull it out. Her head snaps in my direction, her eyes wide. I give a small nod and exhale a sigh of relief that she didn't ignore the message. She closes her jaw and slides the phone back into her pocket without making a sound. When we get to the elevator, she presses eleven. Elias shoots her a quizzical look and she claims she needs a shower. He shrugs and leans his forehead against the cool metal of the elevator car.

Stella isn't in Elias's room when he cracks the door, quietly peeking in. His roommate passes behind us in the hall and mentions that she asked him to sign her out. I follow Elias into his room, and he nose dives into the pile of sheets and blankets on his lowered bed in a huff, narrowly avoiding a bowl of ramen on the overturned milk crate next to it.

Typical boys. Bed on the floor, leftover ramen, and a milk crate as a nightstand. I should take him to Ikea for an upgrade.

I shake my head and laugh lightly before returning to my purpose.

"Elias—" I start.

"Case, I need to sleep," he cuts me off, mumbling half into his pillow.

"Alright… alright… but you're not getting out of this that easily. We have to talk about you and Stella."

He lifts his arm, waving me off. "Yeah, yeah. Later."

I let out an exhausted sigh before picking my way across the floor. Five minutes later, I jam my keys into the lock and push the door in. Jess is on the couch when I step into the kitchenette, her eyes lifting to mine.

"What happened? I thought you were going to talk with Stella?" she asks, concerned.

"She had Elias's roommate sign her out. I'm going to text her."

She sucks in a breath. "I hope she's okay. Let me know how it goes. Maybe I should message her too? Or maybe not. I don't want to overwhelm her. Just let me know what she says."

"I will, Jess," I assure her.

I pull out my phone, intending to start a message to Stella.

MESSAGE: BRETT

Brett: how did it go this morning?

    Casey: piece of cake

Brett: of course

    Casey: u know me

Brett: i do

Brett: whats up for today

    Casey: i think i need a nap

    Casey: lunch with a friend

    Casey: i don't know about tonight

Brett: nice

    Casey: what about u

Brett: class this afternoon

    Casey: going out for Thirsty Thursday?

Brett: whats that

    Casey: i guess maybe a Philly thing

    Casey: just what we call going out on a Thursday

Brett: then yea probably doing that

    Casey: i miss u

Brett: oh yeah?

    Casey: yes

Brett: where'd that come from

Casey: just thinking about u
Brett: well i miss u too Casey
Casey: what... no baby?
Brett: don't like when i use ur name?
Casey: no i do
Casey: u just usually dont
Casey: something wrong?
Brett: not at all
Brett: u like it when i call u baby?
Casey: u know i do ;)

I'm lost in my messages, standing in the middle of the space connecting the living room and hallway when Jess clears her throat, grabbing my attention.

"Hey! So, Bear was going to come over tonight so I can cook him dinner. Do you mind sleeping out? I'm thinking spaghetti and meatballs, maybe a nice salad. Oh, and I guess I probably should pick up wine and something for dessert. I need to take a trip to Trader Joe's this afternoon. Do you want to come?"

I let the surprise paint my face.

"No, I don't mind. I'll see if Ryan is free for me to stay over. Yes! I'll come with you. I could use the fresh air and a walk. That's a little presumptuous for you, Jess. You think he's going to stay the night, huh?" I wiggle my eyebrows at her.

She smiles, a little color coming to her cheeks. "I kinda hope so."

"Text me if it happens." I turn to walk toward my room and return to my phone, leaving Brett's last message unread in favor of sending a text to Stella.

Before I forget.

Casey: free for lunch?

Stella: yeah sure

Stella: when and where?

Casey: probably be hungry early

Casey: been up since 7 haha

Casey: maybe 11:30 dining terrace?

Stella: perfect

Casey: meet u there

* * * * *

At lunch, Stella apologizes for her behavior, though she doesn't need to. I don't blame her for letting loose after our run-in with her ex, though I suspect there's more to that story than just the one party. Placing a hand on her arm, I gently remind her that she never needs to apologize to me.

With a soft smile on her face and sadness in her eyes, she continues to tell me that Alex, her ex-boyfriend, has spent the last week harassing her, attempting to apologize, and begging her to take him back. She was scared and confused and ran full force toward Elias. He just made her feel safe.

I can understand that. He makes me feel the same way.

At first, I suggest that if the harassment kicks up, she should do something about it. Her face falls and something like panic floods her eyes. She seems to want to steer clear of discussing Alex or the situation. I soften and resolve to try my best to just be a sounding board as she weeds through the possibilities with Elias, encouraging her when she acknowledges the damage it could do if things end badly between them.

Not to mention our whole friend group.

I remind her to ultimately do what feels right for her. Jess joins us just as Stella starts asking questions about Brett. She's not a fan of the fact that I ran back to him after Duke kissed me and left me dangling.

I'm not a fan either, Stella.

I shoot her a dangerous look, hoping she'll get the hint to not continue. It doesn't matter, though. Jess's endless chatter fills the space between the three of us, detailing her plans for the night with Bear and professing her hope that he'll spend the night.

I lose myself in my own thoughts, wondering what I would do if I was in Stella's situation and had stumbled upon Brett when I didn't expect to. A shiver runs down my spine. I'm not sure if it's excitement or dread, and I'm suddenly exhausted. I decide to take tonight off from drinking, knowing next weekend will be a big one for everyone with the packed agenda of Halloween parties.

With our food finished, Stella invites us both up to her room. Jess declines, reminding me of our trip to the grocery store. Before Stella can answer, the screen of her phone lights up, displaying *Mom*. She picks up and waves us off, mouthing that she'll catch up with us later.

By the time we've gone to Trader Joe's and trekked to the sketchy liquor store we know will accept our fake IDs, it's close to 5 p.m.

Where did this day go? But also… it's been a long-ass day.

In a daze, I throw some clothes in a bag and walk over to Calhoun without even bothering to ask Ryan if I can stay in his room first. Even if he wants to go out, he'll probably let me stay.

When I get to the sign-in, I finally call him to say I'm downstairs. My skin tingles at the prospect that just maybe I'll run into Duke on Ryan's floor, but Ryan's voice cuts through my daydream.

"Earth to Casey?" Ryan taunts.

The student behind the desk is looking at me expectantly when I glance up. Ryan is on the opposite side of the turnstiles, unexpectedly *not* put together. I notice the bags under his eyes and his usual composed outfit is more of a hurried ensemble of Drexel t-shirt and sweatpants.

"So sorry!" I smile at the student whose face is familiar, but name is not.

I hand him my ID and he waves me off. "Just go. You practically live here."

"Oh, thanks!" I smirk and turn to Ryan. "You look like shit. What's up?"

"Long night."

"What time did you come home last night?" I suddenly remember that I couldn't find him leaving the bar.

"I don't want to talk about it, but I *did* do the walk of shame this morning at 10 a.m., so…" He clasps his hands together in front of his chest. "*Movie night!*"

"Ian will be out. Right? And will Elias be staying with us?"

He narrows his eyes at me, dropping his tone. "Do you even have to ask?"

I giggle and squint back at him. "Well, after last night…" I stop, not knowing if he knows about Elias and Stella, and quickly recover. "Just want to know if I'll be sharing a bed tonight."

"Oh, honey, you and I will be cuddling all night long. Ian is always out, and you know Elias will end up crashing even if he doesn't plan on it. Unless you'd rather snuggle up with him?" he teases, oblivious of my almost slip about Stella.

He curls his arm around my shoulders and ushers me into the elevator. On seven, the floor is empty and my heart sinks. I scan each door as we pass, hoping it will open and Duke will magically appear.

I wonder if Brett's actually going out tonight.

Something sharp twinges in my side, a sign I need to stop that train of thought before I run away with it. By the end of the hall, my face falls until I hear Elias shouting.

"Who's in for *Knocked Up* tonight?"

We round the final curve and see Elias hanging out of Ryan's door, yelling into the hallway. I step up to him, putting my hands on his chest to push him back into Ryan's room.

"Oh, come on. Can't we watch *P.S. I Love You* or something?" I whine.

He ignores me and looks at Ryan. "You let her in here again?" he jokes before hugging me and dragging me into the room. I roll my eyes.

It's like nothing even happened last night.

CHAPTER 29

By Friday afternoon, I'm surprised no one has changed my mind about not going out this weekend. I remind myself that my body needs it if I'm going to make it through Halloween next week.

And my mind could use another night off.

Ryan and Elias decide to take Ian up on his offer to go to the usual house party. Stella went home this morning to take a few days to clear her head.

Probably better for her not to be around this weekend. She needs a break.

Jess is out with Bear. She was disappointed that he didn't spend the night yesterday but thrilled that he asked her to join him for dinner today.

Somewhere around 6 p.m., my phone buzzes in the quiet of our empty suite. I don't know where she goes, but Jess's roommate is literally never here. I think I've seen her all of three times—two of them being move-in day. I set down the vampire book I'm reading to pick up my phone before unlocking the screen to check the message.

MESSAGE: JESS

Jess: its dinner with Bear AND fraternity members

Casey: oh no. im so sorry Jess!

Jess: no

Jess: its okay

Jess: now I can prove i'll be a valuable member

    Casey: give em hell

Jess: thats the plan

Jess: hopefully Bear notices

I'm constantly amazed by her genuine positivity.

After downing a bowl of cinnamon-sugar cereal for dinner and changing into my favorite oversized sweatpants and hoodie, I tuck myself into bed and get lost in the mindless blackhole of YouTube.

At 8:53 p.m., my phone pulls me out of my almost-slumber and back to life with the sound of a text.

MESSAGE: JESS

Jess: can u thank Ian for me for the ID!!!

    Casey: of course!

Jess: theyre going to this whiskey bar in Center City

Jess: Bear asked me to come

    Casey: YES! thats a win

Jess: some of the members were impressed at my ID

Jess: said i was "resourceful"

I laugh out loud, the sound echoing through the stillness of my room. Only a business fraternity would think getting a fake ID as a freshman is "resourceful." To everyone else, it's expected.

MESSAGE: JESS

    Casey: have fun

    Casey: be careful

Casey: let me know when ur coming home
Jess: thanks Casey!

Closing the laptop, I roll onto my back and stare at the blank white ceiling. I bring the phone to my face and scroll through my inbox, passing the last message from Duke four times before finally opening it. It's the message he sent Sunday asking what time our Business exam was on Monday. He didn't even bother to answer after I told him our exam block was 8 a.m. I hover over the reply button, racking my brain to come up with something attention grabbing to text him and surprise myself by instead texting Brett.

MESSAGE: BRETT
    Casey: you up?

Of course, he's up. It's Friday and only 8 p.m. for him. He's probably out.

A crawling sensation forms at the base of my skull. I toss the phone to my side in disgust and shake my head. My fingers feel the vibration before my mind registers the sound. I instantly bring the phone back to my face.

MESSAGE: BRETT
Brett: yeah u?
    Casey: y aren't u out?
Brett: y aren't u?
    Casey: oh come on
Brett: just didn't feel like it
    Casey: r u alone?
Brett: yes
    Casey: want to call me?

The screen lights up with his incoming call.

This is a bad idea.

I debate letting it go through to voicemail. At the last second, I answer, shifting onto my side and tucking my knees up to my chest. With the phone pressed to my ear, nestled in my comforter in a dark room, it feels just like home.

* * * * *

My eyes open at almost exactly 8 a.m. despite not having set an alarm. A faded light streaming through the cracks in my blinds tells me to roll over and go back to sleep. Something in the back of my mind keeps me awake, and my thumb comes to settle on the familiar cool metal of Brett's gold band.

Oh, boy, what am I doing? I need a coffee and a distraction. That'll fix everything.

I pad into my bathroom, sliding the ring from my finger and placing it back in its box in my now-full makeup bag. Grabbing my toothbrush with one hand, I type out a text in the other.

MESSAGE: RYAN

> **Casey:** i'm coming over
> **Casey:** starbucks?
> **Ryan:** y r u up at this ungodly hour?
> **Casey:** better question
> **Casey:** y r u
> **Ryan:** haha yes coffee
> **Ryan:** see u soon

I throw on the first pair of jeans I find and pull out my new sweater before sliding on my coat. On the way to Starbucks, my mind touches on how easy last night's conversation felt with Brett. He was home for the weekend. One of his siblings was in a school play on Friday and begged him to come home. There was no tension, no pestering questions, just us. Almost as if he knows I'm talking about him, my phone vibrates in my pocket as I pull open the door and am greeted by the heavenly aroma of coffee beans.

MESSAGE: STELLA

Stella: i needed this

I'm pleasantly surprised to see her name and make a mental note to text Brett later. At the counter, I place my order and step aside.

MESSAGE: STELLA

Casey: feeling better?

Stella: so much better

Stella: how was ur night

Stella: go out?

Casey: no

Casey: saving myself for next weekend

Stella: oh what did you end up doing then?

Stella: ryans?

Casey: no actually stayed in my room

Stella: alone??

I hesitate, wanting to tell her about Brett but not wanting to make this conversation about me.

I need to tell someone.

> **Casey:** yes alone
> **Casey:** i am capable
> **Casey:** i was reading...
>
> **Stella:** ...?
>
> **Casey:** Brett called
>
> **Stella:** AND U ANSWERED?
> **Stella:** proud of u
> **Stella:** what did u say
>
> **Casey:** nothing
> **Casey:** it was just a normal conversation
>
> **Stella:** i dont buy that
>
> **Casey:** idk
> **Casey:** it felt just like old times
>
> **Stella:** Casey dont do this to the poor guy

You don't understand, Stella.

"Two Grande Blondes for Casey?"

I shove the phone in my pocket and pick up the coffees, savoring the warmth of the cups in my cold hands. Outside, I breathe in the crisp late-October air, noticing the season has fully transitioned to fall as I make my way toward Calhoun. Standing by the entrance, I look down at my thin cream-colored V-neck sweater, adjust my bra to enhance the shadow of cleavage peeking out, and pull the sides of my coat a little tighter across the front. I admire my face in the glass window of the door before pulling it open.

I look good today.

I can't remember the guy's name on duty—*Aaron, maybe*—but he knows me from every weekend I've spent here. He doesn't even bother to take my ID. He lifts his own cup of coffee and brings it to his lips, mumbling something about the seventh floor and pressing the button to buzz me through the turnstile. This early, the elevator is waiting on the lobby floor. I step in and awkwardly shift both coffees to one hand, pull out my phone, and send a quick message to Ryan that I am on my way up.

My nose is still buried in my phone when the doors open on the seventh floor. I don't bother looking up as I walk out and turn right toward the familiar long hallway to Ryan's room. A raspy guy's voice drags my attention away from the screen.

"Hey, Casey." Duke is coming out of his door in sweats and a sweatshirt, the hood pulled low over his eyes.

"Oh, hi," I say passively, putting my phone away and continuing down the hall.

He follows me, I assume in the direction of the bathroom at the very end. I look up when he reaches my side. He pulls the hood back, and I stop, shocked to see the bags under his eyes, dark as bruises. Looking harder at his face, I realize his one eye is completely bloodshot and don't bother to hide my horror.

"What happened? Are you okay?" I ask, turning toward him.

An emotion that looks like shame passes for an instant under the tired and worn-out features of his face.

"Yeah." He gives me a nervous laugh. "Tried chugging a fifth of Jack last night and it… didn't end well."

I tentatively step forward and put a hand on his arm, leaning to get a closer look. He smells faintly of tobacco and something sweet, making my nose wrinkle.

"Your eye…" I stare intently and lift my hand, bringing my fingertips lightly to the space just below the hollow of his eye socket. I don't even realize I'm touching him until his skin warms mine and he pulls back, turning his head to look away from me.

Shit. I shouldn't have touched his face.

I recoil, letting my hand land back on his arm. He looks down into my eyes without tilting his head, as if he doesn't want to bring his lips closer to mine.

"It doesn't hurt really, just looks nasty. You're headed to Ryan's?"

"Yeah. The three of us are gonna get breakfast." I step back, dropping my hand to my side. My fingers start to cool without the warmth of him underneath them. I shift the coffees, one in each hand.

"Three?" He raises his eyebrows, a lilt in his voice making it a question rather than statement.

"Elias—I think you met him a few times?" I turn to continue down the hall.

"Yeah. He's in a few of my—our—classes," he corrects himself.

"Yes. Him."

We're almost at Ryan's door. I pause before knocking. "Well, take care of yourself, okay? Maybe lay off the chugging."

Another nervous laugh. "Yeah. I'm taking a break for a while."

I nod and turn to knock as he continues toward the men's room. I stare at the ceiling above the door, counting the ugly gray and white speckled tiles as I wait for it to open, when I notice Duke stop short and turn back.

"Hey, Casey, think we could grab lunch or dinner sometime?" His voice holds an unexpected nervousness.

"Lunch or dinner?" I raise my eyebrows in surprise.

"Yeah... I mean, I'm not doing so hot in a few of our classes. I was thinking maybe you could help?"

My face settles, and I let the edges of my lips curl slightly. "Sure. Okay. Just text me whenever."

Ball's in your court, Duke.

The door opens to Elias, eyes sleepy, hair more ruffled than usual.

It's like he lives here... He should just switch with Ian.

"Sup, dude?" He nods at Duke.

"Hey." Duke nods at him before fixing his eyes on me. "I'll see you around, Casey." He nods and pads away lightly, concentrating on the floor.

I step inside and close the door gingerly, leaning my back against it.

"What was *that*?" Elias asks suspiciously.

"Oh, stop!" I set the coffee down on the desk just inside the door and slap his arm playfully, moving deeper into the room. "He just wants my help with some classes."

"Sure." His disbelief is on full display. "That's not all he wants."

"'What's that?" Ryan asks, lounging comfortably on his own bed.

I open my mouth to answer, but Elias cuts me off, "Duke wants to have *dinner* with Casey so she can *help him with his classes*." He rolls his eyes.

"Oh, honey, no. Not this again." Ryan's tone reminds me of the times my mom yelled at me instead of my dad. Not quite threatening enough to make an impact. "Remember what happened last time you gave him the time of day?"

"What?" I ask innocently. "I'm just going to help him get his grades back on track. The poor guy doesn't need to fail out just because he had a little too much fun his first few weeks as a freshman. Not everyone is playing catch-up to the party game." I stare decidedly at Elias.

Elias looks at Ryan, ignoring my comment. "Get his grades back on track. Do you believe her?"

"Can we just go get breakfast? I'm starving," I plead in a rush, attempting to cut off the conversation.

"Maybe you should ask Duke to join us," Elias challenges me.

"Maybe I will." I pick up his sweatshirt to throw at him. It lobs him in the face just as he looks up from tying his sneakers.

"Don't take out your sexual frustration on me," he jokes, sliding in both arms and throwing the hood up over his head.

"I knew I never should have told you guys he kissed me!" My cheeks burn deep red at the comment. I turn toward the door, hoping neither of them notice the bright shade of my face.

"Casey, you can't hide from the truth." Ryan's voice is teasing.

If he only knew how much I'm hiding.

I face them, faking confidence. "I'm not," I say, tilting my chin up.

"You definitely are! Forget dinner, just sleep with him already!" Elias taunts me, and I stare at him, angry for putting me in this situation in the first place. He just shrugs with a huge grin.

"I'm not sexually frustrated!" I practically shout and wouldn't be surprised if everyone else on the floor could hear me, especially Duke just down the hall.

"Then what are you?" Ryan presses.

I drop my voice to a barely audible whisper. "I've just never had sex."

Fuck. Why did I just admit that?

For so long I've been fixated on Brett being the first, despite the irreconcilable factor of long distance. Then I thought maybe I had a chance with Greg, but we never got that far. Duke was a strong candidate when I first met him, but after his recent dismissal of my affections, I slid back into the comfortable daydream of Brett and me.

"You're kidding!" Ryan's voice is shocked, and my cheeks grow hotter.

"You haven't?" Elias echoes incredulously.

"I haven't. There, I said it. Can we move on from this fascinating tidbit, please?"

Sensing my embarrassment and a potential impending meltdown, Ryan attempts to comfort me. "We all have our right time. Just don't lose it to that jerk who kissed and dismissed you."

I'm quiet and analyzing his last statement.

Maybe it isn't that big of a deal that I've been waiting? At least not to my friends—the people who matter.

Ryan shoots Elias a look that silences whatever comment he was just about to make.

Instead, Elias says, "I'm just teasing. Come on, we'll make it a project over breakfast. Operation Mate Case!"

A clipped giggle escapes my throat at this ridiculous conversation.

Operation Mate Case? Ugh.

I roll my eyes and quickly shake my head, trying not to laugh. "Absolutely not. We are not talking about this."

"Fine. So long as you give us all the gory details when it does happen." Elias winks and slings an arm across my shoulders, pulling me out the door. Ryan trails behind us, buttoning his coat.

"So does Ian ever come home anymore?" I strain my neck to ask Ryan. "Or should Elias just officially move out of Race and in with you?" I tease and poke Elias in the side.

Ryan catches up, sandwiching me between them. "He spends all his time at Ava's."

Ah. There it is.

CHAPTER 30

Why do they always give freshmen the first class on Monday mornings?

I thought after half a term, I would be used to the 8 a.m. Monday morning start times, but I'm not. Elias and I are settled into our usual cushioned lecture seats waiting for Mr. Finneghan to dim the lights. We battle over the armrest between us, shooting each other dirty looks without a word, until he finally wins. This early, we barely talk. Neither of us are morning people.

My laptop sits open on the pullout half-desk, a blank Word Document open with the date and class neatly arranged across the top. I rub my eyes with a heavy sigh and decide to check my email before class begins. Of the few unread messages, my eyes widen at the one sitting at the top of my inbox.

EMAIL FROM: BCAVIAR@HOTMAIL.COM

SUBJECT: JUST FOR YOU

... Image loading

I catch a glimpse of skin and quickly exit without scrolling through to see if a message is included. A flash of warmth pours over my body. Grabbing a handful of sweater, I pull the fabric away from my chest, letting the cool air from the room rush in and over the heat on my skin. I silently pray Elias didn't see, but I see him pull out his phone from the corner of my eye as someone clears their throat next to me. I drag my gaze in the direction of the sound and try to hide my surprise at Duke standing at the end of the aisle.

"Mind if I sit here?" Duke asks, sliding into the open seat next to me.

I close my jaw and bite my lip as his knee grazes mine. There's not enough space, and I lean awkwardly to shift my bags around my feet to create some for Duke.

"Not at all, please do," I respond from behind the curtain of hair that's fallen in front of my face, even though he's already sitting down.

I feel my phone vibrate and hear a snicker. Turning my head, I see Elias's shit-eating grin. He wiggles his eyebrows at me, stifling a smirk and slinking lower in the seat. I sit up and shift to pull my phone from the back pocket of my jeans, knocking my knee into Duke's again since his legs are spread wide in his seat. The lights dim and the screen at the front of the room illuminates our faces with the image of today's PowerPoint.

"S-sorry," I stammer in a whisper as I bump the small desk and fumble with my phone.

Keep it together, Casey.

My laptop slips, threatening to fall to the floor with the wiggle of the desk from my clumsiness. I slap my hand down on the keyboard.

"No problem," Duke responds quietly, finally settling my computer with his long fingers. I try not to stare at his hand so close to mine on the keys and turn my gaze to read the message that just came through on my phone.

I roll my eyes and shake my head.

"Something wrong?" Duke asks under his breath, studying me.

"No, no. Thank you," I whisper.

He nods, pulling his hand back to his lap. His pinky brushes mine as he does, and I glance over at him. I notice his hand is poised with a pen and actual notebook and smile. While Mr. Finneghan opens class, I scroll through a few more messages, settling on one from Stella before turning my attention fully to today's lesson.

For the next hour, I sit rigidly in my seat, dutifully typing out copious amounts of notes. Elias nods off, assuming he can bum them off me as usual and piece together anything else he missed. I steal a few glances at Duke, scribbling his own notes sporadically, and realize I've spent more than a few minutes silently begging for his knee to fall open just a little further to touch mine again.

As we're being dismissed, I take the time to diligently pack away my things, each in their designated place in my bag. I'm excitedly aware that Duke has not gotten up yet. The seat creaks against his weight before his elbow bumps mine while slotting the notebook into his own bag. He clears his throat again. I look at his face, his eyes holding some glimmer of emotion I can't read.

"Want to grab a coffee?" he asks.

Elias leans in front of me. "I'd love to." He emphasizes "love" and lifts his voice at the end.

My head snaps in Elias's direction, and he smiles in mock sweetness. I squeeze my brows together in annoyance, and his eyes dance in delight.

"Sounds wonderful, Duke. Should we go to Starbucks?" I ask without turning to look at the him.

Again, Elias cuts in, holding my gaze. "Let's!"

What is this, my first date? I don't need a chaperone.

"Stella's going to join." I continue to stare at Elias pointedly. "Maybe you can have coffee with *her*."

Duke laughs wholeheartedly at our exchange and stands up, adjusting his jeans and smoothing his sweater. I turn my head, noticing the shadow he casts over me, and admire the length of his trim body. I realize this may be the first time I've seen him in something other than sweats in a long time.

He looks even better put together.

A flash of self-consciousness about my own outfit passes before remembering that I've made a few upgrades myself. I look pretty put together in my new skinny jeans and navy-blue crew-neck sweater. He swings his peacoat up over his shoulders and steps out into the aisle, graciously gesturing for me and Elias to pass in front of him.

"Maybe I will," Elias says tauntingly, brushing past me. I stare straight at the back of his head as he makes his way toward the doors, side-by-side with Duke.

Elias bursts out into the bright morning sun. The cool October air stings my cheeks and burns my lungs, and I pull my coat closer around me.

"So, Duke," Elias starts, his tone as stern as a father asking for intentions with his daughter. "How's it going?" He switches to playful.

I'm starting to feel whiplash from the abrupt change.

Come on, Elias.

I roll my eyes and let out an exasperated breath.

Duke forces another laugh. "Not so great, man. Not so great."

The two of them walk together ahead of me in the direction of coffee. I pull out my phone to message Stella that we're on our way. Duke tips his head over his shoulder and slows his pace. Flashing him a smile, I stow the phone in my coat pocket before hurrying to catch up. When I'm at his side, keeping him between Elias and me, he continues his thought.

"I didn't do well on midterms." He swallows hard. "Actually, I haven't been doing well in class in general. My parents are sort of on my case." He looks at the ground ahead of his feet.

I've never seen him this beaten up. Except maybe the other day.

The memory of the fracture of veins splashed across the white of his eye makes my chest squeeze.

"It happens," I say before Elias can respond. "You have a couple of weeks to turn it around. Have you tried talking to any of the professors?"

"Not really, no. Not sure what good that would do? It's not like I've made any effort to show face."

"I don't think that really matters. As long as you show interest in making an effort now..." I shrug. "It could help."

"Yeah, or just do what I do and bug Casey before all the tests," Elias jokes, leaning around to look at me and stick his tongue out.

Duke smiles at me hopefully. "I mean, I'm sort of trying to ask for her help now."

"Riiight," Elias drawls sarcastically.

"No, seriously." Duke stops, putting a hand on my forearm. "Could you help me?"

My heart skips a beat, and I have to stop myself from jumping up and down. I control my composure and hope my voice won't give away my excitement, willing my eyes to stare straight at his.

"Of course. I'd love to help."

Elias mocks me behind Duke's back, dramatically mouthing, "I'd love to help!" and rolls his eyes before stepping into Duke's line of sight. "Great! Now that that's settled." He claps Duke on the back. "Duke, how do you feel about Xbox?"

And now I've lost both of their attention.

They gab like girls about the latest games and favorite cheat codes. At least Elias holds the door for me when we get to Starbucks, giving me a slight bow as I walk past him. I raise an eyebrow and shake my head.

He shrugs and whispers into my ear, "I'm just making sure he's the right guy for you."

"Suuure." I laugh and notice Stella already on line.

Her eyes widen when they land on Duke and Elias behind me, both boys moving to find an open table and claiming it as ours with their coats and bags. I sidle up next to her, leaning in.

"He asked me to help him with his classes," I inform her as if it's top secret.

"And you're going to?" she accuses.

I take a step back at the unexpected tone.

Why is she mad? I didn't think she'd have the same reaction as Elias and Ryan.

"What's so wrong with helping him?" I ask, hurt seeping into my voice.

"Casey, what are you doing?"

I don't really understand her question. Pinching the bridge of my nose in confusion, I don't respond.

She pulls me in closer. "He's been hot and cold with you this entire time, and you're just going to let him walk all over you because 'he needs help with class'?" She's practically out of breath attempting to whisper in anger.

"It's not like that."

"Then what is it like? Because the last time I checked, you spent all night on the phone with Brett the other night, and he hasn't done anything but be there for you when you need him."

Shit, I did tell her about that phone call.

I stare at her in shock, feeling her words like a slap across the face before Elias and Duke come up behind us, ending the conversation.

CHAPTER 31

I wonder what the comparison is between the time it takes to form a bromance and how long it takes girls to actually decide if they like one another.

Elias has surprised me all week with his invitations for Duke to join us for everything. Every. Single. Thing. At first, I thought it was his way of poking fun at my crush, but I think he genuinely likes Duke. I shouldn't complain too much. The invites have made Duke feel more like part of our group and not just some guy I am sharing notes with. It's given me the perfect excuse to see him more often in a social setting when clearly my previous efforts were failing.

Sometime between Monday and Friday, while our group was expanding plus one for Duke, we settled on which Halloween parties to attend. It took them until breakfast on Friday morning to understand that I wouldn't be joining them until Saturday. Friday is reserved for my sorority Halloween party. Saturday I'm all theirs for the party hopping.

Late Friday afternoon, I stand in front of the mirror in my tiny bathroom, my hair dripping wet and plastered to my back. My eyes look bigger somehow, innocent against the backdrop of my soft features. A sweet smile spreads across my lips. Combing my fingers through my hair, I pull one side back, exposing the height of my cheek bones, and pucker my lips.

Tonight, I want to be sexy.

Halloween for pledges is like a rite of passage. Each sorority's new pledge class has a theme. It's always a play on words based on the sorority name and usually involves taking something sweet and turning it sexy, like kittens or flight attendants. It's all *very* original. This theme is kept "top secret" until the big reveal during the annual Greek Halloween party at the swankiest Frat on campus.

My class chose the Pink Ladies in honor of our sorority colors. The twenty-seven of my almost-sisters and I spent weeks secretly gathering supplies to piece together the outfits— hacking off skirts, bedazzling bras, and personalizing skimpy jackets.

Tonight, at the party we'll parade down the main steps leading to the basement, with all the fraternity members lined up along the stairs, handing us drinks. The boys will cheer, and the sorority they yell the loudest for wins bragging rights until next year.

I'm excited beyond belief, if not the tiniest bit nervous. To don a costume I would never have given a second thought back in my small town. To have the older sisters paint our faces perfectly. For all eyes to be on us... *on me.*

I'm getting dizzy just thinking about it.

Underneath the excitement, I'm more than a little jealous that my friends have a whole night planned without me, but did I really expect them not to? They even invited Duke. And he accepted! When Jess saw my face react to their plans, she insisted that they'll all join me at midnight once the frat house opens its doors to the non-Greek Life population. Stella rolled her eyes at my neediness. A stab of shame at remembering her reaction pierces my good mood. I try to shove it aside, but it keeps needling its way back in.

Could she be right?

As if on cue, my phone vibrates against the fake granite countertop.

MESSAGE: BRETT

Brett: so do i get a picture of this infamous halloween costume?

I smile and pull my bottom lip between my teeth, feeling overly confident and flirty.

MESSAGE: BRETT

Casey: how about a just out of the shower picture instead?

Brett: even better

Shifting the towel wrapped around my chest a little lower, I loosen its grip and let it fall open, exposing just the right amount of skin to be a tease. I keep my lip between my teeth and lower my eyelids to a sexy smolder. Tilting the phone in my typical downward angle, I capture the perfect "come get me" picture. My face breaks into a wicked grin as I hit send and wait for his response.

MESSAGE: BRETT

Brett: fuck baby

Casey: better than my halloween costume?

Brett: much

Brett: i still want to see it tho

Casey: i have something better

I let the towel drop to the floor and admire the curves of my naked body in the mirror, sinking into my hip and placing my hand seductively over my stomach with my fingers spread wide. Just as I'm about to take another photo, a message flashes across the top of the screen and the phone slips out of my hand. Thankfully, it lands in the mess of my towel and not the tile floor.

MESSAGE: DUKE

Duke: help

Duke: what should i be for halloween?

I swallow hard and attempt to control my wildly beating heart. Staring at my reflection in the mirror, I swear I can see my heart pounding against my ribcage, my chest heaving. Excitement wells up from my stomach, making me shiver. I reach down to grab the towel, clutching it to me.

He wants to know what I think.

MESSAGE: DUKE

Casey: u could be the danny to my sandy

Casey: have a leather jacket?

Duke: yeah let me just dig it out of my closet :P

Casey: haha sorry guess not

Casey: lets see

Casey: naked cowboy?

Duke: wouldn't want to scare anyone ;)

Casey: little cocky aren't we

Duke: i just know what i'm working with

Casey: okay

Casey: have a flannel?

Casey: actual cowboy?

Duke: that could work

Duke: thanks Casey

I start typing a response asking if I'll see him later and to save me a dance. My thumb is hovering over the send button when I realize the text above my response.

MESSAGE: BRETT

Brett: well?

Shit. I almost sent that to Brett. That could have been bad.

MESSAGE: BRETT

Casey: sorry to be a tease

Casey: i gotta get going to my sorority to get ready

Casey: i'll show u my costume later

Brett: u are a tease

Brett: it better be good

MESSAGE: DUKE

Casey: will i see u later?

Casey: save me a dance

Duke: yes

Duke: after ur done with ur fraternity business

Where have you been, Duke? This is the guy I remember from Orientation.

I place the phone gently on the counter, a satisfied smile on my face, and hit the lock button to check the time. Just before 5 p.m. I *actually* need to be getting to my sorority house.

Perfect, it wasn't entirely a lie.

Throwing the towel around my waist, I cross the hall to my room. I pull on the first pair of clean yoga pants I can find and tug my Drexel sweatshirt over my head before tying my hair up in a knot and yanking on my jacket. I grab the bag I packed earlier today with my curling iron, makeup, and brand-new black platform heels with the dainty strap around the ankle. My closet doors are slightly cracked—they won't shut completely with all my new clothes stuffed inside. I catch a glimpse of the light pink silk of the Pink Ladies jacket peeking out as I rush for the door.

I almost forgot my costume.

I pull the doors back and lift the hanger off the tiny hook. The fabric barely covers the hanger. The skirt can't really be called a skirt. It's more like a donut-shaped ring of cloth. When I first put it on, I tried to yank the hemline down, but the only thing that accomplished was exposing my ass from the other direction. I decided on a pair of loose fishnets to attempt to provide coverage.

The thin pink jacket is cropped and exposes the soft expanse of my navel. I bought a bright pink belly button ring for my piercing to match the jacket. Sometimes I forget the tiny piece of jewelry is there. It was my present on my sixteenth birthday after my mom found me trying to pierce the skin myself. Right now it adds the perfect touch to my stomach to quell some of my self-conscious nerves at showing this much skin. But the best part is the padded push-up bra I spent hours meticulously dotting with pink and white rhinestones. It pushes my chest into the perfect eye-catching cleavage.

I pull everything off the hanger and fold it neatly before slotting it next to my shoes in my bag. One last check of my phone and I sprint for the door.

MESSAGE: BRETT
Brett: i love u
Brett: dont forget about me tonight
    Casey: i wont
    Casey: love u

MESSAGE: DUKE
    Casey: try not to start in on the jack until u find me :p
Duke: haha i'll take it easy just for u

* * * * *

The stairwell and basement are packed, like New York City subway packed. I'm shaking in my heels, still shivering from the forty-five minutes we spent waiting outside to be the last girls down the stairs. Around 10:30 p.m., it started to drizzle while we waited, and we all huddled together under the small awning to salvage our hair and makeup.

We squealed at the rain dampening our hair and costumes, thinking about the time it took to get ready. At least half of the sisters are fashion majors and came around adjusting our outfits, lifting here, and taking it in there when we were in our house getting ready. While they did, we formed two lines on the chapter room floor and the rest of the sisters painted our faces with dramatic smokey eyes, long cat-winged eyeliner, and pouty dark red lips. I snuck into the bathroom as soon as they were done with me to send a picture to Brett of the finished product. I didn't wait for his response before flinging the phone on the counter and admiring my appearance in the bathroom mirror.

My phone is now tucked into the corner of my bra as we make our way inside. The sisters made us leave our bags at the sorority house, and I'm just now realizing I don't have my ID or keys to get back into my dorm.

Guess I'll be finding somewhere to sleep tonight.

The sound of the bass from below vibrates up through the floorboards of the tiny hallway we're all wedged into, waiting for our moment to step down the stairs. Our Pledge Mom comes around with a bottle of vodka and plastic shot glasses, pouring one for each of us.

"Drink up, ladies!" She hoists the bottle in the air, and we all cheer in response. "Oh! All my perfect babies. Are you ready?"

The president of our chapter snakes her way through the bodies on the stairs and yells over our heads, "Okay, ladies! Rally chant on three! 1-2-3!"

We clap our hands in rhythm and begin the chant together. The roars from below us grow louder. The first of my class must have come into view of the basement. I'm somewhere in the middle of the group, not first and not last but must be at least a half a foot taller than most of the girls in my pledge class in these four-inch heels.

I take a shaky step and my foot wobbles on the first plank of the wooden basement stairs. Inhaling a deep breath, I hold it for a moment and let it out slowly. Adrenaline pumps through my veins. The fraternity pledge standing at the top of the stairwell catches my eye and holds out a hand to guide me farther into the darkness. His grip is cold, rough, and a little wet. He passes my hand to the next guy down the stairs and a smile splits my face as the full scene comes into view. I pick up the chant and join the rest of my class. Every single person in the basement has their heads turned in our direction. Guys and girls of every shape and size are staring and screaming along with us.

So this is what this feels like. Give me more.

I lick my lips and smile, expecting another hand to meet mine but instead feel a cool can of beer sweating with condensation. The chanting turns to an encouraging demand.

"Chug! Chug! Chug!"

I hear the girl behind me pop her can before I feel the cool liquid spray across my back. I squeal as it hits my bare skin. The guy next to me leans in and pops mine, pushing it up toward my lips. I shift on my feet and glance toward him. He's cheering in my face with a devilish grin. The liquid pours down my throat as I tip my head back. I swallow hard and try not to grimace at the disgusting taste.

"Chug! Chug! Chug!"

There's pressure at my back to keep moving down the stairs and into the sweaty sea of people. The heat radiates through me, warming my cheeks, and my fingertips burn. It's almost unbearable and I yank the zipper down on my tiny jacket, exposing the full design of my bra.

Fuck it.

I press the opening of the can against my lips once again and tilt my head back, gulping down the remainder of its contents. Haze seeps into my vision as the concrete floor comes up beneath me. I drop the can and reach for another in the waiting hands of the swarm of sisters around us. Glancing to my left, I see a slightly raised portion of the basement, bodies lounging on top of each other on a couple of couches surrounding what looks like a stripper pole. The sound of someone speaking through a microphone drags my attention forward.

"And the winner of this year's Greek Halloween is…" He pauses dramatically, waiting for the noise to die down. "The Pink Ladies!"

I hear screaming before I realize it's coming from my throat. The girl next to me swings her arms around me, jumping up and down and spilling my drink on the people surrounding us. The music picks up and she lets go, grabbing my hand and pulling me deeper into the darkness toward what looks like a bar.

As we approach, I see it's lined with shots. Each girl in my class steps in to pick one up and funnel into the circle we've created around our Pledge Mom. With tears in her eyes, she gives a short speech on how proud she is before professing her love for us and cheering. Twenty-seven heads tip back at the same time, swallowing the freezing cold liquor.

At least it's vodka.

I toss the small cup on the bar and grab a second, swallowing it on my own, before following the girls back into the center of the dancefloor. I feel my phone vibrate and ignore it, the music numbing my senses and resonating through my body.

A mix of boys tangle in with our group of girls, grabbing and pulling at our jackets. I feel a warm body curve along the line of my back and hot strong hands grip my sides. Before I know what I'm doing, I press myself back into him, grinding my hips into his. My phone vibrates again as I feel the hand dip dangerously lower.

This is not what I want.

I grip his wrists and yank them away from my body before turning back toward the bar. I find a small space at the ledge and pull out my phone.

MESSAGE: BRETT

Brett: ur fucking hot
Brett: save that for when u come see me
    Casey: u like?
Brett: i love
Brett: thank god ur mine
    Casey: tell me u need me
Brett: i need u
    Casey: and no one else
Brett: no one else

I close the message with a satisfied smile fueled by liquid courage, keeping the phone pressed between my palms. When I lift my eyes to the bar, my vision wobbles and I feel just how tipsy I am. I look out over the crowd and notice it's thinned out a touch. Then I hear more cheering from the steps as another flood of people enter the basement. I touch the lock button, checking the time.

12:43 a.m.

That means the party is open.

MESSAGE: DUKE

    Casey: come find me
Duke: we're on our way

An ache forms between my legs, complementing the heat coursing through my body. I tip another shot between my lips and shove the phone back in my bra before making my way back onto the dance floor.

I find a familiar face and join in on the dancing, angling myself to face the stairs and hoping I'll see my friends as they step down. Another unfamiliar set of hands finds my hips, rocking them back and forth. The fabric of my skirt slips, and I stop moving to readjust it. The hands never move from their place on my sides unlike the last guy.

Little more of a gentleman, this one. Still not the hands I want on me.

I close my eyes and try to relax, my senses heightened, feeling every pulse of the music, every bead of sweat sliding across my skin. Something in me stirs and my eyelids flutter.

When I open them fully, my eyes meet Duke's over the top of Jess's head. He's wearing a dark red flannel like I suggested, a plain white tank underneath, with a cowboy hat and a massive silver belt buckle to top it all off. His gaze is dark, and his face is tight. I watch him drag his widened eyes down my body as he steps down into the crowded basement. I bite my bottom lip and smile when his attention lifts back up to mine.

He's pushing roughly through the mass of people and steps directly in front of me, leaning past to the guy behind me. He's so close. His scent hits me like a wrecking ball, but instead of falling backward, I step forward into him. I can't hear what he's saying, and I don't care, but I feel the hands leave my hips.

Duke rubs my arms and grabs my hand, pulling me back in the direction of the bar. Peering up into his face, it looks more relaxed, his bright green eyes a little clearer.

"Want a drink?" he asks, pointing to the beer can the guy behind the bar is holding up.

"Yes. Not beer."

"A shot for the lady." He leans across the bar to yell into the guy's ear.

"You went with the cowboy look!" I squeal.

"I did. It was a great idea." He grips the shot as the guy passes it across the small space to his waiting fingers.

"Where did you find the hat?" I ask.

"Would you believe me if I said Elias had it?" he teases, and I throw my head back to laugh.

I would absolutely believe that.

"You make a sexy cowboy… I still think you should have gone naked," I tease.

"Maybe I'll show you later." He winks and takes a sip of the can.

I envy his straight face, impressed that he doesn't wince at the taste of the cheap beer. Feeling bold, I pull out my phone, lift onto my toes, and kiss his cheek just as I snap a photo. When I pull the screen down to view, it's the perfect image. His lips are pulled into a surprised "O" with his eyebrows raised. My eyes are closed, and my lips puckered perfectly against his cheek.

"Oh, it's so cute!" I gush.

"Send it to me?" he asks before taking another swallow of beer.

"Now?" I ask, incredulously.

"Yeah, so you don't forget." He places his hand on the small of my back and passes me the shot. I shoot the cold liquid like an expert before slamming the plastic cup down on the bar. He presses into me, escorting me back toward the music and dancing.

I pull my phone out, scrolling through my inbox to find his last message. He spins me around and presses into my back. His fingers brush my hair away from my neck and he dips his head, touching his lips just below my earlobe.

"How much have you had to drink, mister?" I tease.

Not fully concentrating on my phone, I attach the photo without looking and type, *So I don't forget.* I tap the send button just before Duke grabs my phone and shoves it into his pocket. He presses his lips against my ear, reminding me of the first time he kissed me.

Maybe I can go home with him tonight.

"No more. Dance with me," he commands.

How can I resist?

I spot Jess, Ryan, Elias, and Stella across the room and lift my hand to wave. Jess bounces up to me, squealing in delight. Seeing them pulls me out of my fantasy. Jess is wearing butterfly wings and a skimpy dress while Stella's wearing a ripped-up red dress with the word *Wrath* written across her chest in lipstick.

She's gorgeous. I can't stand it sometimes.

Ryan is wearing all black with fake vampire teeth, and Elias is wearing a bright red firefighter hat.

How on point for them.

They come up behind Jess and Stella, enveloping us in a small circle of guys to block out the creeps. I pull Jess to me and yell over the music.

"I left my bag at the sorority house. Don't leave without me. I won't be able to get back into our room."

She beams at me. "Are you sure you don't want to go home with Duke?" She winks, nodding in his direction.

Anticipation heats my cheeks, but I shake my head.

Not like this.

"No. Make sure I come home with you." I squeeze her hand and release her, melting back into Duke and finding a rhythm with his hips.

CHAPTER 32

MESSAGE: BRETT

... picture message delivery failure

Casey 1:13AM: so i dont forget ;)

Brett 1:15AM: so u dont forget what?

* * * * *

MESSAGE: BRETT

Brett 9:16AM: y havent u texted me back

Brett 9:17AM: come on its been 4 days

Brett 9:18AM: in case u forget what?

Brett 9:20AM: baby just talk to me please

Brett 9:25AM: i just want to make sure ur okay

Brett 10:00AM: i kno u had class this morning

Brett 11:47AM: what r u doing that u cant talk to me?

Brett 2:57PM: fine i guess u just dont love me anymore

Brett 3:15PM: if its over then just tell me its over

Brett 3:16PM: i dont understand

Brett 3:17PM: come on

Brett 3:20PM: Casey?

* * * * *

It takes two weeks for me to get over the fact that Jess did, in fact, drag me home on Halloween. I was so close to going home with Duke.

So. Close.

We were standing outside of the frat house in the rain, just Duke and me, waiting for the rest of our group to find their way outside. I was shivering, my teeth chattering in my head so badly I could barely talk straight. He plopped the hat on my head, wrapped the flannel around me, and pulled me close. I leaned my head back to look at him, his face shadowed by the light shining behind him. I could read the desire on his face, see the want in his eyes. His lips were just about to touch mine when Jess danced through the door yelling my name. She yanked my arm, and he hesitantly loosened his grip on my waist and let her pull me away from him.

Jess and I danced down the road, splashing in the puddles and ignoring the stoplights. Not a care in the world. Stella hung back with the boys, staying close to Elias and Ryan.

Out of nowhere, Duke was running toward me, into the middle of the road where we were standing. He scooped me around the waist and wrapped his hand around Jess's arm just as a car rolled through the stop sign from the other direction. She shrieked and hugged him, hanging off his neck for the next two blocks, professing that he saved our lives. I was trying to hide my jealousy when he pulled her arms free and stopped walking. As I caught up, he curled his hand around my waist, drawing circles on the bare skin of my hip. I leaned into him, letting him hold my weight.

When we got to my dorm, he pulled me away and pressed my back against the side of the building. One hand held my waist and the other tangled into my soaking wet hair. He brushed his lips against mine. I could taste the alcohol on his breath as he brought my hips to meet his. Jess split us apart with a sarcastic apology before the kiss could get any deeper. I whispered angrily that I was fine and didn't need her help. She just squeezed my hand and dragged me through the doors of our building while I struggled to turn and watch Duke walk away with Ryan. I guess Elias walked Stella home.

I was even less successful at getting Duke to take me home the next day. I couldn't have been more cliche in my all-white angel outfit consisting of a skintight white skirt and short-sleeved crop top showing off the little wings of my belly ring. I didn't bother with the halo once I found the most perfect feather wings.

Duke showed up wearing all black with a fedora and a fake guitar slung across his back, claiming to be Jason Mraz. He looked like trouble and he knew it. We followed each other around all night, but somehow, we were never alone. Jess would get between us while we were dancing, or Ryan would be there when we went for a refill. Duke ended up having to help Ryan carry Elias back to Calhoun and I slunk home with Jess and Stella, defeated.

Unfortunately, in the light of day, I only get to see Duke in our group outings. I'd be more forthcoming, but I don't want to fall back from the progress we've made, and I feel like I've scared him off before.

I focus instead on trying to figure out what's going on between Elias and Stella. She seems to have softened toward me and will at least meet me for coffee, but I can't say we're back to our easy conversation. She only acts natural when we're in our larger group.

Elias has calmed down from the initial rush of partying to escape the pain of his breakup and is back to himself. In an annoying change of events, he's even waking *me* up for our classes, yelling through the door and driving both Jess and me crazy.

His social side has blossomed, complementing his happy-go-lucky vibe, and it's even more endearing. It's only happened once, but I know I saw his face slip for just a second, making me wonder if it's just a front. I hope it isn't, because he truly is the whole package, and I can't help but think that Maggie made a *huge* mistake.

Maybe he and Stella are actually good for each other.

I'm so glad he's the first person I met.

With Halloween over and a slowdown in my pledging activities as we creep closer to the Thanksgiving break, I luckily don't have to miss out on our group hangs. My stomach fills with butterfly flutters every time my eyes come to rest on Duke across a table, across a desk, across a room.

I almost melted the first time he asked me to go for coffee, just the two of us. It was after our usual Monday morning Business 101. Elias rushed to meet his team for a group project, leaving Duke and me alone packing up after class. Duke helped me pull on my coat and handed me my bag before casually asking if I wanted Starbucks.

I turned left out of the double doors leading outside, toward our usual coffee spot. He grabbed my arm and swung me in the other direction, mentioning the Starbucks on Penn's campus would be quieter. We sat across from each other for hours, through two coffees and a shared blueberry scone. I smiled until my cheeks burned and laughed until my sides hurt.

We've gone to Starbucks alone twice more since then. Both times I felt a wave of excitement as I watched him lean farther and farther across the table listening to me, his hands folded, crossing the midpoint, and entering my space. I kept mine clasped in my lap, ignoring the itch to touch him.

This time it's my turn to play hard to get.

Though I secretly hoped he would lean just a little farther and kiss me.

On Thursday, Ryan sends a group message asking who's ready for dinner. Duke responds immediately that he's in, followed by everyone else. I can't calm the swell in my chest at another night I'll get to see him.

After filling our trays at the dining hall, we find a booth big enough for the six of us and pile in, girls on one side, boys on the other. By happy coincidence, Duke and I are across from one another. My foot grazes his under the table. He lifts his gaze to me and smiles, popping a French fry in his mouth and tapping my foot with his.

"So, who's up to go out tonight?" Elias fills the break in conversation.

Duke looks at me through his lashes without answering.

"I'm staying in, guys," Jess begins hopefully. "Bear is cooking me dinner."

Elias whistles and I clap giddily.

"That feels more intimate than 'just friends'!" I smile and wink at her.

"Oh, stop, guys. As much as I want it to be like that, it really just isn't ever going to happen," she says, sounding discouraged.

"Aw, Jess, you don't know that." I try to comfort her at the same time Ryan says, "Honey, you don't need that man in your life."

Her eyebrows lift in surprise, and she bursts out laughing before pulling her lips into a fake pout. "But I do need him. Ugh, my God, do I need him."

Her comment elicits a laugh from the table, especially the guys. Duke quiets and looks at me, a smile playing on his lips. I can't tell exactly what he's looking at, but he's focused on something below my eyes. I raise my soup spoon, slipping it between my lips and fluttering my lashes quickly. He adjusts in the seat and leans back into the corner. Sliding his foot between my legs, he rests his knee against mine, and looks directly into my eyes.

"I have to spend the night with my roommate. I've barely seen her and I feel bad," Stella interjects, breaking my moment and eyeing Elias.

I turn my head just in time to catch the last glimpse of whatever that was between her and Elias.

Was that another moment?

"Well, I guess that leaves the four of us." Elias looks at Duke, Ryan, and me. Duke still hasn't responded.

This gives me the option of going out to drink with all guys or staying in by myself. Part of me is thrilled at the prospect of getting to be "one of the guys" for a night but part doesn't think I can keep up with the three of them together.

I'm not sure I want to try.

"I don't know, guys. I think I'll just stay in tonight," I say and cover my mouth, faking a yawn. "I'm pretty tired."

I watch Duke pause, seemingly calculating something in his mind before he says, "You know, I'm actually not feeling very well. I think I'm going to hold off until tomorrow."

I hold my breath, waiting for Elias to call him on his bullshit, but he doesn't. He just claps him on the shoulder and cheers, "Tomorrow! Fridays are the best anyway." He then turns to Ryan and says, "So, Caverns then?"

When we leave dinner, Duke hangs back. I turn my head both ways to look for him and slow when I see him a couple paces behind me. We fall into step next to each other.

He bumps into my shoulder playfully. "You still interested in those guitar lessons?"

"If you still want to teach me?" I look up at him and suck in the corner of my lip.

"I'll get my guitar and meet you in Race?"

I smile. "Yeah... Call me when you get there."

"Sounds good," he murmurs with a soft grin.

* * * * *

I'm waiting downstairs when I see Duke walk up the incline from the dirt path connecting our dorms. He called me as he left Calhoun, and I immediately raced downstairs. I notice his heavy hard guitar case held evenly at his side. It's an awkward shape and quite large, but he carries it with ease. I watch him intensely while he gently sets it down. He lifts his head and catches me staring, giving a small wave. I follow the bend of his arm as he reaches into his back pocket, lifting the hem of his sweatshirt just enough to slide out his wallet. He flips open the fold, withdraws the ID, and hands it across to security. She barely glances up, looking only at the name, and lets him through. I can't take my eyes off him as we walk quietly to the elevator. Once inside, I press the button for floor eleven and turn to him.

"So how are you going to teach me if we only have one guitar?"

A slow smile breaks out across his face. "Oh, don't worry. I've got a plan."

My cheeks burn, and I shift my gaze to the floor, a familiar tightness low in my belly.

"What do you want to hear first?" he asks, dragging my attention back to him.

"Have anything original?"

He looks nervous. "I don't usually share those. They're not really finished projects."

"Oh, okay." I pause, thinking what songs I like that feature guitar.

"Pick anything. What do you like? I'm sure I can figure it out if I don't know it." He interrupts my furious searching through the catalogue of songs in my brain.

We arrive on eleven and the doors open. I step into the hall and slowly turn left, waiting for him to follow me.

"Well, I like Jack Johnson and Jason Mraz." I lift my shoulders slightly.

"Perfect. I like Jason Mraz, too. Any specific song?"

"No preference, whatever you want to play." I shake my head innocently.

I fiddle with my keys, fumbling to slide it neatly into the lock, too aware of him standing behind me, guitar case squarely in front of him. I can almost feel the heat of his skin, though I'm probably imagining it. I take a quick breath in and blow it out slowly, fitting the key in and unlocking the door. Pressing the door back with my palm, I step into the small kitchen space. He brushes my arm as he comes through, leaving a trail of warmth, and walks deeper into the room toward the couch. I catch him just before the backs of his legs hit the cushion.

"I-I was sort of thinking we could use my room?" I pause. "Just, ya know… if Jess comes home it'll blow your cover." I dip my head.

He straightens, nods, and swallows. "Right, makes sense."

Picking up the case, he follows me into my room. I lean my back against my open door as he glides past me to lay the case on the unmade bed. He flicks the latches and lifts the top, displaying a beautiful guitar.

He seems more comfortable in here.

"Wow," I murmur under my breath.

His head turns slowly to bring his focus back to me. "Thanks. It's a Taylor," he says fondly, picking up the instrument.

"I don't know anything about guitars. Is that a good one?" I shake my head and lick my lips.

"The best, some would argue."

He strums down the chords with the pick before putting it between his teeth. Lifting his leg to rest his foot on the desk chair, he slings the guitar across his knee to tune the strings. I can't take my eyes off him. He's completely in his element, so comfortable and confident. I'm mesmerized. He tunes the first string using a small black device and then picks up the guitar and tunes the rest while wandering around my tiny room, looking at the pictures on my walls.

"Who are these people?" he asks.

"Friends from home." I'm rooted in my spot by the door, watching his every move.

Pointing to Leila with the pick between his fingers, he comments, "She's pretty."

I smile warmly at the thought of my friends. I can't wait to see them for Thanksgiving in a couple of weeks. I glance at the calendar on my desk.

That's two weeks from now?

Where did the time go?

Now that I think about it, I do remember how excited my mom sounded after midterms, counting down the days until I'd be back. My thoughts wander to how quickly time has gone by and how much has happened.

I've changed so much in the few short weeks I've been here.

"Where'd you go?" Duke asks, picking at the strings lightly.

"Sorry, just thinking about going home for Thanksgiving." I look down at the floor and walk farther into the room.

He looks down at the guitar. "Yeah, that's in a few weeks."

"You're not excited to go home?" I cock my head in question.

His eyes drift back up, and he catches my gaze. "Eh, not so much. Not much to do."

I scoff, "Are you kidding? In Princeton?"

He stops playing. "You really think that fake ID Ian got us is going to work in Princeton?"

I consider the question and frown. "I guess not."

"Exactly." He starts playing again. "So, one song and then it's your turn."

He sits down on the metal chair, propping the guitar on his thigh, and motions for me to sit. I hop up onto my bed and lean my head against the wall. After a couple of warm-up chords, he clears his throat and starts to sing. I close my eyes listening to the soft rasp in his voice accompanied by the light pick of the chords. I'm lost in the melody of the music and don't realize he's come to sit next to me until I feel the mattress shift under his weight. Without thinking, I lean into him.

When he's finished, I open my eyes and peer at him expectantly.

He looks down at my head almost resting on his shoulder and smiles. Taking me by surprise, he kisses my lips while passing the guitar onto my lap.

"Your turn," he whispers. "Sit up."

I lean forward, and he snakes his arms around me, folding his hands over mine and the guitar.

"It's easy. Just let yourself feel the music." His voice vibrates softly against my ear and I close my eyes.

CHAPTER 33

"Nothing happened," I complain to Stella Saturday morning.

I'm surprised she agreed to come over with how little girl-time we've spent together recently. She only said yes when I told her the suite was quiet. We typically preferred the library, but lately there's been less studying and more chatting going on. We both have a few last-minute assignments to finish up, and I assume she didn't want the distraction.

It's only been two days since Duke spent the night in my room without any action other than kissing and snuggling.

I don't know why I can't just be happy with this small step.

Last night when we went out, I drank too much, hoping that we'd end up doing something more. We didn't. The thought that I've come so close to losing myself to him has been eating me alive.

I need to tell someone about it.

The last time I talked about anything sexual with Ryan and Elias, my face was beet red for hours, and Jess and I just aren't like that. I went out on a limb, hoping Stella wasn't still mad at me. Or at least that she'd gotten past it enough to come talk. Unfortunately, I've still only just mentioned that Duke and I haven't done it but can't bring myself to tell her the full weight of why it's driving me crazy.

She's sprawled out on my spare bed, computer in front of her face, working on a paper for Psychology class.

My head pounds with last night's hangover. I swallow hard against my dry throat and reach for a sip of water, concentrating hard on not dropping my laptop off the bed as my fingers grasp the edge of the cup. I stare at my notes on the screen, waiting for her to reply. She doesn't.

"Hello? Earth to Stella?"

"Hmm? Sorry. Maybe he's into guys." She cracks a dry joke without looking at me.

I roll my eyes, annoyed at her lack of response.

"Um, no. He's kissed me, remember?" I lift my phone and scroll idly before throwing it aside to pick at my cuticles. "Ugh, what do I have to do to get him to want me?" I whine.

She turns her head to look at me, wearing something between annoyance and disgust on her face. "Maybe he just didn't want to ruin the moment."

"It was the *perfect* moment to take the next step." I bring my thumb to my teeth and talk around my finger. "He even stayed the night!"

"I don't know, Casey. I don't know why you're even bothering after how shitty he was to you the first half of the term."

"I know. I know. There's just something about him. The first time I saw him, it just clicked."

She lets out a hard laugh. "That's some love at first sight bullshit if I ever heard it."

"What?" My jaw hangs open. "You don't believe in love at first sight?"

"Oh, please." She rolls her eyes. "Do I really seem like the type?"

Turning her attention back to her screen, she murmurs the last few sentences she's written out loud before furiously tapping the keys.

I sigh, breathlessly conceding, "I don't know. I guess not," and lean my head back against the wall. "I thought he'd have tried to come up last night. All he did was text me goodnight after I came inside."

Her head snaps to look at me as if something I said fit the missing puzzle piece forming in her mind. "Wait, what's going on with Mr. Chicago?"

That's not the question I was expecting.

I bring my hands to my head and tug on the roots of my hair. "I don't know. I haven't talked to him in like a week."

"A week?" she shouts and then settles, narrowing her eyes.

"Maybe more than a week." I pull my face into a cringe.

"The two of you haven't talked, or you just haven't answered?"

I groan at how well she knows me despite not having given me the time of day lately. "I just haven't answered."

"Casey, you have to let him go. It's seriously not right. Especially if you and Duke are going to do this awkward high school dance shit."

Her words stab sharply at my insides. My emotions are already out of control as my body fights to focus on recovering from the excess alcohol of last night. Anger at her disappointment spikes like a solar flare through my body.

This isn't about Brett right now. It's about Duke. I don't want to think about Brett.

"Oh, not right... like you and Elias, huh?" I wince, immediately wishing I could take it back.

She sits up, closing the laptop and shaking her head. "Low blow, Casey, low blow."

"Wait. Stella." I shift on the bed, reaching my hand out. "I'm sorry. That came out wrong."

She looks at me and swings her legs over the side of the bed, waiting for me to continue.

"I just hate when… I mean… I know you're right. It's just so hard." I sigh. "You don't understand." I struggle to find the right explanation.

She rolls her eyes while sliding to the floor to pack the rest of her things with her head down and her hair covering her face.

"Listen, why don't you take Thanksgiving break to figure out what you want?" She shakes the hair out of her face and looks into my eyes. "It's not fair to do this to both of them. What happens if you and Duke end up becoming a thing? What do you do with Brett then? It'll be worse than if you do something now. Just… just…" She flexes her hands like she's grasping for what to say. "Make a decision."

I exhale, not realizing I was holding my breath through her entire speech. "I don't understand how you can be so logical about these things."

"Experience. Like I said, fairness and trust. You're being unfair, and you're definitely breaking Brett's trust. Don't be this person, Casey. You're better than that." She spits the last sentence at me.

I'm better than that.

Tears prick at the edges of my eyes. I run my hand across my forehead and pull my fingers through my hair before dropping my hand back to my side.

I don't know what to say.

She turns, taking my silence as the end of the conversation. With her back to me, I feel a sudden surge of dread at the idea of being alone right now.

"Where are you going?" I ask, panic coating my voice.

"To the library. I have to finish this thing."

She slings her backpack over her shoulder and steps through my doorway. A second later, I hear the door creak open.

Ughhh.

I take a deep breath and force it out fast, fidgeting on my bed and itching to get out of my skin. It's stupid, but I'm hoping she won't actually leave.

"Text me later?" I call out to her before the door slams shut.

I close my eyes for a second and realize that was a mistake. Flashes of Brett and Duke appear inside my head. I pick up my phone and see a missed call from my mom and several texts from Brett. I'm tempted to throw it across the room in disgust.

I rest my head back against the wall and bring the phone to my ear instead, letting it ring.

"Hi, Mom."

* * * * *

I spend more time with Duke, Elias, and Ryan than anyone else, and honestly, I don't mind. I like being one of the guys. I've even learned how to play some of the new video games. They've let me play once or twice, but mostly I just watch. And mostly it's just watching Duke.

I tick through my status with the girls like checking statistics on a racehorse you'd bet on. Jess has focused singularly on holding Bear's attention outside of class, and I've barely seen her in our suite the last two weeks. Stella has been standoffish, answering me with one-word texts, and ignoring my coffee invitations.

I don't understand this intense reaction she has to me holding onto Brett. She doesn't even know him. Duke is right in front of us. Someone she could get to know.

I've barely seen her and when I do, it's with the group. I tried to grab her after lunch last week and she purposefully sped up to walk with Elias instead. Her complete dismissal stings more than I want to admit. But I guess it's fair for her to be mad that I'm stringing Brett along while constantly complaining about Duke.

I just don't have anyone else to talk to.

No one else knows about Brett, and it's going to stay that way.

The Saturday before Thanksgiving, I catch Jess on her way out to meet her parents to drive home. She passes my room, her overstuffed purple suitcase rolling along behind her and several bags hanging off her shoulder.

"Need a hand with those?" I call, still folding my jeans and placing them in my own suitcase.

"I got it!" she yells.

I hear something thump on the ground and Jess groans. Padding into the living room, I see her crouched down amid the heap of bags, her purse spilled across the floor. I rush over to grab the Chapstick that threatens to roll under the couch and help her with the rest of the uncollected odds and ends. Standing up, I hold out her tangled headphones and smile. I've never seen her this flustered.

"Feel like I haven't seen you in ages. I miss you." I stick out my bottom lip and try my best at puppy dog eyes.

"I know. I know. It's just this business fraternity, and class, and Bear." She sighs heavily.

"And Bear," I repeat and giggle.

She laughs. "I'm crazy. Aren't I? Like if it hasn't happened yet, it's just not going to happen. Is it?

Her comment hits a nerve. I fight to keep my smile firmly in place while thinking that her point is also applicable to my pursuit of getting more intimate with Duke.

"No, Jess! I wouldn't give up!" I try to convince both myself and her. "I'm just surprised at your 'lack of diversification,'" I tease with a wink.

"I can't help it! Once I see something I want, I have to go after it full force. I've been like that forever, with everything. I'm just not used to not getting what I want. Usually if I work hard enough, it just comes to me."

"Well, I'm sure it'll happen. Just give it time. Think about it over break though, make sure he's something you want to keep spending your time on," I suggest.

Well, aren't I the pot calling the kettle black?

"But when you get back can we *please* go out for a girl's night? I miss youuu," I continue.

"Yes, yes, of course. I miss you too. As soon as I get back, we'll do something."

She adjusts her bags and reaches for the door. I help her settle her backpack more firmly on her shoulder before gripping the edge and holding it open. After a few bumps and wobbles, she's off down the hall.

"Have a nice break, Casey!" she calls over her shoulder and continues to round the corner toward the elevator.

The door closes softly when I let it go to trudge through the quiet empty suite back to my room. I care a little less with every piece of clothing I throw in my bag and finally close the top and pick up my phone to check the time.

One hour until my train.

My anxiety kicks in, making me rush across the hall to grab my toiletries and finish packing when there's a loud knock on the door. I jump at the unexpected sound and drop my makeup bag on the floor. The tiny gold band clinks against the tile. My heart stops at the sight, and my hand goes to cover the gasp escaping my mouth.

I forgot that's where I put it. I didn't even put it back nicely. What's wrong with me?

"Casey! You in there?" Elias yells through the door.

Quickly stuffing the ring back into my bag, I rush out to let him in, not waiting for him to follow me back to my room. He shuffles slowly behind me.

"Thanks for the warm welcome, Case," he says, coming into my room and plopping down on the metal desk chair.

"Sorry, I just want to make sure I don't miss my train. Everything okay?" I ask before glancing at his face for the first time. His features are contorted into a deep frown.

"Not really," he whispers.

Hearing the sadness in his tone, I stop and turn toward him, my face softening.

"What's wrong?" I ask.

He looks like the puppies in the window of a pet store as people walk by—drained of hope. It hits me that this is his first time home since breaking up with Maggie. I cross the room and stand in front of him.

"Stand up," I command.

He stands, and I wrap my arms around his shoulders. He circles his arms limply around me, resting his chin on my shoulder.

"I'm sorry, Elias. I didn't even think…" I trail off, not knowing what to say. "It's about Maggie. Right?"

"It's okay. I know I hide it well—"

"You do!" I cut him off before catching my mistake. "Sorry."

"I just feel like I'm going to go home and not be able to think of anything but her. *And she'll be there.* What if I run into her? What if she asks to see me? I don't know that I'll be able to say no."

Oh, Elias if you only knew. I've been thinking the same thing.

I organize my thoughts around how I'm going to handle my situation with Brett.

"I think... you just need to be honest. Honest with yourself about how you're feeling, what you're thinking. And then honest with her if she does end up wanting to talk. I think for both your sakes you need to try to get some closure. However that may come about, I'm not sure."

"Been talking to Stella, have you?" The lightness in his voice returns.

I pull back in surprise. "Actually, no, I think she's mad at me, but I did borrow her words a bit there."

"She told me basically the same thing you just said." He smirks.

"Oh, so I'm sloppy seconds now?" I step back in mock offense and push his shoulder.

He laughs. "No. I saw her this morning."

"Well you know you can always text me. I know it's not the same as being able to talk in person, but I'm always here."

"Thanks, Casey. Likewise. What time's your train? Can I walk you to the station?"

I pull my phone from the bed and unlock the screen. "Forty-five minutes. I better get going!"

He reaches for my suitcase without asking, hauling it to the floor and wheeling it out of my room ahead of me.

What would I do without him?

Three hours separate me from the familiarity of being home. Dread hits me like a brick wall when I realize I haven't talked to Leila or Greg at all since I left. I pray they'll be around to keep me occupied. I don't know if I can handle all the nights home alone in my room, the computer taunting me and Brett clawing at my carefully constructed boundaries.

"Come on, slowpoke," Elias jokes, standing to the side to let me open the door.

I stop and give him another hug. "Elias. I'm so glad I met you."

He laughs into my hair, arms coming around my middle in a tight bearhug this time. "Me too, Case."

We're both quiet for the ride down to the lobby. My anxiety spikes as I check my phone for the third time and realize my departure is inching closer and closer. When the doors open, I turn to Elias.

"We'll have to hurry."

"We'll make it, Casey. Not to worry," he assures me.

Ahead of me, he pushes through the turnstiles and continues through the doors, pulling my suitcase outside with him. The turnstile locks as I walk into it, banging into my thighs and stopping me short. I let out a frustrated grunt and try again. The commotion causes the Public Safety guard to lift her head. I smile, noticing that it's the same woman who's been here when I've signed in Duke and Stella.

"Oh, Miss Windsor—"

"I'm so sorry, I've got to run to catch a train." I cut her off.

Elias peers back inside, tapping on the window, his hands raised in question.

"This'll just take a minute." She stands, waving for me to stop.

I puff out an exasperated breath and hold up a finger to Elias.

I really don't have time for this.

"Yes, ma'am." I turn to face her, mustering a fake sweet smile.

"Please tell your boyfriend to stop calling the residence hall main line. He's been calling almost nonstop. We really try to reserve that line for emergencies."

CHAPTER 34

It feels strange to wake up in my bed, despite being almost a week since I've been home. My eyes focus on the blank screen staring at me from across the room. Every time I look at it, I'm reminded of the longest train ride of my life. I should have texted Brett right away, but I just didn't want to deal with it.

I don't know how *to deal with it.*

After my train transfer, the time quickly ticked by before I was be in the car with my parents and their incessant questioning. I sent the message—a simple, *I'm sorry, I'm ok, you have to stop calling my dorm.* Not a second after I hit send, Brett called. And called. And didn't stop calling until I finally picked up. I tried to keep the conversation short, but he wasn't having it, and I couldn't find an opening to end the call until my train pulled into the station with a next to dead battery.

I don't know how he does it. It must be something about his voice that melts my walls. I started the conversation ready to tell him I needed space and ended the conversation promising I wouldn't ignore him again. At home, I lasted two days keeping that promise before Duke messaged me about how boring it was to be back at home, and I forgot all about Brett.

Blinking against the image of the computer screen, the smell of pancakes and bacon from the kitchen hits me and I realize the delicious scent woke me up. I stretch lazily before planting my feet on the floor and stretching tall.

"Rise and shine!" my mom calls from downstairs.

I jump at the unexpected sound of her voice. I've gotten used to waking up to a quiet room, no familiar wakeup call or warm breakfast waiting for me. Still sleepy, I run my hands over my stomach, feeling full of Thanksgiving dinner the night before.

"Pancakes!" she calls again.

"Coming, Mom!"

The hallway floor creaks under the weight of my dad's steps before the door cracks open.

"How'd you sleep, bird?" He pokes his head in my room.

"Great, Dad!"

"Good. See you downstairs." He pulls the door shut. I hear the heavy thud of his feet meeting each step on the way down.

Wandering over to the mirror, I glance at my face and rub my cheek. I look different now since it was pointed out last night by my extended family. Despite the drinking and lack of proper nutrition, I've managed to lose weight. Or maybe I've just shed the pudgy layer of "girl" in favor of becoming a "young lady"—as they called me yesterday. Everyone told me I look "more mature." I pull down on my eye and lean into the mirror, looking for the "mature young lady" they saw.

I don't see it. I just feel like me.

I went to bed early last night, dragging my feet up the stairs at 7 p.m. stuffed to the gills with the turkey dinner and all the desserts. I barely checked my phone all day, not remembering where I put it before my family arrived at our house, and not caring when I came up to crash into my food coma.

Now I pull the sweatshirt from the back of the desk chair where I threw it yesterday morning. My phone falls from the front pocket and bounces when it hits the floor, the screen lighting.

That's where I put it.

I unlock it and read through all the messages I missed.

MESSAGE: LEILA
Leila: Tanner's tonight?

MESSAGE: ELIAS
Elias: well… she was at the bakery when I went to pick up the pies

MESSAGE: JESS
Jess: Happy Thanksgiving!!! <3 <3 <3

MESSAGE: RYAN
Ryan: Happy Thanksgiving doll :)

MESSAGE: STELLA
Stella: Happy Thanksgiving

"Breakfast!" My dad's voice cuts through my distracted scrolling.

"Coming! Coming!"

My breath catches in my throat when I see the next message is from Duke.

MESSAGE: DUKE

Duke: Hey Casey

Duke: Happy Thanksgiving

Duke: Want to get coffee when we get back?

MESSAGE: BRETT

Brett: come on

Brett: ur home for thanksgiving

Brett: idk y u wont talk to me

Brett: Casey??

Brett: just call me please

My excitement is crushed by the bit of guilt at continuing to ignore Brett. Stella is more right than ever.

I need to do something.

MESSAGE: DUKE

    Casey: hi! Happy Thanksgiving

    Casey: of course :)

MESSAGE: STELLA

    Casey: Happy Thanksgiving

    Casey: im sorry we haven't talked much lately

    Casey: can we meet up when we get back?

Stella: i'm sorry too

Stella: i was only trying to help

Stella: but i think i came across as a know it all

Casey: no its okay
Casey: i needed to hear it
Casey: ur right. i need to do something
Casey: when do u get back?
Stella: Sunday
Casey: dinner?
Stella: yes please

"*Casey!*" my mom yells, her tone dangerously close to angry. "Breakfast is going to get *cold.*"

I flinch again and type out one more quick message to Leila confirming tonight at Tanner's before placing the phone on my dresser and bounding down the stairs. I sneak a piece of bacon off the plate as my mom carries it to the table from the kitchen.

My dad is staring at me, a cheesy smile on his face.

"What?" I ask with a soft laugh.

"Good to have you home, kid." He looks at my mom.

I reflexively follow his focus. Despite her frosty tone just seconds ago, she's holding back tears. Happy tears, I assume.

"Yes! We missed you!" She smiles.

"Oh, my God, you two. It was like two months." A sudden urge to cry stings my eyes and I laugh nervously. "Ugh... shit... I missed you too!"

"Casey!" My mom is shocked.

My dad cracks, letting out a deep laugh. "Language, you!"

"Sorry, Mom." I shrug, putting on my best angelic face. "Can you pass the syrup?"

Some of the shock dissolves, and she's on the edge of laughter when she hands me the bottle. She recovers, regaining composure.

"So, what's new? Are you ready for finals?" She starts the familiar inquisition and I settle into my plate and a long breakfast, deciding to start with finals and work my way up to telling them all about my new friends.

And maybe Duke.

* * * * *

Knocking on Tanner's door feels weird but walking in without knocking feels worse. I text Leila while standing awkwardly on his welcome mat. I hear her muffled voices behind the door before it unlocks and opens. For a moment, I'm surprised that it's locked, my face pulling into a confused frown. Then I realize I'm at the front door.

No one uses the front door at Tanner's. Everyone uses the back slider.

I shake my head, clearing away my insecurity at how much I've forgotten of my life at home, and force a smile as Leila swings the door open.

"Hey, Case!" She ushers me inside and wraps her arms around me.

"He-Hey, Leila," I stammer, wrapping my arms lightly around her.

Her hair is shorter than the last time I saw her, her cheeks a little rounder. Any other changes are hidden under the oversized hoodie and sweats. I look down at my jeans and fitted V-neck peeking out of my peacoat and realize I may be overdressed. Out of habit, I pulled on an outfit that could be dressed up or down. It was my usual practice in Philly in case of a last-minute decision to go out somewhere.

"What are you doing at the front?" she asks, confused, and takes in my outfit. "You look great though!"

I feel my cheeks heat at her compliment.

I don't think I've ever heard her say something like that to me before.

"Sorry, I don't know how I forgot…"

I follow her deeper into the house and down the stairs to the finished basement where I spent countless nights as a kid. Lounging on one couch are Tanner and Erin. To my surprise, she's cuddled up in the crook of his shoulder, head resting on his chest.

That's new.

Wasn't he with Leila over the summer?

I look across the room and feel a flash of warmth when my eyes meet the weight of Greg's familiar gaze. He hasn't changed at all except for the dark tan in comparison to the rest of us. I give him a half smile and bite my lip reflexively.

"Hey, Case." He lets my name roll off his tongue lazily.

Tanner and Erin turn their heads at his welcome.

"Hey, guys!" I come down from the last step, watching Leila plop onto the couch with Greg, leaving a space between them. I exhale and shake my head again slightly.

Thank God not everything's changed.

"Heyy!" Tanner shifts to stand up, jostling Erin. Her face pulls into a scowl, displeased at being moved from her comfortable position. She doesn't bother to say hi.

And some things will never change.

Tanner moves in to give me a hug. His arms have bulked up, and he squeezes me tighter than he ever has before. I watch Greg stand up over his shoulder, unfolding gracefully from the couch and striding in my direction.

"How's it going, Case? You look great!" Tanner asks into my hair. He releases me and I walk into Greg's arms before answering.

"Th-thanks. It's good!" I say, half muffled by Greg's arms circling me. His familiar scent is mixed with something else. Something that reminds me of summer.

Greg relaxes his arms after a few beats, resting his hands on the small of my back. He looks down at me. "Good to see you." His smile brightens his eyes.

With a small inhale, I catch the sweet scent of his skin and it transports me back to this summer under my deck. I remember his arms around me and the grip of his hands on my hips. It's surprising how familiar he feels and how easy it is to lose myself in him.

Wait. I should be thinking about Duke...

Greg winks and walks backward toward his spot on the couch, nonchalantly patting the space next to him. There's an awkward silence, like I've walked in on a conversation about me and the ending has fallen flat. I ignore it and sit down next to Greg, a little closer than I probably should, letting our thighs press together.

"So, what's everyone been up to?" I look around for someone to start.

Of course, it's Leila. She launches into what I expect to be a full synopsis of everything she's experienced since moving in. I listen intently, reveling in the familiar sound of my best friend's voice, while the others refocus on the TV, having already heard the whole story.

Greg stretches his arm across the back of the couch, encouraging me to lean into him further. At first, I sit up adamantly straight but finally give in and slide into the warm space under his arm. His hand relaxes onto my shoulder and I'm extremely aware of the heat of his hand warming my skin through the thin fabric of my shirt. I pull my focus away from all the places Greg's body is touching mine, and back to Leila.

When Leila went away, she and Tanner fell apart, or to put it more gently, they lost touch. He was going to Community College, which is basically like our high school just in a different building. Erin went with him, not having an interest in any particular thing.

Some people just don't have any drive.

Leila danced over that part of the story very quickly, and Erin barely acknowledged anyone was talking.

No big shock there.

I guess I'm not going to get the Tanner and Erin story tonight. I'll ask Greg later.

Her college experience hasn't been much different than mine, apart from the fact that she has almost all girlfriends and very few guy friends. She's been focused on schoolwork and going out, not much else including a lack of running.

The current outfit choice makes sense.

She explains her classes are definitely more difficult than high school and good grades have never been her strong suit. I feel sad that she seems to have lost a bit of herself while trying to keep up. It must be a new feeling for her compared to our little bubble at home. My mind wanders, taking stock of all that I've been able to juggle—class, sorority recruitment, new friends, Duke, Brett—and my confidence boosts.

I snuggle deeper into Greg and lay my head on his shoulder as Leila starts another story about her and her friend Kimmie getting so drunk at a party that they ended up on a wild adventure, completely missing their dorm while walking home. My eyelids flutter as Greg runs his fingers through my hair. A needling sensation at the back of my head reminds me that despite how good this feels, I have more guys on my dance card than I know what to do with. I swallow and open my eyes to focus fully on Leila.

As the hours pass, I can't help feeling slightly bored at the prospect of spending all night just talking.

Where are the wine coolers or board games or something?

I check my phone off and on, smiling at a picture Duke sends of his dog, and quickly deleting the messages that come in from Brett.

When it's sufficiently late and I'm tired of sitting and doing nothing, I stand up and announce that I have to get home. Greg offers to walk me.

I guess he was looking for the same excuse.

We walk in silence until just before my door. He turns me toward him and searches my face.

"Sorry we didn't get to catch up tonight." I start at the same time he says, "You look great, Case."

I blush through the darkness. "Thanks," I whisper, "So do you. California suits you."

"The city suits you." He looks up at the dark sky, empty but for the stars. "You never belonged here."

I hold back tears that come out of nowhere.

"Really?" I pause to swallow. "You really think that?"

"I do. There's so much more energy in you now. You're so alive." He rests the palm of his hand on my cheek, the warmth searing into my skin through the chill of the night.

"I don't know… Sometimes I'm not sure where I belong," I whisper.

His hand slides down my neck and comes to rest over the left side of my chest.

"Yes, you do, you know it here." He pulls me in for another hug.

I half laugh, half cry into him. "When did you become so philosophical?"

"Are you kidding?" He laughs over my head. "I'm a Lit major. Philosophical is in my blood."

"Why didn't I ever see it before?"

"Pretty sure it was buried beneath Tanner's ego."

I laugh for real this time. He kisses the top of my head, and I pull back and rest my chin on his chest, looking up at his face.

"I missed you, Greg." I shift to lay my ear against his chest, listening to his heartbeat.

"I missed you too, Casey."

We stand there until my fingers and toes are close to frozen. I loosen my arms reluctantly.

"You should go inside." He releases me, nudging me in the direction of my door.

I blow on my fingers, attempting to warm them. "See you at Christmas break?"

"Of course. You think I want to hang out alone with those guys for a whole month?" He jabs his thumb toward Tanner's house.

I smile and hug him quickly before turning for my door. "Don't be a stranger, okay? Text me." The screen door rests against my hip, my hand on the doorknob.

"Hey, Casey?"

I turn back toward him. "Yeah?"

"You still have my hat?" A flirtatious grin splits his face.

My smile matches his. "I do."

He pauses, as if changing his mind, and winks. "Keep it."

"Goodnight, Greg." I turn, pushing through the door and shutting the porch light off on my way in.

CHAPTER 35

The space between Thanksgiving and finals is short. Too short. We all agree.

I saw Erin leaving Tanner's Sunday as I was loading my car to head back to campus.

Of course. The two people I didn't want to see. Why couldn't it have been Greg and Leila?

I smiled and waved. Tanner waved back, yelling across the field that he would see me at Christmas. Maybe I would have been less excited to leave if Greg had been my last moment at home. Now I couldn't wait to get back to campus.

Back to Duke.

When the six of us arrive, the group text bursts into life. We couldn't wait to see each other.

Stella and I are first to meet at the dining hall, thankfully. She sits quietly while I talk through my pros and cons of finally telling Brett the truth. She's not entirely surprised at the fact that my decision is around what to do with Brett and not what to do with Duke. Her theory is that it's much easier to let something go that's abstract and since I've never met Brett, our relationship is an abstract concept. My palms sweat as I listen to her suggest that I call him tonight and have the conversation. She wants me to rip it off like a Band-Aid before we get into finals, so it isn't weighing on my mind. I agree, knowing full well that I won't be calling Brett tonight, despite not having any excuse.

As the rest of our group arrives, we pull the tables around us closer, creating enough space for everyone. While we pick at our plates, we spend approximately five minutes on our breaks before jumping right into complaining about finals. Duke, Elias, and I have ours toward the end of next week, and Stella has most of hers at the beginning except for one on Thursday. Jess and Ryan are sprinkled all over, but we all agree that Thursday will be the night to party since none of us have finals on Friday.

Thankfully, before the madness of exams, we have the week to study with no classes. In my case, I cram studying in between initiation preparation. I spend the entire week shuttling back and forth between my friends in the library and my soon-to-be sisters at my sorority house. I feel myself starting to slip on my studies by Friday—the day before initiation—and decide to map out my last studying blocks ahead of next week.

I've done so well. I don't want to end on a low note. Thank God my finals aren't until Wednesday, and initiation is only one day.

Or so I thought.

What I expect to only be one night of events turns into an entire weekend of sisterly bonding. It starts unexpectedly Friday night with a dark quiet room with secret symbols and passwords and ends with two nights of giant parties full of girls professing their everlasting love for each other.

Though I've never been more excited to feel like I belong, I'm the tiniest bit nervous for my first week of finals. After spending all day in bed recovering on Monday, guilt seeps in, giving me the kick in the ass I need to pull myself together. I meet everyone in the library Monday night with enough supplies that I wouldn't have to leave if not for closing time. I'm apparently not alone. When I arrive, Ryan, Elias, Stella, Jess, and Duke have claimed a study room on the third floor and inform me they've reserved this room all week.

By Wednesday night, Duke and I are lost in our notes, comfortably sitting across from each other at one of the face-to-face desks deep in the back of the library's third floor. Cans of Monster, Red Bull, 5-hour energy, protein bar wrappers, and those pre-packaged hummus and pretzel packs are scattered in the dead zone of shared space between us.

We've been here for hours. Our friends already left—Ryan and Elias to catch the tail end of drinks at the bar, Jess and Stella to get an early night's sleep. Neither of us really need to stay. Our unanswered chemistry keeps us glued to our seats, casting glances and hidden smiles at each other all night.

I don't know how long we've been alone.

I'm not moving until he does.

It's well and truly quiet inside and full dark outside when the security guard kindly informs us that we must vacate as the library will be closing promptly at 2 a.m. He walks away assuming we'll be packing up. I check my phone for the time, but it's dead. I look up at Duke. We hesitate, staring into each other's eyes while figuring out what to do next.

There's no one around, but the energy of the still library compels us to keep quiet while we pack our bags, grab the trash to throw in the bin on the way out, and make our way down the stairs. Duke trails behind me. He hands me my coat as we approach the revolving doors to exit. When we step outside, the crisp night air nips at our noses and chills our exposed fingers.

It's the kind of night that's perfect for snuggling under a blanket with a cup of tea or hot chocolate, your favorite book, or your favorite person.

I don't put my hands in my pockets.

Maybe this will be the night he reaches for me.

We begin the brisk trek back to our dorms.

This early in the morning, the streets of our college campus are empty. All the ambitious students who went to the bars are either passed out or already continuing the party at one of the off-campus houses. Those who have finals—like us—are probably already in bed, having left the library well before closing time—unlike us. We pass the intramural field, with its turf now quiet but lights still blindingly bright. We haven't spoken a word since we left. I'm silently racking my brain for something to say that isn't goodnight.

At the corner by the volleyball courts we stop for a passing car. We're just across the street from Calhoun, the electricity still buzzing between us, begging us to complete the connection.

The car passes slowly. Or maybe it just feels slow, trying to delay the inevitable moment that I have to continue to Race alone.

We cross the street and walk past the first half of the semi-circle and set of steps that will carry Duke to his room. We usually stop at the halfway point, but tonight he keeps walking past the second set of steps to the edge of the dirt path that connects his dorm to mine.

Maybe he doesn't want to say goodnight either.

The butterflies in my stomach flutter. He turns to face me, his back to the street. The light from the field illuminates my face and keeps him in shadow. His head is tilted back, and I think he must be looking straight up in the direction of my room. I don't want to think about turning to go home yet.

"So, are you ready for tomorrow?" I ask sheepishly, shivering.

His eyes are hazy like how they look when he's drunk. "Oh, yeah. Think you've made sure of that."

"Hey." I nudge his arm with a loose fist. "Just trying to make sure you get to next semester," I tease.

He looks down, slightly embarrassed, and then back up at me. "No, I mean, thanks. Thank you." He pauses, searching for what to say next. "Thank you, Casey. You've really helped me the last few weeks. I was really slipping there."

I'm about to respond when the streetlight on the corner burns out and flickers back on.

"Whoa," I say softly, turning my head in surprise in its direction. When I slowly drag my attention back to his face, his gaze is intense.

"Do that again."

"Do what?" I turn my head away and mimic my tone. "Whoa."

This time, I hesitate before turning back, my heart beating out of my chest. Time slows, like I'm moving in slow motion. I swear he can see the way my body reacts to him. Before I lift my eyes to his, his hand is on my face, cupping my chin just under my jaw and tipping my head back. It's strong enough to be playfully forceful. His other hand grips the waistline of my coat and pulls me into him, a surprised sigh catching in my throat. He makes sure our eyes meet before he lowers his head, eyelids closing heavily, and presses his lips against mine.

There's a spark inside my skull and a flash of heat pours down my body. I melt into him, bending my arms to rest my hands on either side of his body. We both breathe in, deepening the kiss, and breathe out sighs of relieving tension. Weeks of buildup release in a rush. His hands climb up my body and lace through my hair, cupping the back of my neck, with his thumbs coming to a point under my chin. He breaks the suction of our lips on his next inhale and tilts my head forward, leaning his forehead against mine.

I hear a sharp inhale before the sound of his voice.

"Do you want to go out with me?" he murmurs.

My eyes pop open, searching what little I can see of his face. His eyes are squeezed shut.

"Like... out-out?" I ask incredulously, looking for the formality of being able to call him mine.

He chuckles, opening his eyes. "Yes, out-out. Will you be my girlfriend?"

The question pierces my soul. I take a deep breath of the chilly air and lean my ear against his chest, hiding my entirely too-satisfied smile.

God, this feels so natural. I knew we'd be perfect together.

"Yes, Duke. I've wanted to be yours since the moment I saw you on that bus." I giggle.

I'm giddy, but his warmth is so comforting. The sound of his heart pounding grounds me, and I memorize every sound, scent, and feeling, knowing I'm going to want to replay this moment forever.

"You had it bad for me, huh?" he teases, resting his chin on the top of my head.

"Was it so obvious?"

"Oh, completely." His confident tone returns.

I push off his chest and look up at his darkened face. Placing my hand on his cheek, I brush my thumb across his bottom lip before bringing my mouth back to his. He wraps his arms around my shoulders and snugs me tightly to him as the wind whips around us, rustling the branches of the trees and sending a whistle through the open streets. His grip loosens, his hands slide down past the hemline of my coat and up under my sweater, coming to rest on my hips. The tips of his frozen fingers thaw against my burning skin. I press the length of my body into him with obvious desire and feel him stiffening under the pressure. He shifts on his feet and again pulls away from me.

"Let's get you inside. Shall we?"

I lick my lips slowly. "Your place, or mine?"

"Yours. No roommate," he says without hesitation and winks, sticking his tongue out devilishly.

CHAPTER 36

Duke takes my hand, lacing his fingers tightly with mine, and leads me up the path we've walked together hundreds of times. We cross the tiny one-way street separating our buildings, completely lost in new relationship babbling, oblivious to our surroundings or the time of night. Tomorrow's early morning final is forgotten.

We approach the double glass doors marking the entrance to my building. It's too late for students to be working the desk so we'll unfortunately have to sign Duke in. He's used to this, though, with the number of times he's come to Elias's after a night out. But tonight, the anticipation has us both in a rush to get upstairs.

He has his student ID ready when the public safety officer looks up, a tired, blank expression on her face.

"Name."

"Casey Windsor," I squeak out a little more cheerful than the time would suggest.

She rolls her eyes. "Room number."

"11-113"

"ID."

Duke hands her his ID. She files it in her rolodex-looking case and tosses the sign-in sheet in Duke's direction. He quickly prints and signs his name. I'm waiting patiently, my blood humming through my veins and sending prickles up and down my arms.

"Go through."

Letting go of my hand, he walks through the turnstile toward the elevator. He doesn't wait for me to swipe my ID and come in. By the time I make it to him, the elevator is waiting. He's standing in the doorway, one arm behind his back, the other outstretched ushering me through.

"Your chariot." He bows.

"Why, thank you." I smirk.

I trail my fingers down his arm and across the lower end of his abdomen just above his belt as I walk by. He steps in after me, back straight and facing the front, presses eleven, and clasps his hands behind his back like an old-time elevator attendant.

"What are you doing?" I giggle from the corner.

"Escorting the lady to her quarters."

"The lady…" I cozy up behind him, sliding my hands around his waist and tucking my thumbs into the front of his belt. "Would prefer a companion to an escort."

Raising his right arm, he coaxes me around to face him. I lift my chin to look into his eyes. They are sleepy behind the smokiness of lust. I kiss his neck on the space just below where his jaw meets the lobe of his ear and am rewarded with a low moan, almost a growl.

The bell sounds, announcing my floor, and the doors open behind me. Duke drives forward, his legs wide on either side of mine, forcing me to walk backward out and down the hall. After a couple of steps, I trip over my feet and can't help but throw my head back and laugh. Squeezing me around the middle, he lifts me off the floor. My legs hook around his hips instinctively. He walks, almost at a jog, in the direction of my suite, his strong arms holding me to him without breaking our connection.

In one swift movement, he sets me on my feet in front of my door, clutches my wrists, and pins them to either side of my head, before crushing himself against me and catching my gasp with his parted lips. I feel my chest meet his with every rise and fall of my quickening breath. When his lips leave mine, they trail along my jaw. My head rolls to the side, exposing more of my bare skin. I feel a whisper of tongue between his lips when he presses his next kiss along my collarbone. My mind is blank except for the singular focus of getting us inside so I can have more.

"Let me get my keys." My breath catches in my throat, forcing a raspy whisper.

He backs up, bending to grab the bag I dropped when he placed me on my feet and holding it open. I reach inside, fishing for the jingle of my keychain. My fingers graze my phone and I press the unlock button, hoping the light from the screen will illuminate the bag to help me find my keys. It doesn't turn on. For half a second, I remind myself to plug it in before I fall asleep and then my fingers feel the cool metal. I pull it free, looking up with a smile and turn to slide it into the lock.

Once inside, we kick our shoes off at the door and leave the lights off, not wanting to create any disturbance, as we navigate through the kitchenette to the door of my bedroom in the dark. Duke kicks the edge of our small side table, dragging it out of place and almost tripping. A stack of books topples over the edge and hits the floor with a smack.

"Shhh… we can't wake up Jess." I stifle a giggle and turn to playfully cover his mouth.

He grabs my wrist before I can touch his face and kisses the soft skin of the underside of my forearm. I bite my lip as a ripple of tingles spreads up my arm from the spot he's kissed, and I reach for the handle of my bedroom door. It creaks open and Duke snickers behind me. I give him a sharp look and he shrugs.

I really should be more nervous.

"You really expect that we'll be able to be quiet the rest of the night?" he asks skeptically.

I catch myself before my knees buckle.

So, this is it. It's finally the night. It's perfect. He's perfect.

I turn to look at him. The light streaming through my window gives my room a romantic glow. There's just enough light illuminating the lines of his face, letting me clearly see his eyes.

"Well, I thought we were just going to sleep," I joke playfully.

He strides toward me, sliding his coat down his arms and tossing it on the empty bed. I feel the heat radiating from him as he brings his hands to the front of my coat, undoing the buttons one by one.

"No, Casey. We're not going to sleep just yet." His tone is dark and hazy, and a matching storm is brewing in his eyes.

I like this Duke. So confident. Tantalizing.

"Oh, no?" I ask innocently.

My coat falls open. He puts a hand against my stomach, dragging his fingers down until his hand is fisted into the top of my jeans, and yanks me forward. I shudder as his fingers brush the sensitive skin just above my panties. I am putty in his hands, letting him move me and touch me wherever he wants. His hands slink down the sides of my thighs and move back up to my shoulders, sliding the coat from my arms and letting it drop to the floor. He stands back to look at me, admiring me despite being fully clothed. I watch his eyes caress the lines of my body and realize he's about to see me. All of me.

He's always seen me, but this is more than he has before.

A sudden uncomfortable feeling takes the place of the swell of excitement from a moment ago.

I have no idea what I'm doing. He is way more experienced than me, even if he did only have sex with that one girl he mentioned when we were texting before school started. Actually, who knows if he's been with anyone since? I'd be naive to think he hasn't.

His fingers lift my chin. I hadn't realized I let my head fall to the floor.

"Casey?" He searches my face.

"Sorry..." I whisper and he scrunches his eyebrows together.

"What for?" His voice sends a shiver down my spine. He tilts his head.

"I-I... I've never done this before." It slips out before I know what I'm saying, my confidence gone.

"It's you and me, Casey. Just let yourself feel the motions. It'll come naturally."

He brushes his lips lightly against mine. The softness of his mouth and his hands around my waist calm the self-conscious feeling building in my stomach. The kiss is chaste and not enough.

I want more.

I lace my hands together at the back of his neck and pull him tighter against me. He tilts his head, opening his mouth wider and letting my tongue dip inside to twist with his. I feel almost breathless, letting loose a sigh. My hands wander down the length of his back, feeling the tight muscles of his broad shoulders and trimness of his waist. Reaching the hem of his sweater, my hands slip inside. His skin is smooth and warm and perfect, and I think about all the times I've caught a glimpse and wanted to run my finger across it.

His teeth nip at my bottom lip, and I groan before he sucks it between his lips, letting it roll out slowly and refueling my confidence. I reach for his belt with our lips still locked and pull it undone, grabbing for the button. He breaks away from me, his lips stay parted, and he stares down at my hands reaching into the space of his open zipper. I curl my fingers around the hard, silky skin and am surprised by the length.

I hope I'm doing this right.

My eyes lift to his, peering through my lashes. His breath is ragged, and a low moan vibrates through his chest as I stroke my hand up and down, flexing my fingers tighter around him. He stops me suddenly, holding my wrist and my hand in place.

"If you keep doing that, I won't last," he rasps.

I release my hold on him, sliding my hands to the hem of his sweater and drawing it up his chest. He reaches both hands behind his head and yanks the fabric over his head, pulling it down his arms before tossing it to the side. My breath comes out in a rush at the ways his muscles flex and bunch without the cover of his shirt. I lay my palms flat against his chest and press up onto my toes to meet his lips.

He stops me again, putting two fingers against them.

"Your turn," he says and licks his lips.

I turn around to face the window and take a shaky breath. Closing my eyes, I cross my hands in front of my waist and grab hold of either side of my shirt. When I open my eyes and let my breath out slowly, I feel calm and collected, almost sexy. I peek over my shoulder, pouring that confidence into my gaze, and meet his eyes as I suck in my lip. He groans and shifts on his feet, bringing his hand to adjust the waistband of his boxers hiding the tip of him from my sight. I smirk and turn my head away, slowly lifting my shirt up my back and letting my hair fall to the side. The sounds he's making behind me are so satisfying. A familiar ache grows between my legs, making my knees weak. I feel an accompanying wetness in my panties and my cheeks heat, knowing what is going to happen next.

I've teased him long enough.

I pull the shirt up over my head and let it fall to the floor before reaching behind my back to unhook my plain black bra and drop it on the pile of clothes.

Shit. I should have put on the lace bra this morning.

Duke comes up behind me, our skin burning against one another, and runs his hands from my shoulders down my arms.

"Turn around, Casey," he whispers, taking a deep breath. "Let me see you."

My breath hitches, and I shift in his arms, turning to face him once again.

He steps back an inch. His eyes travel the length of my torso, landing on the tiny ring in my belly button and back up to stare at my chest. My arms beg to cover me up.

"My God, you're gorgeous." His words float across my skin like smoke, and I blush, resisting the urge to ask, "Really?"

"Thank you," I murmur innocently.

He reaches for my arm to pull me back into him, but it's my turn to push him away. I create a bit of extra space between us while undoing the button of my jeans, slowly pulling the zipper open. I see him watching my hands move across my body and slide my thumbs to my sides, pushing my jeans down over my hips.

Duke falls to his knees in front of me before I can bend to pull the jeans off over my feet. He presses kisses along my stomach, just above the line of my black lace underwear. One hand runs down my leg, grabbing the bottom of my pant leg and sliding it over my foot, as the other reaches up unexpectedly between my legs. I'm knocked off balance at his touch and reflexively place my hands on his shoulders to steady myself. I feel his muscles harden at my sudden touch. He lifts his head, satisfaction written across his face, and pulls the other pant leg, leaving me exposed in just my panties. His thumb massages over me, drawing a moan from my lips.

A wicked grin spreads across his face, and my breath quickens as he gingerly lifts my foot from the floor, running his hand up my leg while massaging me with the other.

"Don't let go of me," he instructs. I nod without a word as he drapes my leg over his shoulder and moves my panties to the side. He leans into me and I suck in a breath and tighten my stomach. His hot breath collides with my wet skin before I feel a brush of his tongue and his lips on me. My legs start to shake at the sensation, and he slides his hands around my hips to grip my ass, holding me to him.

I don't know what he's doing, but it feels amazing.

My breath comes out in a rush. He pulls back and lifts his eyes to mine.

"I'm just trying to relax you," he pants before bringing his mouth back to me.

I roll my head back, lifting to my fingertips on his shoulders and almost collapsing when he sucks my skin into his mouth.

Slowly, he pulls away and moves his hands to grip my hips before straightening his legs to tower over me. I whimper, needing his mouth on me. He dips his head, kissing my lips, then my jaw, and down my neck as his hands slide up my sides and hook under my armpits. I'm weightless for a moment as he lifts and sits me on the edge of the tall bed, parting my legs with his body and coming to stand between them. I reach down to wrap my fingers around him again, leaning my head forward to whisper into his ear.

"Take these off." I tug at the waistband of his jeans and boxers.

"As you wish." He rumbles the words against my chest, sending a shiver through my body.

Duke steps back, yanking his wallet from his back pocket and pulling out a thin foil wrapper. I blush and look away.

At least he has protection.

"You know what you're doing, huh?" I ask to fill the silence, concentrating on the stitches of my bedding.

"A little," he teases.

When I turn my head back toward him, he's completely naked. I take my time admiring the lines of his body while tracing the curve of his chest and abs, and the swell of hard length wrapped in his hand. Excitement and nerves mix dangerously, and I'm not sure if I feel like I'm going to pass out or throw up.

He steps back between my legs, tossing the packet on my comforter, and places his hands on my thighs, squeezing gently. His right hand glides up my thigh and dips between my legs, pushing my underwear to the side. He runs his fingers along my wetness. My stomach tightens reflexively, and I lean into him as he slides a finger inside.

I gasp and squeeze my eyes shut, feeling myself contract around the unfamiliar sensation of something inside of me.

"Feel this?" he purrs. "Now I know how much you want me."

I moan in response, not able to form any words.

He knows exactly what he's doing.

"Say it," Duke commands.

He pumps me faster, curling his finger at just the right angle and drawing a tingling sensation I've never felt before. I open my mouth, but nothing comes out except my quick panting. Lifting my head to his shoulder, I kiss his neck and bite down as the heel of his hand connects with the most sensitive spot on my body. He groans.

"Say it," he pleads through gritted teeth.

"I need you." My voice comes out breathless with want.

I mean every word of it.

"Lie back." He nudges my shoulder.

I slowly lean back onto my elbows and pull my legs up onto the mattress, pushing myself back toward my pillow to lie down. In one swift motion, he climbs on my bed and hovers over me before pressing his lips to mine. I reach for his back, digging my fingers into his skin and pulling him toward me.

"Hang on," he whispers against my lips and sits back on his knees. Leaning, he picks up the foil and tears the corner with his teeth. He notices me watching him pull the condom from the pouch.

"Do you want to do it?" he asks, his voice teasing.

I shake my head. "No, no. You can do it." I take a breath and blow it out hard.

"Nervous?"

"A little..." I whisper

"We'll go slow. You're so wet. It'll be easy," he assures me, rolling the condom over himself. He slides my underwear over my hips and down my legs, my toes pointing to the ceiling as he strips them off. Falling over me, he places one hand on each side of my waist.

"Bend your legs," he continues, talking me through the motions.

I do as he says, curling my fingers around his sides again. He dips his hips closer to my body, pushing my legs farther apart. My breath quickens and the sensation of tears forms behind my eyes. I clench my jaw, looking down the line of my body at him poised just above me.

"Look at me, Casey." His tone is soft, full of emotion.

I blink, focusing on his face and see fire in his eyes. Relaxing, I nod and feel him push against me. I inhale as he eases himself inside slowly and feel the twinge of tightness stretching at every inch. A sound somewhere between a gasp and a moan escapes my throat at the last push of pain, feeling his body fit tightly against mine.

"Are you okay, baby?" he asks.

I barely hear his question, concentrating on pushing away the pain. He drops onto his elbows, letting the full weight of his body press along mine.

"Casey?" he asks again.

"Yes, yes. I'm okay. Keep going," I say with a rush of air pushing out of my lungs under his weight.

He rocks his hips back and forth slowly and my feet lift off the mattress as I tilt my pelvis reflexively at an easier angle. I groan as he fits deeper and bite my lip against the rough feeling of him rubbing against my insides.

"Look at me," he repeats, pulling back a little farther before sliding back into me.

"Duke," I moan.

"Shhh... we can't wake Jess," he teases devilishly before closing his lips over mine to stifle the noises rising and spilling out of me.

I close my eyes as he buries his head into the crook of my neck, breathing heavily and pumping faster. I sink my teeth into his shoulder again to keep quiet and retreat into my thoughts.

This is not what I imagined. It hurts, but it's not excruciating. I understand why people want to do it all the time. I want to do it again, and it's not even over. I wonder when it will be over. Isn't the first time supposed to be quick? Maybe that's just a guy's first time.

"Casey," Duke moans into my ear. "You're going to be my undoing."

I don't even know what that means, but the tone of his voice sends chills through my body. My feet circle his hips, hooking together and drawing him tightly to me. My fingers flex, grabbing hungrily against his back, my nails biting into his skin. I can't control my breathing as he rolls his hips in circles against me. A feeling builds from deep inside, like the anticipation just before the drop of a rollercoaster. My chest rises against him with my next deep inhale.

"Fuck." The word is bitten out, tense. "I can't go much longer."

He looks into my eyes and kisses me hard, crushing his lips against mine and forcing his tongue into my mouth. I rake my fingers across his back as the feeling gets bigger, filling the inside of my body with a growing sensation. My toes curl and my hips push up to meet him.

"That. Don't stop doing that," I moan. "Right there."

"Casey, I'm going to come," he rasps.

"Don't stop, please don't stop," I beg.

The feeling bursts inside me before I know what's happening. My back arches and my eyes squeeze closed, stars flickering across my eyelids. I distantly feel short, quick movements between my legs before Duke buries his head in my hair and squeezes his arms tightly around me as the movement stops. I try for a deep breath but the weight of him, unmoving, on top of me constricts my breathing.

"Duke," I whisper.

"Mmm?" he murmurs, not moving.

"Duke, I can't breathe."

"Oh! Sorry."

He pushes back up onto his palms and my chest rises. I gulp the air, trying to hold onto the tears threatening to spill out of the creases of my eyes. His eyes widen when he lifts his gaze to my face.

"Are you okay?" He raises his eyebrows in concern.

"No, I'm okay." I take a few shaky breaths. "There's just a lot going on right now." I giggle nervously and turn my head to look away.

This feels like the moment I'm supposed to say I love you. I think I do... love him... but I don't think I can say it. I hope he doesn't expect me to.

"Hey, don't do that. Look at me." He brings one hand to my face, gently turning me to look at him. I try for a small quick smile. His face softens, and he leans down to press his lips to mine.

"I'm going to pull out, okay?" he asks.

Oh, God. Is this part going to hurt? I never even thought about this part.

I nod and inhale, expecting to feel the pain, but it's just a pinch and then a feeling of emptiness I didn't know was possible to feel. I watch him lean back on his heels and roll the condom off. He knots it and folds it into a tissue from the box on the back of my desk.

"I'm going to go clean up real quick," he says, climbing down from the mattress.

I make a sound that's supposed to be "okay," and he looks back at me.

"You're sure you're okay?" he asks again.

I nod.

He nods in return. "Come clean up with me."

He holds his hand out to help me down. When I try to sit up, my whole body feels like Jell-O and tingles. My feet hit the floor, and I wobble unsteadily on my legs. Duke grabs hold of my elbow and snakes his arm around my waist.

"How do you feel?" he asks.

I take a minute to internally check myself. There's a different ache between my legs but not bad. I'm tired and wide awake at the same time. But mostly the only thought that comes to mind is—

"I wanna do that again." My face breaks into a smile.

He laughs, a deep belly laugh, and pulls me into him, kissing the top of my head.

"We will." He looks down into my eyes and winks before grabbing my hand and pulling me across the hall to my tiny bathroom.

CHAPTER 37

I wake to the sound of banging on my door with Elias yelling from the other side. I ignore this normal occurrence and blink my eyes a few times, bringing my room into focus.

I had sex last night... I can't believe I had sex last night.

I can't wait to tell my mom and Stella...

And Leila!

I sigh with contentment and shift slightly. Despite the twinge of soreness, I still want to do it again. Glancing sideways, I smile at the comfortable sound of light snoring coming from Duke. He's face down on my pillow, one arm slung over my stomach and the other hanging over the edge of the bed. Heat pools in my stomach and my legs tingle.

I definitely want to do that again.

The bright light streaming through the half-pulled shades makes me wonder how long we've slept. I bolt upright, fumbling for my phone in the mess of pillows and sheets, crammed on the inside of the bed with me. It's still dead.

"Shit," I mutter, shifting Duke's arm off me and working to untangle myself from the sheets. "Elias, what time is it?" I yell back through the closed door.

"7:45 a.m., Casey! We gotta go! What the hell are you doing in there?"

Duke stirs, rolling onto his back and stretching lazily, the relaxed motions of someone basking in rested sleepiness.

Then he notices I'm in a panic attempting to extricate myself from the mess of the bed.

"Hey, you." He smiles up at me, one arm bent propping up his head.

"We have fifteen minutes to get ourselves up and out to this final," I rasp in frustration.

"You look so sexy in my shirt." He ignores me, dragging his gaze down to my chest and back up to my eyes.

"Come on. Come on. We have to go. Help me out of these sheets," I plead before yelling back to Elias. "My phone died! Go and save me a seat. I'll meet you there." I look back at Duke. "Save two seats! I'll grab Duke on the way."

"Why don't you just tell him now?" He grabs my forearm and pulls me down for a kiss. I stop struggling and let the moment bring me back from my manic state.

"Because we should tell him when you're not naked in my bed the morning of our last final before break."

"What better time?" he teases before yelling through the door, "Yeah, she'll grab me on the way."

"Duke," I squeal and successfully make it to a straddle across his hips, still trying to get out of bed.

"Duke?" Elias sounds amazed. "You stayed the night?"

"Yeah, thought I'd sleep at my girlfriend's for a change."

I shiver at the mention of our new label and wiggle my hips. He grins at me deviously, hands gripping my waist. There's hooting from the other side of the door.

"Fucking finally!" Elias yells. "We can all stop being awkward. Now, can we please go and get this over with? I'm starting the party immediately after!"

Lifting my hips easily, Duke helps me off him. I swing my other leg down to the floor with a pout. I pull on last night's jeans, shoving my feet in socks and the first pair of boots I find under my bed. Duke finally rolls out of bed, grabs my phone, and plugs it into the charger, powering it back on. I subtly move toward it while yanking a zip-up hoodie up over both shoulders. As soon as it comes to life, I anxiously press the button to check for missed messages.

A few from Jess, Elias, and Stella. A couple from my mom—probably just checking in. And several from Brett.

With Duke facing away from me getting himself ready to go, I scroll through to the bottom, not bothering to read every message.

MESSAGE: BRETT

Brett 11:01PM: I really wish you would let me know where u r or if ur okay

Brett 11:03PM: I hate when u do this

Brett 11:04PM: stop pushing me away... all u gotta do is let me know whats going on

Brett 12:34AM: I can't take this anymore Casey

Brett 12:47AM: it doesn't feel like u love me

Brett 12:48AM: u just disappear and don't talk to me all day

Brett 2:05AM: ive lost all hope in us

Brett 2:06AM: it hurts to say it but its true

A flash of guilt mixes with the endorphins swimming through my veins after last night, extinguishing the fire burning deep at the memory of Duke being inside of me. I should have figured out how to end things with Brett a long time ago, or a couple days ago at the very least.

I'll call him this afternoon and officially settle this. It's the right thing to do. I can't keep hurting him. Especially not after last night.

MESSAGE: BRETT

Casey: i'm so sorry
Casey: my phone died
Casey: i forgot to put it on the charger last night
after the library
Casey: can I call u this afternoon after my finals
so we can talk?

I don't even know why I'm answering.
I should just wait to call him.
I send the messages quickly and silence the phone. I think
about turning it off, but I'm not expecting a response. It's
early in the morning for him.

MESSAGE: BRETT

Brett: why do u even want to call me?
Brett: u dont care about us anymore
Brett: i believed when u said u want to be with me
Brett: and that we were gona make it work and i
really wanted it to
Brett: but it seems like ur not committed and i cant
do it alone

Whoa. Okay. I don't have time for this right now.

MESSAGE: BRETT

Casey: i know that
Casey: please just let me call u
Casey: we can talk
Brett: u know i love u with all my heart
Brett: why dont u love me anymore
Casey: im about to be in my final

Casey: i'll talk to u later?

This time, I turn it off, grab my bag, and throw it in carelessly, checking for my pens, pencils, and calculator.

"Ready?" Duke is waiting by the door staring at me.

"Yeah... sorry, just my mom worried that her messages weren't going through last night."

"All good," he says with a grin.

He opens the door to Elias leaning on the wall opposite, scrolling through his own phone. He looks up at us with a shit-eating grin.

"You two have a good night?" He wiggles his eyebrows.

"Oh, my God, you're the worst." I breeze past him, shaking my head and hiding a smile while jogging down the hall. "Come on, we're going to be late. Mr. Finneghan's gonna be pissed."

I hear the clap of male congratulations and chatter followed by footsteps bounding behind me.

* * * * *

Two hours later, Elias bursts through the double doors with an exasperated grunt to Duke and me waiting across the hall, smug smiles on our faces. Our business class has weekly quizzes in addition to the midterm and final. It's been a game amongst the three of us of who can finish first since I started helping Duke after midterms. The last person to turn in their answer sheet buys the first round of drinks.

I've never bought the first round.

Until the last few weeks, it had consistently been Duke, but after Duke and I started to spend time alone—studying and not studying—it became a toss-up between him and

Elias. Today, both Duke and I are basking in the sweet afterglow of victory, not afraid to rub it in Elias's face.

"You guys suck!" His tone is joking, but the emphasis on "suck" makes me think he is actually a little pissed about being last.

He slings his backpack off one arm, pulling it forward and yanking the zipper open as he walks down the hall. We take our time behind him, hands clasped tightly.

This might just be the most perfect morning.

"Come on, lovebirds. Let's get out of here," he calls over his shoulder.

I lift my face to smile at Duke and squeeze his hand. The three of us emerge into the fresh morning light of the quad. Elias heads to the cement lip just outside of the science building where students hang out between classes during the warmer months. This morning it's a bit cold to be camping outside for long, but we follow him anyway.

"Close your eyes and hold out your hands," Elias instructs as if we're children getting a surprise.

"Seriously, bro?" Duke asks.

"Oh, Duke, just do it for him." I close my eyes and cup my hands, unsure of what to expect.

I feel cool glass land across the center of my palms and smile without opening my eyes. "Elias, you shouldn't have."

"Okay, now open."

We all look down at the nips of Patron in our open palms. I bite my lip in anticipation.

Duke looks surprised but satisfied. "How did you know to bring these?"

"Dude, with the amount of time you two have spent in the library these days." He shakes his head. "It doesn't matter how much studying you actually got done, there was no way I was going to make it out of that exam before you."

Elias expertly peels the cellophane wrapping from his bottle, pulling the cork with an audible pop.

"Cheers!" Elias raises the nip, tipping his head back and pouring the bottle in his mouth.

"Hey, wait!" I whine, still fidgeting to get mine open.

Duke hands me his, already open, and finishes wrangling with mine. We tap bottles and slug back the prickly liquid, Duke finishing with a thirst-quenching sound of a sigh and me with a pinched face.

Where's the salt and lime when you need it?

"So, what's next?" Elias asks. "It's Thirsty Thursday. We could hit up Caverns and then check out the Party House. A little day drinking slash pregame in my room with Stella and everyone before we go? When's her last final?"

I look at Duke, hoping he'll answer for us.

"Yeah, yeah, Caverns works, but I'm gonna skip the day drinking. I need a nap and to start packing for break. My parents are picking me up on Sunday."

I pout thinking about the month-and-a-half-long break I have ahead of me not seeing Duke every day, but his comment jogs my memory.

"Same here. I need to call my mom and take care of a few things before I start the shit-show. I'm not taking the train until Monday, though. I think Stella's finished at two. Maybe we'll meet you around six. Gives us enough time to get ready."

"Perfect. Duke, just text me when you're headed over so I can sign you in."

Elias pushes off the ledge he was perched on and the three of us make our way back to the dorms. He peels off first, taking the familiar dirt path back to Race, leaving Duke and me standing once again in front of Calhoun.

"Are you really going to have a nap?" I complain, moving toward him for a hug.

"You could join me," he says with a hint of suggestion in his tone.

My heart races and I feel my knees soften.

I absolutely should join him. Maybe I can get him to do that thing with his tongue again.

I smile wickedly and then think about the missed messages from this morning and my conversation with Brett. Unfortunately, I'm going to need all the time I can get to get through this.

"No, we'll never get anything done if I join you," I reply with a hint of disappointment, pushing back from his chest for a chaste kiss.

"Fair point." He kisses me again before nudging me in the direction of the path and heading for the steps.

"Text me when you're headed over to Elias's room?" I call from around the corner.

When he doesn't respond, I assume he's already inside and continue my slow walk to my room, dreading the next few hours of my life.

CHAPTER 38

My mom picks up on the first ring.

As expected.

"Thank God you're alright. I was arguing with your father about getting in the car to come check on you!"

I squeeze the phone between my ear and shoulder and pace the small space between the beds in my room.

"I know. I'm sorry, Mom." I let the remorse seep through my voice. "I was at the library all night studying for my final this morning and—"

She cuts me off. "Oh! How did it go? Ace it per usual?"

I smile picturing her proud face beaming, eyes crinkling at the edges from her wide grin. Stopping to lean my forearms on my bed, I let out an easy breath.

"I was done in an hour. Easy peasy," I say with confidence.

"Great job! Super-duper!" she cheers. "Yahooooo. That's our girl!"

I laugh sincerely at her cheesy excitement. My bent knee bounces, and my foot taps the floor anxiously.

"Thanks, Mom. So, my train gets in at 2:54 p.m. Monday. Are you or Dad picking me up?"

"Both. Dad took off work to come with me. He doesn't want me driving to Newark by myself."

I roll my eyes at their overprotective nature. Newark isn't *that* bad.

"We'll be waiting just behind the taxi line like last time. Call us when you're a couple minutes out from the station and we'll let you know how far back we are."

"Sure, sure, sounds good." I bring my cuticle to my teeth.

"What do you have planned for the weekend? Do you want to come home sooner? We don't mind…" She trails off hopefully.

"No, that's okay." I soften, trying not to disappoint her. "Bunch of us are sticking around campus until the end of the weekend." I skirt any mention of Duke. I want to tell her in person. "I'll just be packing and hanging out. Maybe going to the bar and hitting a couple parties."

"Be careful." Her tone is stern. "And don't drink too much. I want a happy face when we see you."

"Always am, Mom," I promise and mean it.

"I know, I know, but I have to remind you. You know me." I can hear in her voice she's back to smiling.

"Are you guys going out to dinner this weekend?" I ask, continuing the conversation to make up for causing her distress last night. I'm back to pacing, letting my gaze wander over the images of my friends tacked on the wall.

She brightens. "Yes! It's supposed to be a little warmer on Saturday so we're going up to the mountains, have some champagne, and then dinner at the Walpack."

Sunrise Mountain is my parents' favorite spot. It's where my dad took my mom on their first date. They tell the story every time we drive up there of how my mom thought my dad was taking her to the middle of nowhere to murder her. She'd quickly gotten over the fear once she saw the view. They proceeded to finish several bottles of champagne, eat entirely too much at the Walpack following, and not make it home until well into the early hours of the morning. Since then it's been a yearly pilgrimage to go back—a tradition I love being a part of.

"Aww, I'm jealous. I haven't been to the mountains this year yet."

"We'll go again while you're home if we don't start getting snow. They close the park when it snows," she tells me as if I don't already know this from years of experience.

I close my eyes, knowing the conversation is going to end and I'll have to have a tougher conversation with Brett.

"Sounds good. Can't wait." I try for a light tone despite the tightness in my throat.

"Well, alright then. If there's nothing else going on, I'll let you go. Have fun. Be safe. And see you Monday."

I hesitate, grasping at something to say to delay the inevitable.

"I'll probably talk to you later. For sure over the weekend to check in," I reassure her.

"Sounds good. Love you, Casey."

"Love you too, Mom. Tell Dad I said hi and love him too."

"Yup, will do."

"Okay, Mom, love you, bye."

"Love you, bye."

I press the end button and breathe a nervous sigh. Talking to my mom did nothing but fuel my nerves and pull my guilt to the forefront.

One down.

One to go.

I decide on a quick break to mentally prepare myself for this one. Grabbing one of my suitcases from under the bed, I toss it up and flip the top open. At the closet, I start pulling out all my summer clothes and place them inside. I puff out a heavy breath and rifle through the drawers next, finding my favorite pair of jeans toward the bottom. When I pull them free, Brett's navy t-shirt tags along. My breath catches in my throat, and my mind wanders to the image of my bedroom at home. A computer screen lights the darkness, and my fingers are poised above the keyboard, a smile on my face. Something tugs at my heartstrings, and my eyes well up suddenly. I clutch the shirt to my chest protectively.

Maybe I don't have to do this. Brett's like my other half, my best friend. The idea that he wouldn't be there to talk to whenever I want is like picturing living without my right arm. But the comfort of Duke's arms around me... Does Brett really know the real me?

My musings are interrupted by a text.

MESSAGE: DUKE
Duke: I cant stop thinking about u

I can't stop the smile that draws across my lips. Goosebumps raise along my arms.

MESSAGE: DUKE
Casey: me either :)
Duke: can't wait to see you later

My heart races, and I swallow against the swell rising in my chest. The scales tip. My mind is made up that I'll tell Brett the truth. I'll come clean about everything and let him go, however hard that may be. I fold the shirt nicely and place it back in the drawer before picking up the phone. I dial his number, climbing onto my bed, and sink down onto my mattress, hesitating before hitting the final call button. It takes a while for him to answer. I almost think he won't pick up.

"Hey." He sounds disastrous even from that one word.

"Hi," I mumble, unsure of how to begin, hoping he might start for me.

"Where were you last night?" His usually strong, assured voice sounds crushed.

"At the library. I had finals today. My phone died, and I forgot to put it on the charger before I fell asleep," I lie easily.

"You always have an excuse lately."

"I'm just busy. I'm sorry." I barely sound like it.

"Too busy for me?" he whispers.

"I don't know," I say quietly.

"What's going on, Casey?" He goes quiet.

Seconds tick by without either of us uttering a word. I know what I should say, but I'm having trouble forcing my mouth to form the words. I breathe in, holding my breath as the seconds tick by.

"I don't think we should do this anymore." I let my breath out slowly between my parted lips.

"What do you mean?" he asks, distraught.

"I mean things have changed. So much is different. I'm different."

"No, you're not. You're my Casey."

"A lot has happened since I've been here, and I don't think I can keep doing this. It's not fair to you for me to drag this out."

"What are you saying?"

"I think we should see other people." I flush, finally admitting the truth aloud. I'm at a loss for more of an explanation.

"You can't do this. Please don't do this," he pleads.

"I'm sorry. This hurts me too." I start to choke up.

"There's someone else. Isn't there?"

"No," I lie again, not volunteering more.

I feel my heart pounding in my chest. My throat is tight, and my mouth is dry.

He lets out a sinister laugh. "Right. I hope you're happy." His tone grows disgusted. "Because I know I'm not, and I don't know if I ever will be."

It's easier for me to get angry when he sounds like this.

"You can't be happy waiting around for something that's never going to happen. Don't you want to be with someone you can touch and feel?"

"We can make that happen. I know we can."

"I don't see how."

"I'll make it happen. I'll come to you." There's hope in his voice like he thinks this will change my mind.

"Yeah, right." My voice drips with sarcasm. "Why now when you could have for months?"

"Because I can't lose you. Without you, I have no motivation. When you're around, you make every day better and I don't know what I'll do without you. Everywhere I go, everything I see makes me think of you. Everything reminds me of you. It all comes back to you." He sounds as if he's panicking, grasping at anything that will stop me from leaving.

"You can't lose something you never had," I blurt out with spite, hoping it will end this quicker. I can't take much more of the genuine agony I hear in his voice before I'll change my mind.

"Wow. Just wow. Maybe you aren't the same girl," he accuses.

"I'm not. And like I said, I'm doing this because it's not fair to you. I want you to be happy."

"Whatever, Casey. I don't believe you. Just go," he spits out.

The abrupt change in his argument takes me by surprise.

"Fine, I will go," I say with a defeated tone.

This can't be the last thing I ever say to him.

Then the painful fact that I have to hang up without saying I love you hits me like a rock.

"Fine." His tone is clipped.

"Goodbye, Brett," I murmur, not pulling the phone away to hang up.

"Goodbye, Casey."

He doesn't hang up either.

I sit there listening for a couple more beats, working up the courage to end the call. I suck in my bottom lip and bite down hard.

Just do it.

Pulling the phone from my face, I look down at the screen still counting the seconds of the open line. My finger hovers over the end button. I squeeze my eyes and bow my head, feeling the tears creeping their way into the creases. My thumb flexes involuntarily and the call goes dead.

It's over.

CHAPTER 39

I thought I would feel relieved. I just feel awful. There's no better word to describe it. The tone of his voice nearly dissolved my strength. I almost couldn't do it. I feel terrible but I thought I'd feel more broken, like a piece of me was missing.

Why don't I feel lost?

A thought swirling across my mind isn't fully taking shape, but it's there. Swallowing past the bile rising in my throat, I squeeze my eyes shut and throw my head back. I inhale a deep, calming breath, and reassure myself that whatever it is, I'll be fine. I have Duke now.

Mmm, Duke. Duke and his strong arms, soft lips, and rough hands.

All I need is him. I pick up my phone to start a text.

MESSAGE: DUKE

Casey: hows the nap?

Duke: would have been better with u

Casey: tomorrow ur all mine

Duke: i think i can make that happen ;)

Casey: what time r u going to Elias tonight?

Duke: 7 or 8

Duke: we're gonna grab dinner

Duke: wanna come?

My heart drops when it should be soaring.
What the fuck is wrong with me?

MESSAGE: DUKE

> **Casey:** Stella and I are gonna get ready together
> **Casey:** i'll meet u there
> **Duke:** ok babe
> **Duke:** don't be too late
> **Duke:** i'll miss u too much
> > **Casey:** I wont
> > **Casey:** see u soon

I don't know how to end the conversation. I want to say
I love him, but it doesn't feel right. The sentiment is there,
coursing through my body. My heart knows it, but my mind
thinks it feels too soon.

And it definitely feels wrong to say in a text for the first time.

I tilt my head and pull in a breath at the thought. The first
time Brett and I said I love you was on the phone. Not over
text, but still, it wasn't in person. Grasping for a distraction
to my confusion, I type out a quick message to Stella before
I forget.

MESSAGE: STELLA

> > **Casey:** hey how'd finals go?
> > **Casey:** Elias wants to go to Caverns later...
> > **Casey:** ur coming :p
> **Stella:** i am not going to Caverns
> **Stella:** u remember what happened last time
> > **Casey:** oh come on, it wasn't so bad
> > **Casey:** party house then?
> **Stella:** yeah sure

Stella: what time?

Casey: not sure

Casey: i'll ask Elias and let u know

Casey: just come by at 6 and we can go down whenever

Stella: perf

I think of telling her the news about Duke—and Brett—but decide to wait to tell her in person. A few hours won't kill either of us. A shiver rocks my whole body, making me groan. *I hope… It might kill me. Thank God we're on good terms again.*

I shake my head, straighten my shoulders, and message Elias.

MESSAGE: ELIAS

Casey: Stellas not in for Caverns

Casey: party house instead?

I toss the phone on the bed, returning to the task of packing. I don't expect an immediate answer. Elias isn't very prompt.

Pulling out a duffel, I start in on the shoes under my bed, avoiding anything that might trigger any unwanted memories of home… and Brett. A message vibrates through the mattress, startling me. When I pick it up, it starts vibrating constantly. I wonder if it's actually a call as I press the unlock button. It's not, and the messages keep rolling in.

MESSAGE: BRETT

Brett: this really hurts me

Brett: i really loved u with everything I have

Brett: but all i feel now is my heart breaking into pieces
Brett: i don't see my life without u
Brett: nothing i say anymore seems to matter anymore
Brett: it all seems to have disappeared
Brett: i just want to give up
Brett: idk what else to say to convince u
Brett: i wanted the best life for us
Brett: i still know we can have it

My chest feels tight and my thumbs itch to respond, to apologize, or *something.* I try for a deep breath and it catches in my throat, stopping me from filling my lungs. A switch flips in my head and I start to panic, gasping for another breath.

Gently placing the phone back on the bed, I scramble into the kitchen for a glass of water. Jess walks through the door while I have the pitcher in my hand, distracting me. I almost overfill the glass, but she catches me before it's too late. Setting the pitcher and the water down, I stare into the glass, finally catching my breath. I lift the glass to my lips and hold the cool liquid in my mouth without looking at her.

"So, you and Duke, huh?" she teases, wandering around the living room, picking up a few things that my eyes can't focus on.

"Hmm?" I look up at her, not having heard her question.

"You and Duke," she repeats with a smile.

The thought of Duke pulls me back from the edge. A flash of last night, his weight crushing against me, makes me blush deep.

"Oh, my god, you were home last night?" I ask, slightly mortified.

"No, I was with Bear." She smiles. "But I heard you this morning. Elias woke me up as well."

"You were with Bear?" I blurt at a yell, completely forgetting my inner chaos. My excitement for her conjures the same giddy feeling I had when Duke said "like out-out." She chuckles. "Yeah! Can you believe it? Right before break. We both get the guys."

I throw my arms around her neck. "Ah no! I cannot believe it." I am genuinely ecstatic. "Ugh. When are you leaving?"

"Tonight. Bear's gonna drive me home. It's on the way."

Whoa, that's fast.

"Wow! Driving you home already? That happened fast."

"No, I know. But it wasn't fast. He's liked me this *whole* time! He said he needed to wait for me to be officially a member of the frat to ask me out or else it would seem like favoritism if they let me in and we were dating." Her face is pulled into a smile so big the corners of her lips threaten to touch the creases of her eyes.

"Ah! Jess, that's fantastic." I push against the jealousy rising in my chest at how well put together she and Bear seem to be and how potentially fucked up I am.

"Well, we're going out. I was gonna say you should come..." I trail off.

"When we get back, we'll all go out," she promises. "And hey, are you okay?"

"Yeah—yes! I'm just still in shock that Duke and I are together." I pull my face into a composed mask.

She squints her eyes at me skeptically and I smile, hoping it's working.

"Well, okay. But you know you can talk to me, Casey." She turns, walking past my room to hers at the end of the hall.

I bend to put the pitcher back in the fridge and call to her, "I know, Jess! Thank you for being you."

"Of course! Hey, you know your phone's blowing up in there," she calls.

I almost double over from the resurgence of guilt and panic but recover and spout the first thing that comes to mind.

"Yep. Probably just my mom checking how I did on my finals. Thanks!"

* * * * *

Stella knocks on my door at 6 p.m. wearing a jean skirt over leggings, boots, and a deep V-neck sweater that's meant to have a tank top underneath but doesn't. Her thick, long, wavy hair is framing her subtly made-up face. She didn't waste any effort to go glam for our usual haunt.

She's always so fucking effortlessly perfect. Whatever. I can do that too.

I can't hide my lopsided smile as we walk back to my room, The Red Jumpsuit Apparatus "Face Down" playing from my LimeWire playlist.

"Whoa, started without me?" she comments, following me into my room and nodding at the open bottle of Smirnoff and the wet shot glass sitting next to it.

Where do I even start?

The alcohol is slowly hitting me, cutting off the circuits fueling my guilt and leaving me with the excitement of Duke.

The man I'm about to walk downstairs and wrap my arms around. The man who is hopefully going to take me to bed tonight and ravish me.

"Oh, yeah, that." I grab a second glass from the stacks lining the shelf of the empty desk, pouring out two shots. "I called Brett today."

She sucks in a breath. "Bad, huh?"

"I don't want to talk about it. Cheers!"

I hand her one and clink my glass to hers before tossing my head back. This is my third and I'm comfortably warm, my cheeks just on the right side of burning. A couple more and I'll need to take off my own sweater. I chose jeans so I'd be able to keep my phone close in my back pocket all night and paired them with a black V-neck with a zipper down the front and pink bra. I wipe the grimace off my face from the straight shot.

"Did you at least tell him the truth?" she probes with a frown.

"Not the whole truth. But I did tell him that I can't do this anymore. That we need to be over." I choke out the words.

"I'm sorry, Casey. I know that must have been really hard. But you needed to do it, and I'm glad you did." Her face lifts at my response.

"So, are you done hating me?" I tease, my confidence boosted with that last shot.

"I never hated you. I just don't like duplicity. You know that." She winks at me.

"Okay, enough about that." I give her a wide grin and my eyes glisten. "Sooo, Duke and I are official."

"Shut up!" She squeals and hops up on the empty bed. "See aren't you glad you did the right thing with Brett? When did Duke ask you? Last night? What happened after?"

I guess she's not paying much attention to the timeline.

Sitting down in the metal desk chair, I turn my attention to my mirror, twirling the mascara wand in its tube.

"Mmhmm, after the library." I ignore her comment about Brett, opening my mouth wide and leaning into the mirror to work on my left eye first.

"And he just asked you out of nowhere?"

I don't get how she can be so excited when she's been Team Brett this entire time.

I bat my eyes twice, admiring the widening effect the mascara has, and start on the right. "We were outside of Calhoun. A light went out on the corner and when I turned back to him, he kissed me."

"Oh, my God, Casey. I mean, seriously he took his time, though."

I guess she's on Duke's side now? I won't question it.

"Right?" I sit back, taking in the image of my full face. The makeup is covering any resemblance of red splotches from earlier.

"Did you spend the night together?" she teases.

I smile widely, my cheeks burning a deep red.

She catches my eye and narrows her gaze at my lack of response. "Oh, my God! He did. Didn't he?"

"That's exactly what I was saying last night," I purr with a wink. The alcohol is really hitting me.

"Ah! Casey! How was it? Was it good?"

Was it good? I don't have any comparison. It did hurt, but after a little while it started to feel good.

"I think so? I don't really have a comparison." I shrug, but my body reacts to the thought of Duke's tongue sliding across my skin and his hips pressed tight to mine.

"Oh, shit! Wait, was this your first time?" she asks, shocked. "How did I not know this?"

"You got my other biggest secret…" I narrow my eyes at her and tease. "This one just never came up."

She slides off the bed and stalks over to me, pushing my shoulder before wrapping her arms around my neck and looking at my face in my mirror.

"Fair. I'll let it slide. As long as you tell me everything." She kisses my cheek and spins around.

"Okay, okay, but later. All I can think about right now is that we're going home for break and I might die…"

"Oh please, you have the weekend. Just make up for all the lost time." She winks, motioning toward the vodka.

"Go ahead. I need to hold off until we at least get to Elias's or I'll never make it out." I feel my phone vibrate and slide it from its place in my pocket.

MESSAGE: ELIAS
Elias: cme down
Casey: we're coming

MESSAGE: BRETT
Brett: please just talk to me
Brett: i just want to be part of ur life
Brett: just answer me

I swallow hard and look up at Stella. "I think I'm ready…" I make it a question.

She coughs, recovering from the drink. "You look great!"

I pull the zipper down a touch more so the outline of my bra peeks through the opening and pour one more, choking it back quickly.

"Now I'm ready. Let's go."

She stares at me, jaw slack. "I'm not carrying you home tonight," she jokes.

I laugh wickedly. "That's what Duke is for."

CHAPTER 40

MESSAGE: BRETT

Brett 12:23AM: come on... u cant do that

Brett 12:25AM: u cant just call me and hang up

Brett 12:34AM: please just talk to me. i want to know ur okay

Brett 12:47AM: please im really concerned

Brett 1:03AM: i cant take this anymore

* * * * *

My head pounds as I peel my eyes open. The room comes into focus. Its's not mine, but it looks vaguely like Calhoun. There's a water bottle on the chair pulled up to the side of the bed closest to me. I look across the room and realize I'm looking at someone's *Fear and Loathing in Las Vegas* poster. In a moment of panic, I remember I don't have any clothes on. I have snippets of memory tearing them off myself after spilling water down the front. I really only needed to take off the sweater, but off they all went. I attempt to lift my head and search for my jeans, hoping my phone is buried in them.

Too heavy.

I set it back down on the pillow and reach for the water instead. The bottle crinkles when I take a gulp.

"Easy, baby, sip it," Duke coos. He sounds fully awake.

Behind me, he turns onto his side, draping his arm across my waist protectively.

"Ugh, what happened last night?" My tongue is thick, and my mouth tastes rotten. I melt back into him, craving relief from my hangover fog.

"You had a few too many at the party. I tried to stop you, but you insisted we needed to have a good night."

I groan, embarrassed beyond belief. "I'm so sorry," I whisper, desperation in my voice.

"All good. It happens. I got you," he says with nonjudgmental reassurance.

What did I do to deserve him?

More glimpses of memories. Short flashes of myself alone in the corner of a room on the phone with someone. In another, I'm quickly hanging up and turning toward the sound of Duke's voice coming up behind me.

"How did we get back here?" I ask.

"I don't know how you got past me… I found you outside on the way back to your dorm looking for Stella." He kisses my shoulder. "She left early with Elias, but I thought she told you, so I'm not sure why you were looking for her."

I vaguely remember leaving Duke in the kitchen refilling our cups to run to the bathroom. There's a blank space, a gap in time, between the bathroom and being on the street. Dread floods my system.

"I'm sorry. I guess I forgot." I squeeze my eyes shut, trying to forget what little I remember and ditch the effort to find my phone.

Oh, God. Oh, God. Oh, God.

I don't want to know what else I did or didn't do last night. I roll toward Duke, burying my face in his chest.

"You're gonna be okay, babe. Just gotta get you some water and something to soak up the alcohol."

"Can we just stay here for a little while longer?" I plead, not ready to see the light of day.

He tightens his arms around me, breathing into my hair. "Of course," he says, but I'm already slipping back into the welcome darkness of sleep.

The next time I wake, I'm alone in the tiny twin bed. I startle, wondering where Duke went. It's only a little bit easier to lift my head, but I'm successful. I throw my arm over the side of the bed, finding my jeans and my phone still tucked in the pocket. I see several message exchanges between Brett and me, and I quickly read and delete the ones I sent.

I can't ever let Duke find out about this.

Sitting up, I reach for the half-empty water bottle and finish it. The door creaks open. Duke enters my view wearing a towel around his waist, his hair wet. My heart races at the sight of him, and I stare at his abs and the deep V barely covered by the towel.

"Hey, sleepyhead." He smirks at me, ruffling his hair and sending water droplets cascading. "Have a good nap?"

"What time is it?" I try for a smile, squinting my eyes.

"11:45 a.m.," he says coolly after checking his phone.

I see the light and am relieved that it's still basically morning.

"I'm starving," I say, rubbing the sleep out of my eyes.

"Dining hall is open for lunch. I told everyone we'd meet them at one. Can you manage?"

"Yeah, but I need to go back to Race and have a shower."

"I'll walk you."

I nod and carefully move my legs to the edge of the bed, planting my feet on the floor. Slowly, I push myself up to stand, and the room tilts, forcing me to sink back down. I close my eyes, feeling the room start to spin.

"On second thought... Can I just stay here?" I barely mumble as my mouth goes dry.

He grabs the garbage can and slides it next to me.

"Just lie down." He reaches up into the top shelf of his closet, stretching the taut muscles of his sides. My mouth waters. He reaches his arm toward me, holding a new water bottle out.

"Here. I'll grab you a take-out box," he continues.

He turns, bringing his phone to his ear. I roll onto my side, facing away from him, and pull my knees up into a ball. I hear his muffled voice asking if someone is ready to go a little earlier—Elias, I assume—letting them know that I'll be staying here. He laughs and makes an excuse for my lack of attendance before my mind goes blank for the second time this morning.

Duke wakes me this time, informing me that it's 3:00 p.m. and officially time for me to get up for real. My stomach gurgles in agreement. I feel significantly better than this morning as I sit up to take the to-go container.

"So, where's your roommate?" I pull the sheet up across my bare chest and take a bite.

"Oh, he went home this morning."

"Oh, God, you're joking?"

A chuckle rolls out of his chest. "Nope." He sees my horrified face. "It's okay, you were covered. I've had to endure way worse from him more than he has on my account."

I lean to my right, falling back into the pillows, and hide my face. "I'm so embarrassed," I muffle into the pillow.

"What was that?"

Lifting my head enough to look into his eyes, I repeat, "I said I'm so embarrassed."

His back is to me as he turns on the TV and throws in a DVD of *The Office*.

"You're fine. Don't worry about it, Casey." He comes to sit on the bed next to me. "Finish eating. We'll watch some TV, stay in tonight, and snuggle." He nudges my shoulder and repeats suggestively, "Snuggle."

I giggle and let a small moan escape my throat, biting my lip reflexively.

He does things to me. I can't think of anything else when he's around.

The ache growing between my legs is a nice contrast to the pounding in my head.

"Mmm, that sounds nice."

CHAPTER 41

Last night was even better than the first time. It only hurt a tiny bit at the start before his rhythm built, sending tingles that spread throughout my body in waves. His length reached deeper in me and before long, I was squeezing my eyes shut, sparks exploding against the darkness of my eyelids.

I moan deep in my chest and glance over my shoulder. Duke is already awake next to me, scrolling through his phone. Rolling toward him, I snuggle up into his side and rest my head on his chest.

"Hi," I murmur.

He wraps his arm around my back and kisses my forehead.

"Let's go for a walk today," he suggests.

The thought of a walk in the cold makes me cringe, but I'll do anything with him. Something in me releases at the thought, and I let my guard down.

Flipping onto my stomach, I scoot up higher on his chest and press my lips to his. I draw my hand from my side, up along the hardness of his abdomen, onto the swell of his chest, and cup the back of his head, pulling him toward me. His hands wander through the tangle of my hair and rub down my back while his lips massage mine. A satisfied groan escapes his throat and vibrates through my body. I climb on top of him, spreading my knees on either side of his hips and feel him stiffen against the fabric of his boxer briefs as his hands cup my ass.

At the next drawback of our lips, I whisper teasingly, "Okay, but in a little bit."

* * * * *

I return from our walk warm under all the layers. Duke went directly to Elias's room to play Xbox when we arrived at Race. Apparently, there's a new game released that they both couldn't wait to play. I asked if he would be going back to his room to change before we went out. He glanced down at his outfit and asked if his jeans and t-shirt wouldn't cut it at our usual party spot anymore, cracking a joke about needing to change his appearance so I would want to be seen with him. I shoved him playfully in response and he lifted me off the ground, holding me in a big bear hug and taking my breath away with his kiss.

Now in my room, I strip off everything but my t-shirt and jeans and toss the discarded articles of clothing over the spare chair. I check my phone and see I have plenty of time to thoroughly get ready.

Tonight, I want to look drop-dead gorgeous for Duke.

I need him to leave tomorrow not wanting to relinquish the memory of me from tonight. From my closet, I pull out opaque tights to go with my black mini dress and wide waist-cinching belt. I find the over-the-knee boots I've been wanting to wear and finish the look with a light scarf. Turning, I admire the curves of my body in the mirror and smile. Involuntarily, I grab my phone and take a picture.

What am I doing?

Casey: headed ur way
Elias: hurry
Elias: u'll have to catch up
Casey: slow ur roll
Casey: im coming

I hurry down the hall to the stairs, running down them and barging through the heavy door to Elias's floor. I hear the music, laughter, and chatter before I round the corner and think I'm having a bit of déjà vu. The pregame must be in full swing.

I knock hard twice.

Nothing.

I knock a third and fourth time before bringing my phone to my ear.

After a few seconds, I hear, "Hey, baby."

Wait.

My brows knit together in confusion. I pull the phone from my ear and double check that I dialed the right number.

"Duke?" I ask, hesitation in my tone.

"Who else?" I hear his tipsy confidence spilling through.

"Come let me in, please? I'm in the hall."

"Be right there." I hear him yelling to someone in the background before the door opens. "Heyyy." He pulls the door all the way in, arms spread wide.

I laugh and raise my eyebrows. "We're having a good night, huh?"

He pulls me in for a hug, and I nuzzle into his chest, raising my lips to his ear.

"Stay with me?" I pull my head back and search his glazed eyes.

"Of course. Come in! I'll get you a drink."

I follow him the short distance to the small kitchen counter and watch as he dumps way too much vodka into a red cup and tops it off with club soda and a splash of Red Bull before handing it to me.

I don't even feel like drinking tonight. I was hoping Duke wouldn't either. I want to savor our last night before break.

Taking a sip, I try not to immediately spit it out and set it on the counter. He runs his hands down my arms from behind and laces his fingers with mine. I lean back into him. He lets go of one hand, encouraging me to spin, still holding the other, and whistles. The sound pierces through the crowd, and I shush him as people stare. I don't even know half of these people—where did they come from? He pulls me into him, forcing our tangled hands behind my back, and crashes his lips into mine.

"You. Look. Delicious," he murmurs into my ear.

I smile.

Mission accomplished.

Relaxing into the mood, I quickly grab the cup I had intended to ditch and take a small sip of the too-strong drink, letting Duke lead me through the throng of people to where Elias is perched on the arm of the couch. He's wearing sunglasses low on the bridge of his nose, animatedly telling a story to the group surrounding him.

What is he doing with those glasses? I bet they didn't even play Xbox… probably just got right to drinking. We need to go out now or we'll never make it out of here.

I cut through to him, reluctantly leaving Duke's side.

"I wanna dance. Let's go out!" I yell above the music and noise.

"Your wish is my command," Elias yells back and turns down the music a touch. "Kids... We're going out."

Some cheers and a lot of movement later, he's at the door.

"To the Party House!" Elias rallies his followers with a loud cry, pointing his finger to the ceiling.

He's out the door with a sea of people following him down the hall. Duke and I are in the back. I'm attempting to keep up with the group when he pulls me to the side, pushing me against the wall.

"What are you doing?" I giggle at his playful aggression.

"I missed you." His breath is hot on my neck.

"I wasn't gone for long." My breath catches in my throat. I arch my back to press against him, reacting to how close he is.

"It was too long." He presses into me harder so I can feel him beneath his jeans.

I laugh, but it comes out clipped, my breath constricted against his weight.

"You're never going to make it over break." I smile devilishly.

"You're right. I just want you all to myself," he growls.

That's really satisfying.

"Then we better go, so we can come back sooner," I tease and scrunch my hands up between his chest and mine and push hard.

He jerks back, surprised at my matched aggression. The surprise in his eyes turns to raw desire and he kisses me hard, nipping at my bottom lip. He grabs my hand and pulls me away from the wall to follow the group down the hall. His grip is strong as he wraps my arm around his waist. He releases my hand and rests his arm across my shoulder before planting a kiss on the top of my head. I look up at him and tickle his side. He wiggles against my touch, stares down into my eyes, and winks.

"Sooner is good. The things I'm going to do to you tonight." His voice is on the edge of a slur already.

I narrow my eyes and lean into him. "Easy, Casanova. We have to make it back first."

CHAPTER 42

It's freezing cold for an early December night and later than I want it to be.

It was a mistake to forgo the jacket. But also worth it to watch Duke rake his eyes up and down my curves.

We're finally heading back up 33rd toward the dorms. The streets are practically empty with only a few students huddled together walking quickly and a few more outside smoking. I snuggle in closer to Duke's warmth and watch my breath come out in a puff in front of my face.

I told Duke when we left that we're staying in my room tonight. It's closer with an en-suite bathroom versus his shared spaces—just in case. He's intoxicated enough that he didn't argue and couldn't care less. I just focus on navigating the sidewalk, letting him lean on me enough that we're moving slowly. With my arm around his waist, my fingertips are exposed and numb. Every few feet, he plants a wet kiss on top of my head. It's only slightly annoying. I see my tall dorm clearly, cutting across the crisp night sky.

We're almost there.

I don't notice the figure pacing back and forth near one of the parked cars until we round the corner of the walkway toward the entrance of my building.

I hear a choked voice. "Casey?"

Stopping a few feet short of the lighted entrance, my feet freeze mid-step as I see the figure walking toward us. I stiffen and squint against the dark, avoiding what I already know, searching for it to be anyone else looking for me this time of night.

Sensing my fear, Duke steps slightly in front of me, encouraging me behind him by moving our clasped hands to the small of his back. "Heyyy, I think you have the wrong girl." Duke holds our ground.

Faded orange light splashes across the face of the man still moving toward us. "No. You have that backward. You have the wrong girl. This one is mine," he spits venomously. His tone is even and ice cold.

I recognize the voice before he comes into focus, the light fracturing the features of his face into an unrecognizable mask until he emerges fully into the light. An audible gasp escapes my throat.

"Brett," I whisper under my breath.

It's a jarring experience when two worlds collide. Two separate lives, kept in their separate boxes, unexpectedly merging. Like tectonic plates creating a deadly earthquake.

I don't have a plan for this. This wasn't supposed to happen.

I step out from behind Duke and in front to face him. Putting my hands to his chest, palms flat, I plead, "Let me handle this."

"What's going on? Who is this guy?" Duke questions, half accusingly in his inebriated state.

I grasp for a soothing tone. Thinking back to that Welcome Session luncheon when this all started and how naive I was to think I could have both.

"Just some guy," I say, backing away toward Brett. "It's going to be all right. Just give me a minute."

Peering over my shoulder, I see Brett is fidgeting and antsy. He's fumbling with something in his hands, but it's too dark to tell what. I reassure myself, with a quick breath, that I know this man inside and out.

I can defuse this bomb.

Turning ungracefully on my heel, pulling my shoulders back and lifting my chin, I glide toward Brett, feeling a tug deep inside as I move farther away from Duke. When I'm within feet of Brett, the rigid lines of his body soften.

I never imagined this would be the way we met.

"Hey, baby," he murmurs.

His voice hits me somewhere almost foreign. He reaches for my hand to pull me into a hug. I let him, but it feels awkward. Stiff and forced. He can feel it too and lets go, inching backward.

"What's wrong? Did you forget about me?"

"Never, my love." I'm stalling, trying to create time to figure this out.

I draw my fingers across his jaw like I've wanted to do since the first time I saw his picture on the tiny precious screen, now carelessly stuffed in the back pocket of my jeans, probably lifeless.

He's different than I imagined. Not in a bad way.

Slightly shorter, narrower. But his face is exactly the 3D version of his pictures. His eyes are warm and inviting, the curve of his lips enticing. They're parted in anticipation. I find myself oddly drawn to him.

He's waited so long for this.

I could have been waiting too, but I made a choice to share the innermost pieces of me with the real world, with the man now standing behind me. I've bared my true self to

Duke, exposing my rough edges, like pages of a book torn from their source.

Except this one. I've kept this one perfectly hidden.

An itching feeling crawls across the inside of my skull. I search Brett's eyes for a modicum of understanding, but it's not there. The only thing living in the deep pools of dark brown is raw desire, bordering on possession. He's searching my face, confused at my lack of affection nor display of any emotion toward him.

"Casey?" Duke calls from behind me. "Is everything okay?"

"All good, Duke. Please. Just give me a minute." I keep the calm softness of my voice, hoping to avoid an escalation by either guy.

Cracking at the sound of my voice, Brett buries his face in my neck, breathing in the scent of my hair and crushing me to embrace him. Instinctively, I wrap my arms around him, feeling the strong muscles of his back and tips of his hair brushing against my cheek.

"What the hell, man!" Duke booms, his anger rolling off him.

I hear footsteps and can anticipate what's about to happen before I'm ripped out of Brett's arms and Duke is in his face. This close, I can see the height difference, Duke towering over Brett by almost a full head. He doesn't take a swing, but the tension of his bunching shoulders shows he wants to. I stumble backward, two sides of my brain warring with each other.

This will not end well.

Brett is not one to back down in a fight, rather he winds up. Or at least that's how it was every time we'd had an argument.

"What the hell?" Brett shouts back. "I should be asking you the same. Back the fuck off." He puts his hands on Duke's chest, just as I had moments ago, and pushes. "I saw you kissing my girlfriend just now. Falling all over her. Pulling her along like she's a lost puppy! Well, she's not! She's spoken for," he continues and pulls his shoulders back, puffing out his chest.

Duke whirls on me, recalling my earlier comment and something long forgotten. "Just some guy? *Just some guy?* Is that true?" He throws his arm out behind him, pointing at Brett's chest. I hear the hint of betrayal seeping into his voice.

"Duke. Please," I whisper, sounding defeated, pathetic, even to myself. "We dated for a while. Online. I ended it when I came here..." I trail off, knowing I shouldn't have just lied and not wanting to add the next statement that may completely seal my fate. "Or I tried to," I murmur under my breath.

"So, it's over? You and him?" Duke asks, softening the tiniest bit and giving me hope.

"Yes," I answer.

At the same time, Brett screams, "No! It's not over, it'll never be over." He steps past Duke to capture my sight and continues, "You and me, we can have everything together. What about all our plans and dreams? What about our life together? Does it mean nothing to you? Till death, remember, baby?"

I try to hide the panic on my face, taking a shallow breath and holding it for a few seconds.

Duke is studying me, waiting for what I have to say in response.

Brett is ruining everything.

I swallow hard and pull my face into a scowl. Anger creeps up from my toes, grips my insides and spills out of my mouth. "It was all just a fantasy, Brett, an online fantasy."

He rushes forward and grabs my hands, pleading, "I'm here now, though. We can make it work. We can make anything work. Don't just abandon me."

His hands are hot in mine, warming my fingers and thawing some of my fury. I bite my lip at the idea that he's actually here, standing in front of me. I can't stop my shoulders from slouching in certain defeat. He's chasing me like I've wanted all along, begging me to help him make this work.

"Don't touch her." Duke pushes between us. "Just back up." His tone is oddly calm.

I stare at the lines of his back and then down at my empty hands.

"Casey, just tell him," Brett begs over Duke's shoulder, staring straight into my eyes.

I back up, away from both of them.

I need space. I need time. I need to clear this fuzziness out of my head.

Crouching into a ball, I lay my head in my arms, wrapping my hands over top and tug on the roots of my hair.

This is an absolute mess.

A voice cuts through the distant testosterone-fueled argument and interrupts my panicked thoughts.

"Excuse me, is everything all right out here?" The public safety guard. She must have watched as Duke and I approached and got suspicious when we hadn't entered the building after a while. "I'm going to need to see some IDs, please."

I stand up slowly, not wanting the blood to rush to my head too quickly. It doesn't matter. I'm already seeing stars. Making my way toward her, I pull out the contents of my pocket, grappling not to drop anything. I sort through my license, credit cards, and dead Blackberry, finding the student ID just as I'm in front of her.

"Hi. I live here," I say in a daze. "I've got this covered." I hear myself on the edge of breaking as if I'm experiencing the scene as a third party. Duke and Brett are still in each other's faces, inching closer and closer to a physical fight.

"Sure you do, honey." She gives me the skeptical side-eye. "I'm calling for more security. Just a moment."

"No, no, don't do that," I beg, but she's already on her radio.

I turn back to the two men who are now yelling, fighting over protecting me from one another. I stand rooted in my spot, starting to shake. Tiny white spots float across my vision. I look up at the sky and realize the spots are flecks of snow. I turn my head back to look at Duke. My teeth chatter in my head, and I ball my hands into fists and sink my fingernails into my palms. I watch as Duke draws his arm back to take a swing.

Oh, God, Duke, please don't...

I shake my head, silently pleading, and hear a muffled voice beside me. I ignore it, focusing on the scene in front of me.

They're too close to the road.

I see headlights cutting through the flurried haze, coming in our direction, just as Brett steps off the curb. My feet are running without my mind telling them to. The blaring light glints off something shiny.

I don't want anyone to get hurt.

What was that in Brett's hands before?

I'm just about to reach them, yelling to them to stop fighting, when several things happen at once. The guard yells, distracting me from the flash of metal I see Brett pull out of his pocket. I wedge myself between the two men, my back to Brett, pushing Duke as hard as I can back toward my dorm. I hear the squeal of tires and feel something hot spill down my chest despite the frigid air. I'm jolted by the feel of arms squeezing around my waist, dragging me sideways before the concrete comes up beneath me too quickly. There's a sharp pain on the side of my head, but all I can focus on is the unnatural crunching sound of something heavy hitting metal. The pinpricks of snow melt on my skin as my eyelids flutter.

"Brett!" I yell out.

Everything fades to black.

CHAPTER 43

I see the faint glow of light through the lids of my eyes. They're heavy. It takes force to open them. When I do, my sight is blurry. I hear the clang of something constantly coming apart and meeting again. It's a foreign sound I've never heard before and can't place the source. I see bright fluorescent light mixed with flashes of blue and red swirls and blink a few times, attempting to clear the cloudiness. When I open my eyes wide, I'm staring at the ceiling of the inside of an ambulance.

My mouth feels dry, and my tongue sticks to the roof of my mouth. Everything feels heavy, like the fatigue of muscles after being worked out for too long.

No, that's not right.

It's more of an ache, like what I imagine it'd feel like to be hit hard with a baseball bat, repeatedly. I try to lift my head to look around and then I feel it. Searing pain in the left side of my chest. Pain so sharp it makes my ears ring and my vision blur again. I attempt an inhale and feel my chest squeeze. The sound of hospital monitors fills my head. There's a bump, the ambulance shakes, and I realize we're still moving. The weight of someone's hand on mine, their thumb stroking the back, accompanies a soothing hazy voice.

"Everything will be okay."

There's constant chatter threatening to drown out the voice, but I need to know where it's coming from. I muster the courage to turn my head again slightly toward the pain but toward the sound of the voice. I have to squeeze my eyes shut just to bear it. When I lift my lids again, I focus on the lines of Duke's face, his radiant eyes and soft lips. He smiles lopsidedly.

Next to him is a paramedic, his blue-gloved hand pressing firmly on a pad of gauze just below my shoulder. It's too close. I can't get the full view of the pad to grasp the extent of the wound. He's watching a screen, flickering with my heartbeat and other vitals, and talking to the driver.

My voice comes out in a rasp when I attempt to speak. "What happened?"

"You were hit by a car. There's a very deep cut we're trying to stop from bleeding," the paramedic answers.

I scrunch my face in confusion, furrowing my brows.

"I tried to get you out of the way…" Duke adds, seeing my frustration.

A glimpse of memory. I see the shiny metal of a pocketknife in Brett's hands as I ran at him. I remember the whites of his eyes as recognition set in that the car would hit me first. I feel the knife slice across my chest as he wrapped his arms around me to try to drag me out of the way, and I hear the clatter as it hits the pavement despite the noise of all the commotion.

"There wasn't enough time for me to get to you," Duke clarifies.

He seems oddly sober for how drunk he was a short while ago. Then I realize I have no idea how long it's actually been. I look at his face. The left side is puffy and red. His eye is bloodshot, and there's a split on his bottom lip. I try to reach my left hand toward him and am instantly reminded of all my potential injuries.

"Don't try to move, baby." He squeezes my hand again.

I wince and exhale through my teeth. "What happened?" I ask, repeating myself.

"He kept insisting you two were together. That you were in love and you would run away with him."

I don't respond, keeping my face as blank as possible.

"He kept trying to get to you, repeating over and over that I'd never understand what you have. I couldn't let him get to you."

He looks down, his chin touching his chest and back slouched. He brings his forehead to the back of my hand and rests there for what feels like forever. When he looks up again, his face is stricken.

"I hit him first…" He pauses again, searching for a way to continue. "He kept coming at me, but I was able to push him back."

I'm having a hard time connecting the dots.

"It was too late. There was nothing I could do." His face drops again. "I didn't even see him step back into the street, maybe he even slipped."

My lips part to ask the unthinkable.

"All I could see was you standing between me and him." He swallows so loudly I can hear it. "It was dark. I'm sure they never saw you two in the street."

"No. No, no, no."

Brett was trying to save me.

"I should have tried to stop the car, the only thing I could think about was his arms going around you and I panicked. I didn't realize he was trying to help you. The car hit him from the side before he could let you go."

I see tears forming along the bottom lid of his eyes. He blinks and one escapes, rolling down his cheek. I suck in my bottom lip and bite down hard. Squeezing my eyes closed, I can't form a response. My own tears rise and promise to spill over.

"He's not dead. He's in the ambulance ahead of us. We're on our way to UPenn Medical." His tone holds the slightest amount of disgust.

He's hiding how he really feels.

It doesn't matter. Duke's here. I'm alive. And Brett... is still ruining everything.

A machine screams through the haze in my mind. It's a faraway sound. Muffled and easy to ignore with the comfort of familiar darkness seeping in.

* * * * *

The next time I open my eyes, I'm in a hospital room on an uncomfortable bed, wearing one of those ugly polka dot gowns. Needles and tubes connect to various parts of my body, the tape pulling uncomfortably at my skin. I glance groggily around the room and see Duke curled in an armchair in the corner. Light streams through the plastic blinds, despite being pulled closed, creating patterns on the thin hospital blanket that's thrown over him. A pillow is wedged between his head and the back of the chair. I smile.

He stayed.

There's no sign of my parents. I assume not much time has gone by or they'd have been here by now. Though I guess it is light out. An alarm goes off in my head at the thought. I pray someone has called them. If I could find my phone, I'd check in with them myself.

Twisting my head slightly from side to side, I see my phone plugged in and lying on the rolling table to my right next to the standard pink water pitcher and the TV remote. It's just out of reach.

If I stretch, I could probably make it.

I lift the fingers on my right hand, testing which movements hurt and which don't. I feel a slight twinge but it's manageable. I keep reaching and touch the table edge. Using only fingertips, I attempt to pull it toward the bed, but I don't have enough of a grip and the table pushes farther away.

Duke stirs from the noise. "Oh, hi! You're awake."

He flops the blanket down and unfolds his limbs from the chair. I admire his grace as he comes to a standing position.

"What do you need? Let me get it for you."

I try my voice again, unsure what to expect. "I just want my phone. Check in with my parents."

It comes out cracked but understandable. He nods and walks toward the table. His eyes look a little disappointed when he hands me the phone.

"What?" I pull my brows together.

"Your parents got here while you were still being evaluated in Emergency. Your mom *was* here." He looks around the room as if just realizing it's just the two of us. "And your dad went to check in at the hotel."

"Oh… How long have we been here?"

He glances at the clock. "Well, they found a few cracked ribs during the X-ray and you needed stitches for a few of the cuts, especially the one on your chest." He points at my shoulder as if I can follow his gaze. "And they've been monitoring you for signs of a concussion. It's been… just about six hours." He moves back toward the chair but turns on his heel before reaching it and looks intently into my eyes.

He has something else to say.

"Thank you," I whisper before he has a chance to open his mouth.

Tears prickle my eyes. His face relaxes, shoulders sagging. I hadn't even noticed the tightness. He drags the chair across the floor to sit next to me. Leaning his forearms on the bed beside me, he rests his hands on my thigh. I feel the warmth through the thin sheets and blankets. It's comforting.

"Casey, you have to tell me the truth."

I blink my eyes closed and breathe in lightly through my nose. When I open them, he's studying my face.

"We were together." I pause, looking for his reaction. His face is blank. I start over. "His name is Brett. We met online at the end of senior year. It wasn't anything at first. He just…"

I search for the words while I stare at his face. He's silent, his eyebrows pulled together and his lips pursed.

"Well, I guess he satisfied something in me I didn't know was missing," I continue at a whisper. "He wanted to know me, the real me."

He looks skeptical.

"The real you?" His tone is soft and sharp at the same time.

"In high school…" I stop to swallow and wet my lips. "I was basically invisible."

I close my eyes, trying to organize my next thought and take a shaky breath.

"I had friends—or I knew a lot of people—but no one really needed me. I had all these desires and aspirations for who I wanted to be, but I never felt like I could tell anyone or just be that person. I guess I thought I would just be made fun of or laughed at. People always judged me." I rush the explanation and pause before adding, "Except him."

He frowns, bowing his head and puffing out a breath. When he lifts his head, his gaze is softer. "I know what that's like," he murmurs.

I scoff, but it comes out as more of a cough. "Sure you do." I roll my eyes before continuing, "You're like the perfect guy. You're cute. You play soccer. You play guitar. I mean, Christ, Ava knew it the minute she laid eyes on you."

It's his turn to roll his eyes. He squeezes my thigh gently, shaking his head.

"Ava..." He sighs. "Just forget her... I was never part of that group. I did those things because I liked them, but I didn't fit in. I wasn't outgoing. I had four best friends in high school. That's it. I've never even had an official girlfriend before you..." He glances away, his cheeks flushing.

I reach for his hand, and he looks back up at me. I wonder about the girl he had been consistently having sex with and decide I don't actually care.

I get to call him mine now.

"You just seemed so confident when I met you," I say, staring deep into his eyes.

"I was barely keeping it together that day on the bus. Between you and Ava, I've never had that much attention in my entire life. I didn't know what to do."

"Yeah, well, I didn't know what to do either." I shake my head, clearing the memory of my first taste of boldness that day, pushing Ava out of the way of what I wanted. "Brett brought out this confidence in me. I thought I needed him so I could be that person. I never had that confidence with anyone else."

"That's not true. You chased me for how long until I finally opened my eyes and saw you right in front of me?" His lips spread into an encouraging smile. "That takes confidence."

I shift my eyes away from his.

He's never going to understand.

"I can't explain what it was," I continue, still not meeting his eyes. "At some point, we thought we'd be together. Like really be together. We talked about meeting one another. He wanted me to go to the University of Chicago—where he goes—but I just couldn't do it. My parents don't even know. No one knows really, not even my best friend from home. Just Stella."

The words are pouring out of me. I lift my eyes back to hold his. He patiently waits, giving me room to continue, like he somehow knows I have more to say.

"Toward the end of the summer, I started to realize that I was about to come here. I was about to start college, and I could be whoever I wanted. It wasn't worth all the nights on the computer, the loss of friends, and missing out on all the real-world stuff. I tried to let it die out. It just never quite stuck."

My shoulders inch up in an involuntary shrug and I wince.

"So, when he says it wasn't over… He told me you called him begging him to come find you," Duke states, with a question in his voice.

"No," I respond quickly, "That didn't happen."

I don't think.

"How can I believe you?"

I don't know.

A flash of guilt, or maybe dread, washes through me. Then an idea comes to mind.

"Here. Look at my phone. Look at the last few messages he sent me. He's out of his mind," I say, holding out my phone to him.

He grips the edge, pulling it into his hands and scrolling through. Something changes in his eyes. His face softens even more. I let out an audible breath. He nods while reading, a resolve washing over him. He looks up at my face and lays the phone down next to me.

"Okay..." He nods. "Okay. I believe you." A nervous smile creeps onto his face, and he blows out a puff of air. "Last night..." He shakes his head. "I didn't expect our last weekend here to be like this."

I attempt a laugh. "Me neither."

He kisses the back of my hand, gingerly avoiding the IV.

"I'm sure your mom will be right back." His eyes light up, and his lips spread into a wide grin. "I think she likes me." He winks.

"What makes you think that?" I giggle.

"Well, at first, she was worried, but then I told her I was with you the whole time. She gave me the side eye..." He raises an eyebrow at me. "I guess you haven't been talking about me *too* much—"

"I have been!" I cut him off. "I told her about you. I swear."

He laughs, holding up a hand. "I know, I know. By the time they brought you to this room, she was thanking me profusely, telling me to take the chair, tucking me in." He smirks.

My cheeks heat at the thought of my mom tucking him in. He stands from the chair and leans to kiss my forehead before pulling back and looking intently into my eyes.

"If you're okay, I'm just gonna go down the hall for some more ice?"

I try for a nod, despite the ache. "Yes." I smile.

I should say it now. Now would be a good time to say I love you. Right?

"Right. Okay. You rest. I'll be back."

He turns to walk away, leaving me to stare at the muscles of his back bunching under his shirt, now stained with blood. Mine and maybe some of his.

"Duke?" I whisper, unsure if he will hear me.

"Yes?" He turns his head so he can see my face without moving from the door.

My heart pounds and the monitors jump. I suck in as much of a breath as I can and open my mouth to speak.

"I love you, Duke."

CHAPTER 44

DUKE

I close the door gently, though I have the urge to slam it, my emotions fighting with one another. A huge grin splits my face, and my chest warms at the memory of saying the word "love" out loud to Casey. The thought keeps me from completely boiling over with rage at this Brett guy.

I peek through at Casey before pulling it completely shut. The last glimpse I see of her, she picks up her phone, her face draining of what little color it has.

I won't pretend to completely understand this situation. But I trust her. I know I do.

I love her. And I love that she waited to tell me until now, though not the ideal situation. I think I knew I loved her as the words were tumbling out of my mouth, asking her to be mine.

The hallway is long. The corridors connecting each wing are separated by locked doors that require a badge to get through. I don't need to go that far or stop at any of the nurses' stations along the way. I overheard a few of them talking about the hit and run that was brought in. I've walked this hall several times since they brought Casey back from getting stitched up, each time inching closer and closer to his door.

When her parents arrived, hospital security had to physically stop her father from bursting through to him. Since then I've paced this hall every hour, trying to make up my mind.

I shove my hand in my pocket, gripping the knife I found lying next to Casey that I picked up off the pavement.

He was going to kill her. Or me.

I feel my face pulling into a scowl. I've never been so angry in my entire life. I finally worked up the courage to get the girl and I almost lost her.

My eyes glaze over the white hallways. Each door looks the exact same except for the numbers on the black and red plates next to each. I remember the warmth of her cheek under my palm, the frozen tip of her nose grazing mine when I kissed her. I can hear her giggle when I asked if she would go out with me. A tingling sensation wells up from the base of my stomach as I remember the several nights we spent together after, and I have to adjust my jeans. Her body fits perfectly with mine.

Why did I wait so long?

But it's more than that. She brings out the best of me. She challenges me to be better, smarter, more organized. She makes me want to be something or someone great. Before her, I was headed down a path I never thought I would take.

My eyes catch the number for his room, and I stop short in front of the door. I debate about knocking versus barging in and decide he doesn't deserve the courtesy. I inhale a deep breath, collecting my thoughts.

I saw him when they loaded him into the back of the ambulance. He looked beat up but not critical. It was a small street. The car wasn't even going that fast, even though he took the brunt of the hit. Probably a few broken bones and some cuts and bruises.

A small price for almost killing my girlfriend or me if he had had the chance.

If the angle had been different, he could have plunged the knife deep into the soft tissue of her body, hitting veins or organs. Luckily, it looked like just a surface wound, overlooked as the result of her being hit and attributed to the shattered glass of the mirror and headlight left on the road after the car drove off. She needed nothing more than stitches but has a scar she'll have to wear for the rest of her life—reminding her of him every time she sees it.

That bastard.

The thought makes my anger flare again and I swallow it before pressing down on the handle and pushing inward.

He turns his head, eyes focusing on my face when I step through the door and close it behind me. He smiles, pulling at the splits in his lip and drawing fresh bright red blood to the surface.

"What do you want?" He looks back at the TV.

The lower half of his left leg is bound in a cast. Bandages cover several patches of skin on his arms and the side of his head, I assume from road burn. A bruise is blooming around his left eye from my fist connecting with his face before he was hit. I can't stop the satisfaction coursing through my veins at his beat-up state.

"I want you to back off. Leave my girlfriend alone." I spit the words at him.

He mumbles.

"What was that?" I ask.

"She's not your girlfriend." His voice rises sharply.

"She sure as shit isn't yours. I don't care what you think is going on with you two, but it's over."

He laughs—a sinister sound, more like a cackle. Almost fake. I squeeze the knife harder in my pocket.

"What's so funny?" I snap.

"*You* have no idea what Casey and I have. It's not over." He's calm and collected, pronouncing every syllable. I grit my teeth together.

"Dude. She wants nothing to do with you. Get that through your head." I can barely talk around the emotion squeezing my throat.

He turns his head and looks me dead in the eyes. "And you need to get through your head that she'll never be yours. Not completely, at least. I'll always have a piece of her."

I take a step closer to the bed, clenching my fist at my side and then flex my fingers. I try for a steadying breath but fail. "I want you to leave her alone. *She* wants you to leave her alone."

He rolls his eyes. "I'll believe that when I hear it from her."

"That'll never happen. I'm not letting you near her." I step forward.

"You can't stop me," he taunts.

"Watch me," I threaten, letting my anger coat my words.

"You want to try again?" His smile widens. "Look how that worked for you last time."

"But here's something you don't know..." I pull the knife out, holding it flat on my palm. "The police may not know your full intention, but I do."

He flicks his gaze to my palm and scoffs. "What do you think that proves?"

"All it takes is one phone call and they'll be all over your ass before you know what happened. They'll start asking questions. Casey will tell them how obsessed and insane you are." I shove the knife back into my pocket.

A slow smile spreads across his face. "You really think that some part of her won't resent you for putting me away?" He licks the cut on his lip. "Besides, now your prints are on it too."

"You sick son of a bitch—"

A hard knock interrupts me and a nurse comes into the room. "Mr. Caviar—oh!" She almost bumps into me, looking up from her chart. "You can't be in here. Family only. You're not family. Are you?"

"No, ma'am. I was just leaving."

She shuffles over to check the machine monitoring his vitals, busying herself with changing IV bags and checking dressings.

I take one last long look at him before walking out the door. He doesn't look back at me.

Rage boils my blood, and it takes every ounce of effort not to stomp back down the hallway. My mind races.

I'll show Casey the knife. Prove to her that he was going to do far worse damage. And I'll never see this asshole again. I just have to find the right time.

When I come back through Casey's door, the room is dim. The nurses must have turned off a few lights while I was away. Casey is sleeping, her face peacefully tilted to the side. At least she looks comfortable. I search for her phone, thinking I'll just check in with her mom—wherever she is— to let her know Casey woke up. At first glance, I can't find it. I move around the bed to where I was sitting before I left and notice her hand tucked up by her chest, gripping the phone protectively.

Slowly, very carefully, I wiggle the phone from her grasp. She doesn't stir and I think they must have given her another dose of pain medication. I tap the lock button to bring the screen to life. I'd asked Casey to take off the lock code so I would be able to keep in contact with her parents while she was asleep. I stare at the screen and jump when the door creaks open, almost dropping the phone.

I hold up a finger to my lips as her mom enters the room, motioning to be quiet. She nods and walks to Casey's side, lightly rubbing her fingers over the back of Casey's hand. I slide her phone in the pocket with Brett's knife and shuffle next to her mom. Leaning a little to the side, I whisper, hopefully loud enough for her to hear.

"Casey was awake for a little while."

Her head snaps up to look at me. "When?" she asks at full volume.

"A few minutes ago. I went to go ask for more ice," I lie and realize the bucket sitting on the table is empty. "I guess the nurse just hasn't brought it down yet," I add quickly, hoping she doesn't notice.

"Next time call me," she commands.

I nod, guilt replacing the anger swimming through my veins. Turning back toward the chair, I pull Casey's phone from my pocket as my back is to her mom. I think to put it down on the table next to her bed. I don't know what makes me do it, but before I can put it down, I scroll through her inbox, looking for the messages she showed me from Brett. I look up, concentrating hard on the hospital chart on the wall.

They're gone.

CHAPTER 45

BRETT

From behind the sliding glass doors of the discharge lobby, I watch him wrap his arm around my girlfriend's waist, escorting her toward the waiting car.

It's been four days since I laid eyes on her. Four days since I first smelled the sweet vanilla of her shampoo and felt the soft curve of her back under my palms. Four days since that bastard made me almost lose her again. These have been the longest four days of my life. Knowing she's been just down the hall with no way to see her, to touch her. It's agony seeing her now with him so close, touching her where I should be, marking his scent all over her. I can't stand it.

It won't be for long. She'll come back to me. She always does.

His hand grazes the edge of her phone, already slipping out of her back pocket after getting up from the wheelchair. It's just enough to tip it over the edge of the thin cloth. It spills out, tumbling onto the concrete behind her. Neither of them notices. Her head is down as she prepares to slide into the back seat.

Come on, baby, turn around. Look at me. Just once.

She doesn't look up. I see her disappear behind the door, his hand extended to steady her. I can see her parents in the front seat—her dad behind the wheel, her mom turned, checking as she gets settled. He bends in after her and a fire ignites inside me. My palms itch. The view of the back seat is dark, but I can barely make out his arm draped across the back of the seat and Casey leaning into the crook of his body. The lights flicker on as the ignition catches.

Slowly, I make my way in the direction of the car, her phone still forgotten on the sidewalk. No one is around to pick it up. The car pulls away from the curb. I'm still far enough away that I don't think they'll recognize me. I hobble on the uncomfortable crutches to face the building, regardless. I hear the engine pass behind me and groan while turning back toward the edge of the sidewalk. I'm standing over her phone, trying to determine the best movement to bend and retrieve it that will cause minimal pain. Just then, a nurse walks through the door several paces ahead of me. She turns her head before crossing the street and notices my struggle. I catch her eye and flash a helpless smile. She hurries over and bends to pick up the phone.

"Here ya go!" she says with a glint in her eyes.

"Thank you so much. I'm so clumsy." I let the charm drip from my voice.

"Don't mention it." She looks me up and down. "You should try to be more careful in your condition." She winks.

"I should." I should offer more banter, but I can't stop focusing on Casey's phone burning in my palm.

She frowns. "Well, take care, then!" She steps off the curb in the direction of the car park.

"Thanks!" I call after her.

Alone again, I glance down at the blank screen of the Blackberry and tap the lock button, expecting there to be a password. There isn't. I scroll through the contacts— addresses and phone numbers—and then the messages and emails, everything unprotected. A huge grin splits my face in half. I look up as the white of the taxi comes into view. The driver sees me and pulls to the side, back passenger door in front of me. He hops out and comes around.

"Hey, man, let me help you."

He opens the door. I shift both crutches to one arm and hop on my good foot toward the edge of the curb, lowering myself into the backseat. He stashes them in the trunk and slides into the driver seat.

"So where to?" he asks.

"34th and Race."

"You got someone there to help you?"

"Nah, I'll be fine."

We ride in silence on the short trip back to her college campus. The street where the accident happened is still taped off. He drops me on the corner and helps me out of the car. I begin the slow trek to my car, cursing the stupid cast the whole way.

At least it isn't my driving foot. This shit has to go.

I throw the crutches into the trunk and rifle through my duffle bag for my knife, cursing out loud as I remember that asshole picked it up off the street. I hop around to the driver's side and fall in, leaving the cast outside and begin picking at the hard plaster. It's not working. I bang my hands against the steering wheel in frustration and sift through my glove box searching for something, *anything*, that will get this damn thing off.

Fuck it. I'll find something when I get there.

I lift my leg into the car, settle it into a comfortable position, and slam the door closed.

I set Casey's phone down in the cup holder, next to the stale cup of coffee from days ago, and put my own phone to my ear.

"Hello?"

"Hey, Kate, I need a favor."

"Anything."

"Can you get me directions to Spencer Street in Stanhope, New Jersey?"

"Of course. I'll text you the route."

"Thanks."

I hang up and throw my phone on the passenger seat. I pull down the visor and check my face in the mirror, admiring my now-black eye. My phone beeps and vibrates. A slow smile tugs at the edges of my lips.

I turn the key and the engine rumbles to life.

"I'll find you, Casey. I'll always find you."

ACKNOWLEDGMENTS

A SPECIAL THANK YOU:

To my husband, for the countless late nights, snappy remarks, and tears that you had to endure… all while raising our newborn from the start of this journey.

To my parents, for instilling the idea in me that I can do anything I set my mind to.

To my #pettybookclub—Torri, Ebony, Dani, Steph, and Juliana—for your constant support and all the laughs that kept me going when I hit my low points. So thankful to have met you all.

To my editor, Jess, for putting up with me while I navigated my first book. I couldn't have asked for a more perfect match. You've been my guiding light and voice of reason.

AND TO ALL MY EARLY SUPPORTERS, THIS BOOK WOULD NOT HAVE BEEN POSSIBLE WITHOUT YOU:

Jack and Jacqueline Connelly

Tammy Connelly

Jessica Connelly

Sean Connelly

Stefani Pritchard

Rick, Wendy, and D Karp

Stephanie Schiel

Gail Habecker

Gwen Carpenter

Kelly Falcone

Shannon Huber

Jessica Fleischman

Lindsay and Joe Assini

Ryann Harmon

Brian and Lizzie Luciani

The Gabel Family

Sue and Pete Buonpane

Devon Ikeler

Whitney Lott

Jennifer Humphries

Lauren Buonpane

Nicole Beckmann

Lauren Rutkowski

Courtney Brooks

Gina Sosik

Peter Colesworthy

Grant Conselyea

Kelly Moser

Miki Mladenovic

Steffani Marsh

Kayla Santos

Desiree Andrese

Shamia Campbell

Brigitte Van Praag

Alli Smith

Kristina Blair

Cynthia Vorst

Jack Marron

Mike and Jane Marron

Luke and Katie Marron

Russ and Roisin Marron

Grandma and O.P. Marron

David and Patrice Marron

The Cross Family

The Hatfield Family

The Carpenter Family

Gail Hatfield

Kimberly Rooks

Kyle Peach

Doug and Shannon Gausepohl

Nicholas Falato

Brian and Marissa Ninni

Anthony Cistulli

Victoria and Alex

Megan and Chris

Anissa and Jarred

Marie and Joe

Ben Crater

Diego and Ryan

Nicholas Navaro

Dennis and Theresa Freshnock

Jeanne Moir

Paul Najemian

Adam Najemian

Janine Roukema

Joanna Cortina

Gina Betkowski

Jessica Stewart

Allison Tegano

Alicia Rivera

Ashley Harnish

Anna Rose

Jacqueline Viens

Xiemel Akbar

Brittany Heap

Juliana Pappas

Linda Phelps

Laura Stuart

Ted Ypsilantis

Alexander Grullon

Haley Noble

Caitlin Isasky

Sabrina Pusatera

Alysha Zimmerman

Jessica Lui

Shanice Anderson

Sakshi Mahtani

Aysha Lakhani

David Ngo

Yazmin Velazquez Rivera

Lei Wang

Eric Koester

Michelle Buonfiglio

Andrea Guzman

Dotschi Schloh

Kara Scott

Laura Cakolli

Maria Seabra

Eduardo Saldivar

Joseph Weisberger

Michelle Cheng

Nina Stelmakh

Zach Mayfield

Olivia McDonnell

Lisa Pridgen

Amy Pontrella

Demara White

Colleen Dean

Nancy Krivda

Walter Ingman

Jaquelin Wood-Luna

Made in the USA
Middletown, DE
13 May 2021